LABOR ON THE MARCH

LITERATURE OF AMERICAN LABOR

Cletus E. Daniel and Ileen A. DeVault, Series Editors

Between the Hills and the Sea
K. B. Gilden

The Diary of a Shirtwaist Striker
Theresa Serber Malkiel

Industrial Valley
Ruth McKenney

In the LITERATURE OF AMERICAN LABOR series we bring back into print some of the best literature that has emerged from the labor movement and related events in the United States and Canada. We are defining literature broadly; the series encompasses the full range of popular writing, including novels, biographies, autobiographies, and journalism. Each book includes an introduction written especially for this series and directing the reader's attention to the historical context for the work.

We believe that the titles in the series will be particularly useful to students of social and labor history and American studies. Our hope is that, both individually and collectively, the books in this series will contribute to a greater understanding of working-class experiences in our culture.

LITERATURE OF AMERICAN LABOR SERIES

LABOR ON THE MARCH

EDWARD LEVINSON

With an Introduction by
ROBERT H. ZIEGER

ILR Press
ITHACA, NEW YORK

Library of Congress Cataloging-in-Publication Data
Levinson, Edward, 1901–1945
Labor on the march / Edward Levinson ; with an introduction by
Robert H. Zieger.
p.   cm.
Includes bibliographic references and index.
ISBN 0-87546-340-1 (paperbk)
1. Trade-unions—United States—History.   2. Labor movement—United
States—History.   3. Working class—United States—History.
I. Zieger, Robert H.   II. Title.
HD6508.L48   1995
331.88'0973—dc20   95-5512

This new edition of *Labor on the March* is designed by Lou Robinson.
The text, with the exception of the front matter, is reproduced from the
original edition, published by Harper and Brothers in 1938.

Cover photo courtesy United Mineworkers of America

Copies of this book may be ordered through bookstores or directly from

ILR Press
School of Industrial and Labor Relations
Cornell University
Ithaca, NY 14853-3901
607-255-2264

CONTENTS

To AGNES MARTOCCI

ACKNOWLEDGMENTS

THE organizing and writing of this book, begun and completed while the events it describes and discusses were occurring, were made easier by the help of good friends. I am indebted, for assistance with various details, to Leon Climenko, Hyman Goldberg, Len de Caux, Vin Sweeney and Herman Wolf. I am particularly grateful for the generosity of Daniel L. Horowitz, who placed the result of many months of work on sit-down strikes at my disposal, for the assistance of Miss Evelyn Edmunds with the manuscript and of Miss Catha Levinson with the index.

A section of Chapter I has appeared in *Harper's Magazine,* and part of Chapter IX in the *Survey Graphic.* To the editors of both, my thanks for permission to reprint. Much of the material and observations was gained first hand from attendance as a newspaper man at the Atlantic City and Tampa conventions of the American Federation of Labor and the Committee for Industrial Organization, and in Flint, Detroit, Pittsburgh, Johnstown, Youngstown, and other cities when they were the scenes of C.I.O. strikes and negotiations. For having made these assignments possible and for having displayed a keen and liberal appreciation of the necessity for "covering labor" in its recent momentous struggles, I am indebted to Harry T. Saylor and Walter Lister, editor and city editor, of the *New York Post.*

Responsibility for the accuracy of the book, its emphasis on certain events, and its point-of-view is exclusively my own.

New York
December 1937   Edward Levinson

INTRODUCTION

THE DEVELOPMENTS of the 1930s seemed tailor-made for a reporter of Edward Levinson's background and experience. Though only thirty-seven when *Labor on the March* was published, he had logged almost twenty years as a journalist. A reporter of the old school, he substituted early immersion in the rough-and-tumble of urban and industrial life for a college education. At age eighteen, he began writing for the socialist New York *Call*. He then worked for papers in Denver and San Francisco, returning in 1922 to New York as night editor of the *Call*. Soon after, he joined the editorial staff of the *New Leader*, a New York socialist weekly. In 1932, he managed Norman Thomas's Socialist Party presidential campaign and soon thereafter joined the then-liberal *New York Post* as its chief labor correspondent.

One of the topics Levinson followed closely was professional strikebreaking. In 1934, he published two articles in the *Post* based on interviews with Pearl L. Bergoff, whose "detective bureau" contracted with employers to wage war on union organizers. For more than a quarter of a century, Bergoff had recruited goons and thugs to break up union meetings, smash picket lines, and create confusion and mayhem among union supporters.

In 1935, Levinson expanded and updated this newspaper material, publishing *I Break Strikes! The Technique of Pearl L. Bergoff.* This richly documented exposé convincingly recorded the heavy dependence of some of the nation's most respected corporations on Bergoff-provided violence to thwart collective bargaining. Levinson's book helped spur the creation of the La Follette's Civil Liberties Committee. In turn, the committee's exposure of antilabor practices provided organizers with invaluable help in building industrial unions. Declares historian Jerold S. Auerbach, "Levinson nearly did for strikebreaking what Upton Sinclair had done for the meat-packing industry by publishing *The Jungle*," whose revelations of abuses in the nation's slaughterhouses thirty years earlier had led to passage of pure food and meat inspection legislation.[1]

But the revival of the labor movement claimed most of Levinson's attention. Just as reporters in the 1960s accompanied the civil rights activists venturing into the South, so Levinson and his colleagues followed union organizers into the grim steel towns of Pennsylvania, the textile villages of the upland South, and Michigan's and Ohio's auto plants. The surviving black-and-white newsreels somehow capture their experiences as no Technicolor print could. The hulking factories dominate the urban skyline. Cloth-capped workingmen face tin-helmeted National Guardsmen. Truncheon-wielding police wade into picket lines as clouds of tear gas swirl past the defiant union banners. Massed thousands of jubilant workers celebrate union victories.

This was Edward Levinson's world. He covered the strikes and riots and demonstrations. He reported on the more mundane doings of union conventions and collective bargaining sessions. He

---

1. Jerold S. Auerbach, *Labor and Liberty: The La Follette Committee and the New Deal* (Indianapolis and New York: Bobbs-Merrill, 1966), 50.

rubbed elbows with the Socialists and Communists and old Wobblies whose radical commitment steeled the fledgling industrial union movement. And as a union advocate, he hailed the birth of a vast new labor movement, arising triumphantly from the ashes of half a century of bitter defeat.

For throughout the 1930s, industrial workers were on the move. Stunned by the collapse of the economic boom of the 1920s, they turned to the picket line and the ballot box for redress. Yet neither the established labor movement, as represented in the American Federation of Labor (AFL), nor the traditional Democratic Party initially either sought or particularly welcomed this surge of working-class activism.

But after six years of depression and three years of increasingly violent and frustrating labor conflict, a new workers' movement emerged. Founded in the fall of 1935, the Committee for Industrial Organization (CIO) was designed to tap into the unfocused militancy of working people and to revitalize the labor movement. Thus, the CIO's ambitious and innovative founders, notably John L. Lewis, Sidney Hillman, and David Dubinsky, sought initially to prod the lethargic AFL to reach out to mass-production workers. In response, however, AFL leaders declared war on the CIO. The split in the labor movement soon pitted worker against worker in workshops and union halls across the country.

Meanwhile, worker activism, along with pressure from other disaffected Americans, pushed President Roosevelt to the left. In the 1936 election campaign, the president vowed to drive the money changers from the temple and to bring to heel the "economic royalists" who ran the nation's banks and corporations.[2]

---

2. Roosevelt's acceptance speech at the 1936 Democratic national convention, Philadelphia, June 27, 1936, as quoted in Arthur M. Schlesinger Jr., *The Age of Roosevelt* vol. 3: *The Politics of Upheaval* (Boston: Houghton Mifflin, 1960), 582–84. Roosevelt borrowed the phrase from journalist Stanley High.

With du Pont, General Motors, and other industrial giants openly financing his Republican rivals, Roosevelt turned to a working class that was politicized as seldom before. And the new CIO delivered, pouring over half a million dollars into the president's campaign and mobilizing thousands of blue-collar voters. "The C.I.O. was out fighting for Roosevelt and every steel town showed a smashing victory for him," boasted CIO head John L. Lewis.[3]

Organizing victories followed political triumph. In Flint, Michigan, occupation of the auto plants forced General Motors to recognize the United Automobile Workers. A new steelworkers' union wrested a contract from its ancient enemy, US Steel. Rubber workers, electrical workers, longshoremen, miners, tobacco workers, and others brought unionism to the heart of the industrial economy for the first time. Senator Robert M. La Follette Jr.'s special investigating committee exposed the violence and espionage at the heart of corporate America's antiunion strategy.

Union fever ran high. In elections conducted by the new National Labor Relations Board, workers overwhelmingly voted for union representation. Sit-down strikes, *Time* magazine declared, had replaced baseball as the national pastime. "There is an awful power and might in this age-old drive for freedom," wrote Mary Heaton Vorse of the industrial union surge. "It is like a force of nature[,] irresistible as a tide."[4]

But labor organizing has never been easy in the United States, and the late 1930s were no exception. A series of bitter setbacks followed quickly on the heels of the remarkable victories in the spring of 1937. The so-called Little Steel companies—each a large

---

3. Lewis's remarks in minutes of CIO meeting, November 7–8, 1936, Katherine Pollak Ellickson Papers, Archives of Labor and Urban Affairs, Wayne State University, Box 14.
4. Mary Heaton Vorse, *Labor's New Millions* (New York: Modern Age Books, 1938), 58.

and powerful corporation in its own right—squared off against the CIO's steelworkers' union in a violent strike. Before the walkout sputtered to a close in the summer, eighteen steelworkers were dead and the Steel Workers Organizing Committee had to admit defeat. The new United Automobile Workers, it is true, did follow success with General Motors with a similar victory over the Chrysler Motor Corporation. But Henry Ford stepped up his campaign of terror against activists in his far-flung industrial empire. In May 1937, when UAW organizers tried to pass out leaflets at the gates of Ford's huge complex outside Detroit, local police watched with detachment as Ford's thugs assaulted them.

No chronicler could have hoped for a more dramatic story or for a more vivid and robust cast of characters. Of course, FDR himself commanded public attention as no other president before or since. Corporate America contributed an ample supply of villains: septuagenarian Henry Ford, retaining his reputation as public benefactor even as his hired thugs brutalized union adherents; Republic Steel's Tom Girdler, holding high the banner of rugged individualism in his lethal crusade against the new steelworkers' union; a thousand straw bosses violating elementary rights of democratic choice.

But it was the ranks of labor that provided the most vivid and distinctive presences in that turbulent decade. The bespectacled William Green, AFL chief and defender of the old order in the unions, provided a perfect foil for the fiery activists of the CIO. The Longshoremen's Harry Bridges combined a breathtaking Aussie-bred radicalism with sharp-tongued attacks on union rivals and employers alike. The Clothing Workers' Sidney Hillman, thoughtful and ambitious, brought the accents of New York's Jewish garment workers into the central arenas of industrial relations. And in every industry, the 1930s cast forth a new generation of activists eager to challenge the corporate establishment, often in the name of bold political agendas.

It was the CIO's founder, John L. Lewis, however, who commanded the greatest attention. It was Lewis who delivered the punch that decked the Carpenters' William Hutcheson at the 1935 AFL convention and thus, in effect, launched the CIO. It was Lewis's portentous rhetoric, salted with classical, Biblical, and Shakespearean references, that spread the CIO message. It was Lewis's bushy-browed visage that filled the movie screens and the front pages of America's dailies. "Lewis," declared journalist James Wechsler, "was [the CIO's] founding father, its emotional symbol, its commander-in-chief."[5] Added another writer, he was "the Babe Ruth of the labor movement."[6]

Labor on the March captures all this. But Edward Levinson was more than simply a splendid journalist. He was a student of the rich and distinctive history of the labor movement. He collected its stories and cherished its relics and legends. Thus his readers gain access not only to the stirring events of the 1930s but also to the whole legacy of trade unionism in the United States. From its opening paragraph, a poignant account of Samuel Gompers's death in 1924, *Labor on the March* links the struggles and follies of labor's past to the epochal developments of the 1930s. Levinson takes us back to 1887, into the ornate new headquarters of the Knights of Labor, built during an earlier (and, alas, short-lived) time of labor advance. We join him as he follows veterans of the 1892 Homestead steel strike in their search for the neglected graves of victims of Pinkerton violence. His accounts of the confrontations between the CIO's young industrial unionists and the AFL's leaders, unable

5. James Wechsler, *Labor Baron: A Portrait of John L. Lewis* (New York: William Morrow, 1944), 72.
6. Heywood Broun, "Mr. Lewis and Mr. Green," *Nation* (Nov. 28, 1936), 634.

to remember their own youthful dissidence, capture in sharp detail the human reality behind the headlines.

Despite the impressive achievements that Levinson recorded, by late 1937 the CIO juggernaut seemed to have stalled. The fragile economic recovery of 1935–37 gave way to a sharp downturn. Unemployment soared. Employers fired union members and slashed wages. Meanwhile, conservatives rebounded from earlier defeats and dealt the seemingly invincible Roosevelt a series of stunning political and legislative setbacks. With international tensions mounting and with both the New Deal and the industrial union movement apparently stalled, it was easy to believe that this latest outburst of worker activism might yield no more permanent results than had earlier episodes in the 1880s and during World War I.

Labor on the March, however, displays no doubts. It celebrates the birth and early successes of the CIO. It is an ebullient chronicle of industrial unionism's triumphant breakthrough, as well as a richly detailed account of the conflict between new unionists and the guardians of AFL traditionalism. Dutifully recording the difficulties faced by the new industrial unions, it is not an analytic assessment of the problematic aspects of organized labor's rebirth. Written before the full impact of the "Roosevelt Recession" became clear, it stops short of the setbacks and controversies that marked the CIO in the years immediately preceding World War II. Feisty activists and confident union leaders fill its pages.

Modern readers will no doubt note the absence of themes that have occupied the attention of more recent historians. Sharing the class-essentialist assumptions of CIO leaders, Levinson dealt with the experiences of African-American workers only in passing. He gave even shorter shrift to the problems and prospects of female workers. Hailing the NLRB as an effective instrument of workers' choice, he little dreamed that increasing legal enmeshment might prove confining as well as liberating. Imbued with the ecumenical leftism of his times, he dismissed concerns about Communists' role in the new unions and paid little attention to the implications of rising international tensions for the CIO. Disdainful of the AFL's initial caution and negativity, he hardly noticed the old federation's increasingly successful ability to compete with the CIO.

For Eddie Levinson, the CIO capped fifty years of labor struggle. Thus, *Labor on the March* captures the fighting spirit of the CIO and brims with the promise of a bright future for the new labor movement. It is a book born of a period of sharp class conflict, and it brilliantly depicts the words and deeds that made this a time of naked confrontation.

In his preface to the 1956 edition of *Labor on the March*, UAW president Walter Reuther—himself one of Ford's victims at the battle of the Overpass—paid tribute to Levinson's achievement. Noting that only two decades had passed since the stirring events chronicled, Reuther remarked that "today, they are as far away as the Whiskey Rebellion, the Dred Scott Decision or . . . the Haymarket riots." For Reuther, in the wake of the reunion of the AFL and CIO in 1955, the rise of the CIO had been one of the epochal events in American history. It made possible "the passage of American workers from across the railroad tracks into the centers of brightly lit cities" and provided the "improved income of millions of wage-earners [that] has made the 1950's as unlike the 1930's as the 20th century is unlike the 19th century."[7]

Forty years later, rediscovering *Labor on the March* excites different reflections. After two decades of relentless attacks on organized labor,

---

7. Edward Levinson, *Labor on the March* (1938; reprint, New York: University Books, 1956), xii.

the percentage of union membership has shrunk to less than half of what it was at the time of the merger. Despite the steady erosion of standards for a majority of working people, a probusiness ideology that equates absence of worker representation with social progress prevails. Labor laws, initially passed to bolster collective bargaining, now impede union organizing.

True, modern-day employers defeat organizing drives with sophisticated public relations and legal pettifogging rather than tear gas and brass knuckles. A globalized economic order poses challenges that even a John L. Lewis would have found daunting. Corruption, inertia, and lack of imagination and commitment have robbed unions of the vigor and public sympathy they could claim in the 1930s.

Even so, reading *Labor on the March* does more than provide a window into the past. It is a reminder of the conflictual nature of workplace relations and of the inequalities of wealth, status, and power that have pervaded life in the United States. When he wrote in 1956, Walter Reuther was too complacent about the permanence of the gains working people had made since the 1930s. As a once-powerful labor movement struggles to regain strength and relevance in the vastly transformed economic and political environment of the 1990s, we may wonder if the struggle for democratic representation and workplace security must be won again. In view of the economic and social changes since the depression, *Labor on the March* can provide no detailed tactical blueprint for accomplishing such a project. But perhaps, by highlighting a moment of worker empowerment, it can both remind us of the persistence of workers' struggles and inspire us to renew the battle.

University of Florida
December 1994   Robert H. Zieger

PART ONE

REVOLT: LEADERS, ISSUES AND EVENTS

1.

THE LEADERS OF LABOR

I

SAM GOMPERS was eighty and almost completely blind when he died in San Antonio. But to the last breath he displayed the perseverance with which he had battled all his life for a labor movement in the image of his own very practical dream. Premonition of death came to him while he was in Mexico City, where he had gone to reap the homage of the peons and laborers whom he had befriended for many years. He insisted he must die on 'American sod, and a sad entourage of American labor leaders rushed with him over the border back to the "native soil" of this London-born builder of the American labor movement. Early in the dawn of December 12, 1924, just before the end came, Gompers called the elders of the movement to his bedside. To James Duncan, octogenarian president of the granite cutters union, he murmured a command: "I have kept the faith. Tell them I expect them to keep the faith." Duncan promised. William Green and the others nodded in consent. Each placed a shaking hand on the hot brow of the shriveled body and whispered, "Good-by, Sam." Then the physicians and nurses made a final effort to prolong life. Needles pierced the dry skin, stimulants were administered, but the heart would not respond and at 4.10 A.M. the Grand Old Man of American Labor died.

A huge bronze casket on a gun carriage and a military escort took the body of labor's leader to the railroad station. Another artillery caisson and more soldiers met the body in Washington and brought it slowly through the streets of the national capital to the building of the American Federation of Labor. Here the official family of the Federation, Gompers' closest friends and associates,

[3]

gathered. Several felt unusual responsibilities weighing down upon them. Who was best suited to keep the faith, as Gompers had enjoined? Within a few days the choice would have to be made. Matthew Woll's claims were perhaps best. For more than a decade he had patiently borne the title of Crown Prince. Gompers had entrusted him with certain significant tasks at the convention of the Federation just ended. So also had the Grand Old Man singled out Green, giving him his opening address to read to the delegates. John L. Lewis, for several years estranged from the eldest labor statesman, had been handed the gavel to preside while Gompers was being renominated and reëlected for his last term. Duncan felt that the duty of carrying on belonged to him, the oldest of the remaining leaders. Daniel J. Tobin's long years in service and his eloquence gave support to his ambitions. Thomas A. Rickert, manipulator of Federation inner circle deals, was also not unwilling. The multiplicity of candidates gave still other members of the Federation's executive council of nine hope that, in the closeness of the contest, the lightning might strike near them.

When Lewis, the miners' president, arrived at the Federation headquarters to pay his respects to the departed leader, Green made his way to his side. Green, who was then secretary-treasurer of the United Mine Workers of America, had a particularly pressing problem to pour into his friend's ears that day. Other candidates were also soon to seek a word with Lewis. Theoretically, the miners' leader was not the one appropriately to designate the inheritor of Gompers' position. Gompers had been a craft unionist, deriving his power and building the Federation policies around the corner stone of exclusiveness, organizations of skilled workers. Lewis came from the miners, an organization which knew no craft distinctions and which served the coal-mine laborer equally with the mine electrician, machinist, and carpenter. Yet Green knew that with so many candidates in the field the votes and influence of the miners' union— largest in the Federation—would perhaps be a deciding factor. Green, himself a member of the miners' union, spoke to his president, and Lewis agreed to meet him that evening at the Raleigh Hotel.

A group of mine union officials was gathered around Lewis in the

Raleigh that night. Green arrived and the two stepped to a far corner of the lobby.

"Should I run?" Green inquired.

The question was not unexpected, and Lewis answered directly.

"Yes," the miners' president replied. "There are so many candidates, the United Mine Workers will have the balance of power. Your election is reasonably certain."

Lewis outlined the results of his canvass and discussed his plans for the forty-eight hours which would intervene before the executive council of the Federation convened to choose a new president. Green listened intently. He contributed a few suggestions. They talked for an hour and then returned to the other mine-union leaders in the center of the lobby. One non-miner was among them. Matthew Woll had arrived and was waiting patiently to see Lewis.

Lewis approached the president of the Photo Engravers' International Union.

"I think I know what you are waiting for," said the miners' president to the Crown Prince. "I am compelled to tell you that you have no chance whatsoever to be elected."

The funeral train departed for New York late that night. The Gompers' casket was placed the next morning in the auditorium of the Elks Club, where Gompers had found comforting friends in the years of abuse and bitter invectives from big business which had followed the warm salutes for his World War services. At noon December 19th the funeral was to take place.

On the evening of the 18th, Green again sought out Lewis. He found his chief at the Cadillac Hotel. In the presence of Philip Murray and other miners' officials Lewis delivered glad tidings.

"After the funeral tomorrow, the executive council will elect you president," said Lewis to Green. "The votes are available. Your election is certain."

Eagerly, shaking with emotion, Green grasped the hand of his chief. The eloquent one-time coal-digger from Coshocton, Ohio, trained in speech by many lay sermons in his local Baptist Church and by several years in the Ohio legislature, could not immediately find words for his gratitude. Finally they came. Warmly, he gave profuse thanks and vows of unceasing loyalty. Lewis would never

[5]

have cause to regret his choice, Green declared. To Lewis the moment was also an important one. Even then his ambition had built up a vision of a more powerful labor movement which would cut across narrow craft lines and bring powerful unions of steel and auto workers to stand beside his own miners' federation. Lewis himself would have wished to be president, no doubt. But the respect with which the craft-union leaders regarded him was matched by their fear and distrust of his brusque, dominating personality. But Green in a position of influence might serve the purpose. He had previously committed himself to industrial unionism. American labor could go forward.

A cold drizzle of rain enveloped the Gompers funeral procession as it traveled through Manhattan to Tarrytown's Sleepy Hollow Cemetery. A few feet from the graves of John D. Archbold, former head of Standard Oil, and near the tomb of William Rockefeller, the Grand Old Man of Labor was buried. A little more than a decade later, John D., Sr., himself joined the company.

The mourners turned back to the city, where the executive council gathered again at the Elks Club. Woll was placed in nomination, as was Green. Duncan, persisting in his futile hope to the end, nominated himself. He pleaded for a single term in the presidency so that he might round out in glory his long years with the Federation. Defeated, he resigned his vice-presidency in pique. He died soon after. Woll was counted out, and Green was elected amid open and concealed anger at the "ruthlessness" of John Lewis who had robbed the Crown Prince of his heritage.

John Lewis watched protectively over his new president in the years that followed. The convention of 1925 brought a nominating address in behalf of Green to which the miners' president gave his oratorical best. That year and each of several years after that, efforts were made to form blocs against Green and unseat him. Always the menacing shadow of Lewis halted the attack. Green stayed in the presidency.

But the decade that followed Green's succession to Gompers' post wrought great changes in the power and prestige of the miners' union. The collapse of Coolidge normalcy and prosperity struck heaviest blows to the miners. Markets dwindled; mine-pits closed;

[6]

the industry, particularly the bituminous section, became a battleground of ruinous competition and price wars; employers broke
contracts freely; miners by the hundred thousand joined the unemployed, stopped paying dues, and then dropped out of the union
entirely. The touching scene of devotion to the mine union and its
leader enacted in the Cadillac Hotel back in 1924 became dim in
the memory of William Green. Labor politics are no less pragmatic
than those which deal in public office. Green continued to hold the
presidency, but now the base of his strength and with it the object
of his allegiance had shifted from the miners to the building-trade
craft unions, the teamsters, electricians, carpenters, and machinists.
The miners no longer had the votes.

Thus it was that the great crisis which beat down upon American
organized labor from 1934 to 1938 found Green the champion not
of his "own people," of the industrial unionist miners and their
program, but rather of the craft unionists. He found himself carrying out the command of the dying Gompers.

II

Craft unionism was "the faith" to which Gompers had referred.
Its triumph for fifty-four years in the councils of the American
Federation of Labor was in a large degree attributable to this immi-
grant cigarmaker. Gompers felt that the strength of the skilled
workers lay in organizing by crafts. His early manhood, the 'eighties
and 'nineties, was the day of the skilled worker. Gompers was one
himself. Mass production and the straight-line process were unknown. Corral the skilled of one particular craft into a union,
Gompers urged, and the workman was in a position effectively to
negotiate for himself. To the devil with the unskilled and unorganized. "Their lack of organization stands out as clearly due wholly
to lack of courage, lack of persistence and lack of vision," he said.
Let the craftsman concentrate on his own hours and pay, and in-
cidentally make his union hard to get into. In Gompers' vision, the
aim of his movement was simply to gain "more and more—and then
more." Gompers mistrusted politics and government. Social insurance was socialism and paternalism. He preached that the craft
unionists should stand on their own legs. This he called "volun-

[7]

tarism." The Gompers policy attained a great measure of success for the crafts—the "business organizations of labor," they were called—and there grew up around him a hierarchy of hefty-paunched labor politicians with big watches and the eternal cigar. Their loyalty to old Sam was loyalty to themselves and their jobs. The years rolled on and Gompers grew old and grizzled. The number of skilled workers declined; the whole picture of industry changed. But the old Federation set its face against these changes; it became a static institution, administered by men much interested in proprietary rights represented by "jurisdictions" or claims which they had staked out for themselves, in salaries, expense accounts, and the dues that made these possible. Gompers, despite his narrow vision, had some intellectual power and could grapple with an idea. His successors inherited the constricted vision but not the intellect. They were, almost without exception, of small caliber. Some were energetic and rapacious. Some were indolent and their rapacity correspondingly clumsy. Some were small-time routine business men helpless and terrified in a crisis. The membership of the Federation began to fall; its strength and prestige dwindled. Before the depression of 1929 struck the country, the Federation had been sliding back. During the depression it was prostrate.

Then, suddenly, came the NRA with its labor provisions. Hundreds of thousands of men and women who had never before belonged to a union, and for whom there was no union, began clamoring for organization. Then it was that agitation for new-type industrial unions, based on labor solidarity rather than craft distinctions, took on force. The old-line leaders of the Federation drew back in fear that their unchecked power of decades would be broken. Alien elements—the unskilled and unorganized, despite their "lack of courage, lack of persistence, and lack of vision,"—pounded on the doors of the craft unions. They raised such a din and cry that the leaders of the Federation were terrified.

Meanwhile, a spokesman for these masses had appeared within the ranks of the Federation itself. John L. Lewis gathered around him a group of other believers in industrial unionism and together they gave to the clamor of the unorganized, seasoned leadership and strategy. Citing the example of his own United Mine Workers,

[8]

which had in 1934 again become the largest union in the Federation, Lewis proposed simply that the craft unions surrender their self-arrogated and never-enforced jurisdictions over the millions of unorganized and the few thousands of organized workers in steel, automobiles, radio, electrical supplies, rubber, aluminum, and cement. He proposed that the workers in these industries, largely machine-tenders and semi-skilled, be permitted to band together in new, inclusive, industry-wide unions at low rates of dues. Only thus, Lewis argued, could these workers be won for trade unionism and only thus could they present closed ranks to the concentrations of capital which had for years placed the divisive craft-union structure at a disadvantage. Lewis said he would leave the craft unions undisturbed if they would surrender their paper claims to the unorganized millions.

Paper claims! Unorganized millions! The words caused the elders of the A.F. of L. to quiver with rage. For they knew that the slightest move in the direction Lewis proposed would end their control of the Federation. And they feared that powerful industrial unions, once on a sure footing, might be as inconsiderate of the crafts as the craft-union leaders had been of the unorganized. In the historic Federation convention of 1935, Lewis amassed the support of 1,028,000 unionists for his program, as against 1,802,000 for his craft foes. The enrollment of half a million steel-workers and as many automobile unionists alone would shift the balance of power. For more than fifty years the craft leaders had ruled the roost and had diligently taught their members that any influx of new unionists into their unions would involve a threat to their jobs. Now the thing the leaders dreaded was about to happen and they were compelled to fight for their lives.

III

If the contending leaders could be gathered round a table, grouped for a photographer, the contrasts would be instructive. On the right is William L. Hutcheson, his huge frame well filled out, proof of a fondness for beefstakes and beer. Clamped between his teeth is an excellent cigar. It is he, the boss of 300,000 carpenters, who constructs the underpinning of intercraft deals, the hotel-room horse

[9]

trades by which jurisdictions are parceled out and withheld. Beside him is his yoke fellow in arms, Daniel Joseph Tobin, Irish-born boss of the teamsters. He has a paunch, too, but is not so tall. Like Hutcheson, he is a dictator, but he has a skill in swathing his dictation in sentiment and blarney. How moved he is when he recalls the dear departed, how effective on a platform when he beseeches the A.F. of L. founding fathers, the spirit of the illustrious dead, to hold up the unsteady hands of the living craft unionists.

There is a long resolution to be drafted in good English, and so the scholars of the A.F. of L.—John P. Frey and Matthew Woll—are present. Frey is tall and straight for his sixty-seven years; Woll is squat, florid of face, and fifty-seven. Frey is conservative in business man's gray; Woll is wing-collared. On the table in front of Frey repose several thick volumes, including the full minutes of the 1881 convention of the Federation of Organized Trades and Labor Unions, and a copy, with supporting arguments, of the charter granted by the National Forge of the Sons of Vulcan to its Paducah, Kentucky, local in 1863. Thus equipped, he is ready to play his accustomed rôle, to decipher the scrolls, producing ancient precedent for modern problems, and historical allusions sufficient to revive old fears and mistrusts. Woll, trained for labor leadership by a law course, is ready to connect the precedents with the current dangerous trends of Communism and to combine all in correct and stilted verbiage.

At the extreme end of the arc from Hutcheson is the abomination of the stand-pat unionists, John Llewellyn Lewis. The cold gray eyes of the miners' chief gaze with disdain on the circle. Woll is speaking. Lewis does not face the rest, but glances over his shoulder. Bushy brows and heavy jowls make caverns for his eyes. His head is surmounted by a generous crop of banked, wavy black hair, thinly streaked with gray. Reading from left to right from Lewis, there would be David Dubinsky, the young leader of the garment workers, rough-edged of language and shrewd enough as a politician to choose the right time to fight. Beside him is Sidney Hillman, president of the Amalgamated Clothing Workers, for twenty years outcasts from the A.F. of L. Neither Hillman nor Dubinsky has the girth of Hutcheson and Tobin. Both discovered socialist economics in youth, but trade-union activity has absorbed their interest. The fourth of the Lewis supporters in the picture, the tall man with the sharp bespectacled face, is Charles P. Howard, president of the International Typographical Union.

Last of all these worthies is the presiding elder who sits in the center, his head cocked in the direction of Hutcheson. His soft hands are peacefully arched on the table, his stomach slightly rounded, his face pinkish in contrast with the ruggedness and pallor of Lewis. William Green, the president of the A.F. of L., once a coal-digger, appears to have been a long time out of the mines. His tailored clothes stamp him as one with a small city banker. Woll has finished with his warning of the danger of appearing to drift in the direction of Moscow, and Green, in gentle words, is supporting his point of view, spreading the oil of conciliatory righteousness while he accepts the policies of the crafts which maintain him in office.

These are the surfaces of the personalities. The conflict over industrial unionism affords an excellent opportunity to probe beneath, to study the variations of opinion and of strategy which these men represent.

IV

If the Messrs. Woll and Frey delight in resolutions and bleary-eyed researches that uphold and glorify the ancient and honorable dogmas of craft unionism, it is their colleagues, Hutcheson and Tobin, leaders of the carpenters and teamsters, who most vigorously translate those dogmas into action. But the dogma undergoes a curious sea change. You may fight industrial unionism to the death, but that need not prevent you from trying to snatch workers in other trades and incorporate them into your own union. This has been known as craft-union imperialism. Its prize is dues; dues-paying members furnish the sinews of war. If a structural-iron worker can be technically declared a carpenter, so much the better for you if you are running the carpenter's union. To prove such a technicality may involve a ferocious battle, and it is in just such battles that Hutcheson and Tobin have won their spurs. "Once wood, it is always the right of the carpenter to install it,"

[11]

says Hutcheson, "no matter what the material is." A wag has said, "God created the forests and He gave them to Bill Hutcheson." To that appraisal, we may be certain, Hutcheson would not object. By degrees this labor boss has gathered in not only cabinet makers, mill carpenters, furniture workers, but members of the machinists' and coopers' unions as well. Nay, more; he has annexed bridge workers, brewers, longshoremen, metal lathers, and sheet-metal workers. Hutcheson is a genius at this business; he can make two carpenters grow where there was but one, and if it were necessary he doubtless could find reasons why Jim Farley, the former gypsum salesman, or Frances Perkins might be called carpenters—provided they could and would pay dues. No jurisdictional fight has ever been finally settled unless it was settled Hutcheson's way.

Hutcheson is an autocrat inside his organization and runs it with the craft unionist's "proprietary interest" which President Green has endorsed. He allows a convention every four years, but by constitutional law anyone who so much as ignores the rap of his gavel is subject to expulsion from the session. His history includes some curious chapters. In 1916 in New York City 10,000 striking carpenters had returned to work victorious and with a wage scale of $5.50 a day. Hutcheson voided the agreement and signed a new contract with the employers for $5.00 a day. When there were objections from the sixty-five local unions involved, he suspended all but the one headed by the notorious Robert P. Brindell. He then recruited strike-breakers. In Chicago in 1924 the unions defeated the Landis award, an attempt to turn the carpentry trade of the city into an open shop. Soon afterward Hutcheson signed an agreement embodying the terms of the award. A referendum in 1937 to enlarge Hutcheson's powers was carried, but when the results of the poll were published local unions found that 6,000 votes—enough to decide the issue—had been wrongly counted. Efforts to obtain a recount were unavailing.

When he speaks—and Hutcheson can roar and bluster—he expects to be heard; his 300,000 members and his 3,000 votes in the annual Federation conventions are regarded with a good deal more than gravity. He is a Republican and supported Coolidge in 1924 after the A.F. of L. had endorsed La Follette. In 1932 he was chairman of Hoover's labor committee, and in 1936 performed the same office for a man by the name of Landon. When the Federation executive council gave perfunctory support to the reëlection of President Roosevelt, Hutcheson resigned from the council rather than be compromised. If he has any positive social beliefs, they have never been discovered. During the chance absence of most of the delegates from the Federation's 1935 convention, he steamrollered defeat of a proposal for a federal constitutional amendment safeguarding social legislation. At the convention of 1936 he voted against demands for shorter hour legislation, evoking the Gompers philosophy of "voluntarism."

Between Hutcheson and his colleague, Daniel Tobin, president and lord of the teamsters, there is a deep spiritual affinity. True, Tobin cannot control as many A.F. of L. convention votes as Hutcheson, and occasionally is forced to compromise; but he is stentorian in his devotion to the Gompers faith, and as a spellbinder he leaves the carpenter boss far in the rear.

"To us was given a charter . . . " he declaimed in an indictment of industrial unionism, "and Gompers, McGuire, Duncan, Foster, and the others said: 'Upon the rocks of trades autonomy, craft trades, you shall build the church of the labor movement and the gates of hell nor trade industrial unionism shall not prevail against it.' "

No one belabors Communists more lustily than Tobin, and he has a constitutional provision to bar them from his union. He seems to be less successful in keeping racketeers out. In November, 1933, he agreed to let the Cook County, Illinois, state's attorney supervise Chicago teamsters' elections and pass upon all candidates for office. It will not do to imagine him as one whose heart bleeds for all those who labor. On the contrary, in 1934 he referred to the new unionists as "rubbish." "The scramble for admittance to the union is on," wrote Tobin in the heyday of the NRA. "We do not want to charter the riffraff or good-for-nothings, or those for whom we cannot make wages or conditions, *unless we are compelled to do so by other organizations offering to charter them*

[13]

under any condition. . . . We do not want the men today if they are going on strike tomorrow." Strikes he denounced as "unholy conflict," a surprising statement for even a conservative labor boss.

To understand better the Tobin psychology and the operations of his union, let us sit in on a meeting of the general executive board of the International Brotherhood of Teamsters. The setting is Miami's Hotel 'Alcazar during the cold winter of 1933. Tobin, who as teamster-general receives $20,000 a year, plus expenses, is in the chair, and present are six loyal vice-presidents who are justly rewarded with $12,000 a year, also plus expenses. A report is received indicating the depression has made serious inroads on the union. Few of the members have ever been to Palm Beach and since the resort is only sixty miles away, it is voted to adjourn for the day. Reconvened, the board hears that charges of racketeering are being made against some of its leaders. The board, says the minutes, "advises publicity of the situation by purchasing of space in newspapers not conducting attacks on any individual officer." Tobin reports gloomily that though the entire labor movement favors his appointment as Secretary of Labor, it is not likely that President Roosevelt will give him the post. The board, nevertheless, has received letters from several local unions which "requested the board to take proper care of the general president financially, should he be selected as Secretary of Labor." (As Secretary of Labor, Tobin would have received $5,000 a year less than as head of the teamsters.)

"Suitable action" embodying the substance of the letters was taken, the minutes declare.

Tobin reports that he is tired and worn out by his efforts as chairman of the Roosevelt labor committee and "that he would like to go away somewhere across the water where he will not be bothered for a while by the political situation or by the work within the organization." The board votes to pay his expenses for a two or three months' vacation trip. The board then decides not to try to organize the New York taxi-drivers because they are a difficult and unreliable crowd of men. The charter of the local union of Jersey City bus-drivers is revoked because of their failure to pay dues. The treasury is being depleted, and therefore it is decided that no locals are to be permitted to strike where conciliation or arbitration is offered. (Thus, the board decrees compulsory arbitration.) The board then adjourns "subject to the call of the general president whenever absolutely necessary."

We now turn to John P. Frey and Matthew Woll, the intellectuals, the thinkers of this group. Frey is the leader of the molders and for years edited their Journal. Once a proud and vigorous organization, the molders have lost ground. Changes in industry combined with a flabby, wobbling policy have dragged this union down to a membership of 22,000 as against 57,300 in 1920. More recently Mr. Frey has given his efforts to the presidency of the Metal Trades Department of the Federation, a convenient catch-all for a number of craft unions. But here, too, something seems to be amiss. The Newport News Shipbuilding and Drydock Company, frightened by the success of an industrial union in Camden, New Jersey, opened its doors to Frey and his crafts—and its yards are still unorganized!

But that fact does not disturb Frey as a philosopher. He is, in truth, the philosopher of a movement that has no philosophy. Whatever may be granted to Gomperism as a practical, craft-union tactic for its day, no serious student can ascribe to it any long-range program or vitality. Yet over its dry bones Frey broods tenderly. He has been the researcher and historian of the A.F. of L., the delver in the cemetery of labor's dead hopes. He can rattle the bones of the Knights of Labor, denounce viciously Daniel De Leon's Socialist Trade and Labor Alliance—which vanished long ago—and he can take to task the Industrial Workers of the World with great bitterness.

When he approaches the present day Frey is less clear in his perceptions. One can get a perspective on the railway troubles of '77, but a current general strike, that's another story. Still he apparently is aware of some social manifestations of the day, for he claims to have detected a resemblance between the industrial unions Lewis proposes and the labor organizations of Fascist Italy and Germany. A diligent researcher, Frey discovered in 1933 the interlocking directorates of banks, and presented this interesting fact as labor's explanation of the depression. His book on labor injunctions is almost exclusively a compilation. Until a few years ago Frey's understanding of economics and labor's needs, profound though it is, did not lead him to favor unemployment insurance. He dislikes altercations and was upset by a reception he received in Butte in 1934. A strike was on, called by the Union of Mine, Mill, and Smelter Workers, an industrial union, which the A.F. of L. tolerated as long as it was weak. Frey went out to explain why certain craft unions had signed an agreement in behalf of the skilled workers, leaving most of the strikers out in the cold. To his great distress, when he had spoken only an hour and a half, a motion was made to put him out of the room. According to Frey, the whole trouble was that the Butte miners hadn't heard a logical argument for years!

Matthew Woll deserves attention, not because he is an active force, but because at the early age of fifty-seven he is an A.F. of L. tradition. During decades as president of the Photo Engravers' International Union he was a faithful understudy to the Old Man. He wanted to succeed Gompers as president of the A.F. of L., and Gompers smiled on the ambition; but Lewis did not.

Forced to play second fiddle, Woll has done the best he could. He became acting president of the National Civic Federation, from which position he waged relentless war on the "reds" and provided Monday-morning copy for indifferent city editors. He accepted the presidency of the International Sportsmanship Brotherhood, organized to coördinate the welfare activities of non-union employers. He devoted some time to the Workers' Education Bureau, threw Brookwood Labor College out of the fold, and reduced labor education to the humiliating and innocuous point where its main sources of financial support became the Carnegie Foundation and John D. Rockefeller's General Education Fund. He gives more time now to his business, which is the presidency of the Union Labor Life Insurance Company, than to the labor movement proper. And an enterprising business it is. A few years ago the company called for the celebration of "Matthew Woll's Birthday Month," during which time it was to be the duty of the loyal laborites to subscribe to a policy with the company.

The truth is that Woll is through. At the 1935 A.F. of L. convention, a growl from Lewis hastily led him to resign his presidency

[16]

of the National Civic Federation. There is nothing more important ahead. He continues to find a vehicle for his thoughts in the Hearst press and in the columns of *Liberty*—where he must suffer intensely the necessity of limiting his contributions to seven minutes, twenty seconds' reading time—and he has his mission to urge employers to save the nation "from impending social revolution." But that is all.

Room now for the gentleman from Coshocton, Ohio, William Green, president of the American Federation of Labor, inheritor of the Gompers purple, and most obliging of men. He has been called the diplomat of the labor movement; if he is, he is a diplomat without cunning. Lewis has been forceful and domineering, Green has been ingratiating. Up to the time of his election to the A.F. of L. presidency he had offended fewer people at the top than any other leader. He is an Odd Fellow, and an Elk, and a leading member of the Baptist Church of his home town. In Indianapolis, where Green and Lewis made their offices when both were officials of the United Mine Workers, the business men preferred Green. They called him more "human," a "better balanced person," more ready to listen to reason and persuasion. With these resilient qualities, Green has given the A.F. of L. the negative Gompers policies without the fire and wit of the craft unionists' patron saint.

Of his sixty-five years, Green has spent some fifteen in the coal mines. Early in his manhood he became a district officer in the Ohio section of the miners' union. He soon graduated to the Ohio legislature, where the nicety of parliamentary relationships first gave him lessons in diplomacy and obscured the closer realities of economic life. The circumstances of Green's elevation to the executive council of the Federation are indicative of his progress. When John Mitchell quit the council in 1912, the place was offered to John P. White, president of the United Mine Workers, with the qualification that he must take his place at the bottom of the list and become the eighth vice-president. The miners' union objected, insisting that the second vice-presidency, which Mitchell had held, was the only place on the council that would adequately recognize its standing. While the row was on, council members went to Green

[17]

and, as a result of private discussions, prevailed upon him to accept the place at the bottom of the list. It was a start, at any rate.

Green was an industrial unionist before his elevation to the presidency of the Federation; he is now the front man for the crafts. He was a dry before, and a wet later. For the rest, he might be considered an unusually articulate Babbitt with a minute deviation to the left, which places him far to the right of, say, the Federal Council of Churches of Christ. On his acceptance of the A.F. of L. presidency Green announced he would "support the right and oppose the wrong." He has since endorsed "progressive conservatism"; spoken for a big navy at an exercise laying the keel of a battleship; told the cadets at West Point—where he was given honors equal only to those previously accorded Queen Marie of Rumania—that he was opposed to giving "unreasonable employers" the use of the military; and pledged the aid of the A.F. of L. to Kerensky in his efforts to overthrow the Soviet government.

Within the fold of the A.F. of L., until Lewis focused attention upon the organization of the unorganized, Green's diplomatic talents had been occupied with a year-round, year-in-and-out effort to keep peace between the warring craft unions. He had cemented peace frequently, only to find that his cement, when it dried, was dirt and water. He liked to disclaim the power that the prestige of his office gives him. Thus he pleaded with the industrial unionists that he was powerless to do otherwise than carry out convention decisions. And at the conventions he remained silent. It was Green's unpalatable job in 1935 to jam a limited charter and executive council control down the throats of the few automobile unionists whom the craft-union policy had been able to attract. He was not so fortunate when he tried to administer the same medicine to the Akron rubber-workers. Yet Green continues to shoulder the burden without complaint. Personally he would prefer to compromise the differences; fervently, piously, he appeals to the spirit of labor unity. But something always seems to go wrong; his hopes are dashed. The presidency of the Federation has lost influence during his incumbency, things are not as they might be; but still he has his job and that's a comfort.

[18]

V

And now, moving from the center of the group toward the left, we may inspect the leaders of the great rebellion now in progress. Lewis of the miners, Howard of the typographers, Dubinsky of the ladies' garment workers, and Hillman of the men's clothing workers are the insurgents; and Lewis outranks them all.

Lewis' is a strange story. See him sitting on a platform, his heavy jaw thrust forward, his stony gray eyes fixed, his hair like horns. When enraged he can roar like a bull. In some respects he is like an old-time actor. Nobody relishes a big scene more than he does. To get the center of the stage—and appear to hold it with main strength—and then set off elaborate oratorical fireworks is his particular pleasure. His vocabulary is orotund and there is no public figure alive who can wring the withers of our language as Lewis does. Sometimes the heavy forefinger is raised in solemn warning, again he waves his arms aloft in defiance of all the powers of darkness. A Kansas strike is referred to as an "embroglio" to the astonishment of his delegates; he plucks his jaw and mutters "methinks."

During an NRA-code hearing he took on Patrick Hurley, former Secretary of War, as an adversary. Hurley had once been a member of a miners' local; now he was arguing for the employers. "It is a source of pride to the United Mine Workers when one of its sons carves for himself a place in the nation," said Lewis, "but it is a matter of regret and shame when one of our number betrays his brothers—for thirty pieces of silver." Hurley, enraged, rushed down the aisle with a demand for retraction. With a nice eye for distance and with theatrical deliberation, Lewis turned to the stenographer. " . . . and betrays his brothers," he repeated. "Strike out 'thirty pieces of silver.'" These are examples of Lewis in action. Over a period of eighteen years he has been variously described as a master of dissimulation, a calculator of icy coldness, a betrayer of labor, the savior and defender of the same.

Such contradictions deserve some analysis. By inheritance—so far as office goes—Lewis has always been an industrial unionist. His union, the United Mine Workers of America, not only claims but enforces jurisdiction over all men who labor in or about the mines. Yet he was for years at one with the ruling group in the A.F. of L. in social blindness and lack of interest in the unorganized. And that's what makes the old guard in the A.F. of L. so boiling mad today. Once they all slept comfortably in the same bed, and now this bull of Bashan threatens to wreck everything.

Lewis was born in Iowa on February 12, 1880. After fifteen years in coal and metal mines, he became legislative agent for the Illinois mine workers. Nine years in various labor positions preceded his election as president of the United Mine Workers. He has held the job since 1919. He was damned for yielding to a federal injunction against the bituminous strike in 1919—he said he wouldn't fight the government—but he got a 27-per-cent wage increase for his men. In the 1922 hard and soft coal strike he insisted on fighting for the *status quo* and no more. His policy in subsequent coal strikes continued to be negative, and the miners' union began to slip. The non-union Southern mines were allowed to remain in that condition; the union in West Virginia and elsewhere went to pieces. The economics of the industry were against it.

From a membership of 400,000 in 1926, the miners' union dropped to 150,000. Internecine wars and rebellions kept the union in convulsions while Lewis busied himself with roughshod politics, choking off protest and witch-hunting for Communists, as all his critics were labeled. Lewis' prestige within his own union and with the A.F. of L. craft leaders sank to a low ebb. So sage a prophet as Benjamin Stolberg wrote that if one counted slowly, he could begin to count Lewis out.

A change began to be visible in 1932. He showed no great passion for teamster Tobin's desire to be Secretary of Labor, nor did he, like the other craft leaders, sulk at the selection of Miss Perkins. With the election of President Roosevelt in 1932, Lewis saw hopes for a thoroughgoing, nation-wide effort to stabilize and revive the "sick" coal industry. He helped initiate the NRA, and fostered the Guffey Coal Act. With the Recovery Act a law, he moved energetically to take advantage of it. He began patching up old feuds, he roused his organizers to action, he dispatched men to the Southern non-union mines and the "captive" coal pits of the steel companies.

[20]

The miners responded to this treatment, and today, out of 620,000 coal miners in America, 600,000 belong to the union and there is a substantial treasury. The climax to all this bewildering activity was the 1935 convention of the A.F. of L., held at Atlantic City, where Lewis set the assemblage on edge with his defense of industrial unionism and ferocious attack on the crafts. Before the convention was over he had knocked carpenter Hutcheson down in a fist fight and received a telegram from an enthusiastic member of Hutcheson's union: "Congratulations. Knock him down again."

How to reconcile these tactics with those pursued during the '20's is difficult, if not impossible. Was it the desperate weakness of his own union that woke him? It is possible that his desire for the broader organization of labor was induced, in part, by the fact that his own union was menaced at strategic points by the open-shop steel industry. He could see that the worst failure of the NRA, even before the Blue Eagle was decapitated by the Supreme Court, had been its failure with the labor unions. His own industrial union might indicate a solution, but such a solution meant a war with the crafts. He must have thought and calculated a long while, but he made his decision at last. And the war was on.

Closely associated with Lewis in the attempt to unionize mass-production industries are Hillman, Dubinsky, and Howard. The organizations which they lead are among those which have done the most in asserting the right of labor to a voice in industry. Charles P. Howard is the head of the typographical union and has seen his following establish a more effective control of working conditions than any other union in the Federation. It happens that his is a craft union, and it is often argued that this fact is an inverse proof of the industrial unionists' basic contention. The highly skilled and completely diversified tasks of the printing industry are suitable for craft organizations, whereas the semi-skilled and unskilled workers in mass production can never be so divided. Howard has steadfastly supported the position of Lewis and his associates, and none of them can argue the case for industrial unionism as clearly and ably as the typographical chief. He lost a chance to become a vice-president of the A.F. of L. because of his stand, and though his own union has no immediate stake in the fight, he is committed on the issue.

David Dubinsky, alone among the industrial unionist leaders, is a Socialist, though he comes to that distinction only by meeting the modest qualifications of the dwindled corps of old guard Socialists. He is president of the International Ladies' Garment Workers Union. Sidney Hillman, head of the Amalgamated Clothing Workers, was a Socialist also in his youth, but he is given too much to a desire for immediate results to give serious consideration to radical politics.

Dubinsky is an organizing genius. His union was the third largest in the Federation and has managed to penetrate the most distant fringes of the women's garment industry. Italians, Jews, Negroes, Spaniards, Puerto Ricans, and small-town American girls are enlisted in its ranks. This organization has its own songs, slogans, and literature, and spends more money on labor education and recreation than any other union. Dubinsky had escaped to America after a Siberian exile. He learned labor politics in the cutters' union, composed of the skilled key men of the ladies' garment industry. The organization he now leads has 252,000 members, the semi-skilled members far outnumbering the skilled. It took a small revolution in 1934 to elect Dubinsky to the executive council of the A.F. of L., where he was considered rather an oddity since he was the executive of a large international and got only $7,500 a year for it.

Hillman and his Amalgamated were kept out of the A.F. of L. for twenty years, outcasts beyond the pale. Back in 1914 his union of men's clothing workers revolted against the ossified conservatism of the United Garment Workers and struck out on its own. He came to attention through his brilliant leadership of the famous Chicago struggles of the clothing workers in those days. He has been an active figure in a number of enterprises, is chairman of the board of the Amalgamated Bank in New York and a director of the Amalgamated Trust and Savings Bank in Chicago. He had much to do with selling President Roosevelt the labor sections of the NRA. Dubinsky and Lewis took most advantage of them. The history of the origin of the NRA must give due attention to the

[22]

hearings before the Senate Committee on Manufactures which Hillman helped bring about in 1931. It was then that Hillman proposed an economic council and a plan of industrial codes, though he wished them limited to regulation of hours and wages. The fair-trade practices he would have left to the Federal Trade Commission. For two years, most of the time as a member of the NRA's labor advisory board, Hillman shuttled by train and plane between Washington, where he gave his time to the entire labor movement, and the men's clothing centers, where he guarded the interests of his own union. Of the several leaders of labor called to the White House during the NRA period, few remained as long or were listened to with as much receptivity as Hillman. In the end his fear that business domination of the code authorities would nullify the labor safeguards was proven true. Never an extremist who fights for all or nothing, Hillman turned his attention to winning by the power of organized labor, through industrial unions, the gains which the NRA tried to accord by political fiat.

These are the outstanding leaders of American labor: Hutcheson, Tobin, Frey, Woll and Green, who are attempting to hold the fort against the onrush of new leaders and new policies; and Lewis, Howard, Dubinsky and Hillman, who have stormed the ramparts, made effective advances, and brought about the greatest labor upheaval the American nation has known.

2.

"THE AMERICAN SEPARATION OF LABOR"

I

THE American Federation of Labor came into being as a dual organization, displacing the Noble and Holy Order of the Knights of Labor from its position as the first popular movement of American labor which enjoyed a period of continuous organization and had followers as well as leaders. Historian John P. Frey never fails to point with warning to the "failure" of the Noble and Holy Order as an effort to establish industrial unions. But like many other historians with a purpose, Frey finds in the Knights just what he needs to prove his case.

The Knights lend themselves to that kind of treatment. The organization came into being in 1869, fostered by Uriah S. Stephens, a philosophic, religious-minded Philadelphia tailor. It aimed to bring all workers, regardless of advantages in jobs or crafts, into a single organization. The slogan was "an injury to one is the concern of all." When in 1886 the Knights reached the peak of their strength, they had three-quarters of a million members. The Order had engaged in bitter strikes, taking the measure of Jay Gould once, only to retreat before him in the great Southwestern railroad strike. Its militancy and its early naïve faith in secrecy and ritual rigamarole gave the red-baiters of its day plenty of ammunition. The elder Allan Pinkerton, originator of the business of labor spying, proclaimed that he had learned from his stool-pigeons that the Knights were an amalgamation of the Paris Commune and the violent Molly Maguires of Pennsylvania's anthracite fields. More dispassionate observers and historians have termed the Knights an expression of Socialism, which was then being vigorously propagated by newly-arrived German Americans, a revulsion against Socialism in the form of non-political "pure and simple" unionism, and reformism with panaceas of education, coöperation and other short-cuts out of the wilderness of low wages, long hours, unemployment, poverty, and depression. The Knights were not any of these, but had elements of all. Its confusion was abetted by its leaders. The man who succeeded Stephens as the Order's Grand Master Workman and remained to bury the organization was Terence V. Powderly, a passionate conniver, an interminable letter-writer, and a windy orator. He had no idea that lasted more than six months on where the Knights were going or where they ought to go.

But the Knights deserve a place in history. It was a completely authentic American labor movement, thrilling in its huge dimensions and in the fervor it aroused among the masses for its noble slogan—the solidarity of all Americans who labor. Only the recent growth of the C.I.O. has equaled the Order's phenomenally quick growth. In 1879, the Knights had a membership of 9,287. In July of 1885 it reported 111,395 adherents, and when another twelve-month had rolled around it had achieved a dues-paying following of over 700,000. Wherever organizers went hundreds and thousands of workingmen, tradesmen, and farmers signed up. The Washington *Gazette* predicted, with disapproval, that the Order would probably name the next President. Rumors gave the membership as 1,000,000 and some went as high as 2,500,000. So great was the progress of the Order in February of 1886, that Powderly called a halt on further enlistments until the gains already made could be consolidated. From July to November, some 800 new "assemblies" were formed. It was the period of "the great upheaval." Railroad men, horse-car drivers and conductors, collar-and-cuff makers, curriers, glass-bottle blowers, and textile-mill hands revolted in a series of strikes. The eight-hour day was their first demand, and on May 1, 1886, 190,000 struck in a concerted movement to reduce the hours of labor. Some 150,000 gained their objective without a strike, and about 50,000 of those who had been forced to fight it out on picket lines returned to their jobs victorious. There was debating, violence, and generally a storm of combat in the nation. That unskilled laborers, and foreigners—Swedes, Bohemians, Poles, Norwegians, and Welshmen—

[25]

took part in the battles; that the Knights accepted women and Negroes into their ranks; that Socialists took part—all this added to the heat of the attacks and counter-attacks. A staff of investigators for the *New York Sun* gave the leaders of the Knights even greater power than they claimed for themselves:

"Five men . . . control the chief interests of 500,000 workingmen, and can at any moment take the means of livelihood from two and a half million souls. . . . These men compose the executive board of the Noble Order. . . . They can stay the nimble touch of every telegraph operator; can shut up most of the mills and factories, and can disable the railroads. . . . They can array labor against capital, putting labor on the offensive or the defensive, for quiet and stubborn self-protection, or for angry, organized assault, as they will."

Politically the strength of the Knights was attested by its success in compelling Congress to outlaw the profitable business by which steamship lines recruited and transported alien, unknowing strike-breakers and low-scale workers under contract to specified employers. The Knights influenced Congress in other ways, and forced a number of state legislatures to curb the ruinous competition of prison labor.

The Knights heralded the arrival of an organized working class and, for the first time, placed the unskilled worker on a plane of equality, perhaps of leadership. It was the period of the "robber barons" in industry, with their corruption of politics, their juggling and watering of stock, their milking of railroads. The impact of the Knights' army of more than a half a million brought a social war whose effects were felt in every city and community. Sympathy strikes and flying squadrons which closed down plants were commonplace, almost as frequent as the employers' use of police, militia, and Pinkerton thugs for violent repression.

Just before the arc of the Knights' strength had begun to slope downward, in the winter of 1886, Powderly and other officials purchased a headquarters, a brown-stone mansion at 814 North Broad Street, Philadelphia. It cost about $50,000. The stable and much of the furnishings went with it. Up a wide series of brownstone steps one came to carpeted halls and stairs and thence to "a large stained-glass window representing the four seasons." The banisters were wood of "unusual thickness," and a bronze figure surmounted the newel post. In the rooms were large mirrors in carved walnut frames, mantels inlaid with marble, fine curtains of lace, elaborate frescoed walls, and three "immense old-gold satin tufted battings" several inches deep and bordered with satin hangings. "This room," said the Knights' *Journal*, "which is to be occupied by G. S. Litchman and his corps of assistants, many of whom are ladies . . . is partly separated from a small reception room . . . by huge veneered and highly polished double columns. A magnificent chandelier. . . . The reception-room opens through sliding doors . . . upon what was formerly a picture gallery. . . . The floor is inlaid with hard wood . . . solid marble wainscoting about three feet deep."

Then there was the north room, with more mirrors and hand-made lace curtains, large easy-chairs covered with red velvet, and a massive sofa. A rear north room contained another sofa, a "large leather one," and a wine-cooler. And in back of this was the dining-room, "lighted through an octagon-shaped dome" from the center of which was suspended a "double revolving chandelier with twenty-four highly polished and ornamented brass burners. Around the base of the dome, carved in wood, a deer with real antlers, a boar, ducks, fish, and other specimens of game . . . eight carved columns . . . four massive pedestals of marble." This was the meeting place of the Knights' general executive board. Upstairs there were eight carpeted large rooms, with curtains, hangings, mirrors, and wash-stands, and bathrooms "fitted up in the most complete style." There was another floor with a billiard-room and "a billiard table covered with marble." The entire building was "heated by steam" and there were "registers in every room," also "electric call bells, messenger calls, and burglar alarms."

The officers of the Noble and Holy Order of the Knights of Labor saw nothing wrong in providing themselves with such comfortable headquarters for their undoubtedly arduous labors. If they had been squandering the poor man's money, as was soon charged, Litchman would not have been moved to spread the spendthrift details in the *Journal*. Nevertheless, troubles were beginning to accumulate for the leaders of the Knights from other directions, and Litchman's faithful, proud description was broadcast in a manner to give the humble sons of labor pictures of Powderly with his walrus mustaches, and other labor leaders lounging decadently on thick piles of satin while near at hand were Litchman's corps of assistants, "many of whom are ladies."

The peak strength of the Order came after the depression of 1884-85 had lifted and prices had begun to rise. The decline of the Knights was almost as swift as their growth. The 728,677 members of 1886 dropped to 548,239 a year later. More fell by the wayside each year, until only 100,000 were claimed in 1890. The last available figure, in 1893, placed the membership at 74,635. A precise explanation of why the Knights appeared when they did, and why they declined, has yet to be offered. There are some good explantations of its collapse. Powderly suggested them in a melancholy letter written in 1893. He said the Order had taught reforms which it could not bring about. "Advocating arbitration and conciliation, advising against strikes, we have been forced to yield our time to petty disputes. . . . While not a political party, we have been forced into the attitude of taking political action." He added, and with truth: "but through all the turmoil and misunderstanding the Order had stamped deep its impression for good upon the records of the world, and should it collapse tonight those who survive it may point to its splendid achievements in forcing to the front the cause of misunderstood and down-trodden humanity."

The misconception that the Knights of Labor was a great futile experiment in industrial unionism arises primarily from its underscoring of the solidarity of skilled and unskilled workers. The Knights' "assemblies," local unions of a specific craft which nevertheless admitted workers of other callings, have been offered as proof of the industrial-union character of the Order. The fact is that the assembly was composed of workers in a given craft and that others who were admitted to membership were "sojourners," temporarily accepted into the ranks so that they might absorb its principles in a sympathetic atmosphere and then go forth to organize others in their own trade. Some of the assemblies, clinging to the craft exclusiveness which the Knights did their best to dissipate, refused to admit sojourners. In 1886 there appear to have been 1,088 trade local unions and 1,279 "mixed assemblies." Most of the latter were in small and newly penetrated communities where no craft had sufficient members to establish its own local. The locals were tied together in district assemblies. Alongside of these were also trade districts, comprised of locals of one trade in a geographical area. There were glass workers' trade districts, and districts of miners, shoemakers, printers, government employees, leather workers, and railroad men. Some of the trade districts were national in scope, or professed to be. At the top was the Grand Assembly with its general executive board. This was dominated by the mixed locals and the district assemblies.

This cumbersome, somewhat conflicting set-up, bears no similarity to the industry-wide unions which have been created by the current movement for industrial unionism. Structurally, the Knights' form of organization was closer to that of its successor, the American Federation of Labor, than to the Committee for Industrial Organization. The Knights had mixed locals, and the Federation had their equivalent in the federal labor union; the mixed districts of the Knights were similar to the city and state federations of the A.F. of L.; the Knights had their trade assemblies, and the Federation its national and international trade unions. The difference was in the domination of the Knights by the mixed and trade assemblies, and in the rule of the Federation by the trade unions. Basically, the difference was that the Knights, suffering from a confused leadership and burdened further by misapplied shibboleths of education, politics, and coöperation, tried to organize all workers; the Federation decided to take the easier course and strike out for a selected group of craftsmen, the "aristocrats of labor." As part of its revulsion against the Knights, it eschewed politics, coöperation, and other "excess baggage."

II

Samuel Gompers, resentful of the Knights' interference with his plans for an exclusive, "responsible" craft union of skilled cigarmakers (although a majority of the cigarmakers, if one counted the unskilled home-workers, were opposed to him), Adolph Strasser, another cigarmaker, whom Gompers termed his Bismarck and who called the home-workers "tenement-house scum," and P. J. McGuire, carpenter, better equipped mentally but less determined a politician than Gompers, were the spearheads of the dual movement which set itself up against the Knights. Had the Knights possessed some real leaders instead of a collection of floundering windbags, pulled here and there by scheming local labor politicians and doctrinaires, some compromise might have been worked out and the interests of the craftsmen fused with the high ideal of the Knights.

But this was not in the cards, and on May 18, 1886, craft-union leaders among the steel workers, tailors, carpenters, printers, furniture and cigarmakers, met in a war council in Philadelphia. Gompers was proud of this group: "men of good presence and exceptional ability . . . practically every man wore a silk hat and a Prince Albert coat. . . . Each was a dignified and self-respecting journeyman" (an aspersion on the rag, tag, and bob-tail he saw in most of the Knights) "yet we were all poor." The frock-coated labor leaders drew up a "treaty of peace'" which they presented to the Knights. The proposed treaty was in reality an ultimatum calling on the Knights to surrender. Briefly, the "treaty" demanded that the Knights should not initiate any new members of assemblies in industries where a national or international union existed, without first obtaining the consent of such unions. The Knights were to bar all members expelled by the craft unions; they were to revoke the charters of assemblies in trades where national unions existed; organizers were to be forbidden to "tamper with the growth" of the trade unions, and no union labels were to be issued in competition with the existing or future labels of a national trade union.

The Knights scornfully rejected the proposed "treaty," and at Columbus, on December 8th, the American Federation of Labor was born. Rejecting the completely theoretical "centralized control" of the Knights, the Federation stressed autonomy of its affiliates. This was of a piece with the sectarian craft exclusiveness of the trade unions. Even so it was not exclusive enough for the railroad brotherhoods, who have to this date remained aloof from the Federation.

Jurisdictional rights and grants became the corner stone of the Federation and its units. Socialism and other forms of political action—even to favoring shorter hours by legislation—were made taboo. At the top there was created an executive council whose duty was to watch over legislation, extend aid in organizing the unorganized, carry on proper boycotts and raise finances for the prosecution of strikes.

These limited constitutional rights which Gompers inherited when he became president of the Federation did not prevent him from building a strong personal machine. Butressed in office by the support of the crafts and their jurisdictional rights, for which he waged ceaseless war, Gompers was permitted to build a machine of organizers who served also as political fence-builders, discipliners, informers, and errand boys. Thus fortified within the Federation, Gompers sought to cultivate public esteem and employer friendliness by an alliance with the National Civic Federation. This historic puller-of-fangs of American labor was the brain child of Ralph M. Easley. Mark Hanna gave his blessing, J. P. Morgan and August Belmont put up the cash, and Easley set out to bring together for public discussion and secret co-operation the "reasonable" men among the labor leaders and the capitalists. Gompers swallowed the bait and remained an official of the Federation until his death.

III

A number of basic industrial conflicts soon tested the efficiency of the Federation policy of drawing the craftsmen apart from their less-skilled brothers. First came the Homestead lockout of 1892, which dealt the Federation's Amalgamated Association of Iron, Steel and Tin Workers the first of its blows. The Amalgamated was in its day the strongest of the craft unions, yet its membership was but 24,000 of a possible 100,000. Its rollers and heaters were an aristocracy which felt it had won hereditary and permanent advantages. The skilled steel workers of the 'eighties would come in top hats and Prince Alberts to collect their wage and from it distribute a share to the gang of laborers who worked under them. Laborers could join certain subordinate lodges, but few accepted this left-handed invitation. With the blindness that marked the entire with-

[31]

drawal of craft unions from the rest of the working class, the members of the Amalgamated disregarded the changing techniques of the industry which was making skilled labor of diminished importance, or the concentration of ownership of their industry into ever fewer hands which were soon to set up a united front of owners against the divided house of steel labor.

Few of the hundreds of "bohunks" which Andrew Carnegie, in a mixture of little altruism and much desire for profit, employed at Homestead were members of the Amalgamated. Only 800 of the 2,000 eligible workers had been attracted to the union in 1892. Most of them were English-speaking rollers, heaters, and nailers. They were imbued with the idea that with their skill withdrawn, the mills could not operate. The benevolent Carnegie had gone to England for the grouse season and to avoid implication in the job of demolishing the union which he had assigned to Henry Clay Frick, the "Coke King" who had but recently smashed a coal-miners' strike. The battle lines were drawn: on the one side a new Goliath of capitalism, the Carnegie Steel Company, Ltd.; on the other, the Amalgamated Association with its handful of skilled steel workers.

The Homestead mill management told the union in February, 1892, that it would have to take a cut in wages. What was really intended was that no new contract should be signed. Negotiations dragged, and in May the company said that on June 24th the union could take the new scale or leave it, and that after that date each worker would be dealt with individually. Meanwhile, the Homestead mill was turned into a fortress. Amalgamated men, angered, burned Frick in effigy and turned a stream of water on men sent to extinguish the fire. The entire working force was locked out of the plant. The skilled men now called upon the Hunkies and Bohunks for help, and together the 800 skilled union men and nearly 2,000 others held a meeting at which pledges of solidarity were asked and given. The company's answer came on July 6th when several barge-loads of Pinkerton men came down the river from Pittsburgh. For thirteen hours the Pinkerton men and the workers exchanged fire. Seven steel workers and three Pinkerton men were killed. The barges were burned, the Pinkertons captured and deported. Pennsylvania national guardsmen appeared on the scene. Soon two steam-boats full of "black sheep" entered the Homestead mill under protection of the militia.

The lockout turned into a losing strike. There were indictments of strikers and arrests by the score. The public sympathy aroused by Frick's and Carnegie's use of the armed Pinkerton agents proved to be of short duration. The *New York Daily Tribune* declared that the head rollers on strike were really sub-contractors, that some of them made as much as $13,000 a year, and that they employed less skilled men. In August the semi-skilled men and day laborers needed additional argument to keep them from returning to work. By October 13th some 2,000 strike-breakers had been introduced into Fort Frick. A month later the laborers decided the strike was lost. Within a few days the Amalgamated men who had remained in Homestead voted 101 to 91 to give up the fight, and the American Federation of Labor had sustained the most disastrous defeat in its history.

The rout of the A.F. of L. in steel was completed in 1901, under circumstances that cast a great shadow over the Federation. The membership of the Amalgamated in 1901 was down to less than 14,000. President T. J. Schaefer had come to the realization that something would have to be done at once if his organization were not to be irretrievably lost and the Federation barred forever from the most important industry in the nation. The fear was given solid basis when in February of 1901 the United States Steel Corporation completed its merger of Carnegie steel and ten other companies, appearing before an amazed world as the first billion-dollar corporation. Schaefer and the Amalgamated resolved that a strike in one plant of the merged corporation would have to be the signal for cessation of work in all of its subsidiaries. He presented demands to two subsidiaries, American Sheet Steel and American Steel Hoop, insisting on contracts for all their mills. He was turned down, and 38,000 workers of both companies answered a strike call. A week later a deadlock with the American Tin Plate brought out 8,000 more mill hands, skilled and unskilled. J. P. Morgan, Judge Elbert H. Gary, and Charles M. Schwab, acting for the Corporation,

[33]

proposed settlement in some of the mills of the three companies. The Amalgamated rejected the offer and proposed instead that contracts be signed in some mills, that union wages be paid in all, and that no restrictions be placed on its right to approach workers in those mills not under contract. The Corporation terminated negotiations.

Desperately, Schaefer urged Gompers to call all the unions of the Federation into emergency conference. To this Gompers said "no," and the Amalgamated thereupon decided to act for itself. A strike against all the mills of the Corporation was ordered for August 10th. Some quit in plants where the Amalgamated had contracts with the managements, which made Gompers extremely angry and served as a partial alibi for his failure to muster the Federation's full strength for the crucial contest. The hands of Ralph Easley and the National Civic Federation were already at work before the contracts had been broken, however, and these dexterous hands, it developed, played a part in depriving the steel strikers of the A.F. of L. support they should have had.

Henry White, a discredited former official of the United Garment Workers, wrote to Gompers that if the steel union would drop its demand for recognition (which was the basic point at issue), the strike could very likely be settled. White said that Easley had been in touch with influential heads of the Corporation. A conference between Gompers, John Mitchell, the leader of the United Mine Workers, Schwab, Gary, and officers of the Amalgamated was arranged. The upshot of the matter was that Gompers traded Schaefer's hope to unionize steel for a promise that Schwab and other steel magnates would lend their support to an eight-hour bill then pending in Congress. (Almost twenty years later, steel was still operating on a twelve-hour day.) The settlement of 1901 sealed the doom of the American Federation of Labor in steel. The American Tin Plate Company received the right to fire union men. A most humiliating clause provided that "non-union mills shall be represented as such, no attempts made to organize, no charters granted." Michael F. Tighe, then a vice-president of the Amalgamated, later its president, said that the Amalgamated from 1901 on followed a policy of "giving way to every request made by the subsidiary companies of U. S. Steel when they insisted on it."

Within the ranks of the Federation, the fiasco brewed bad medicine that for a time poisoned the whole body of organized labor. Schaefer launched charges that Gompers and Mitchell had failed to give proper support to the strikers. Mitchell, he said, had volunteered to enter the situation as an aide, but had remained to engineer a disastrous settlement. Mitchell denied he had ever given more than moral support, and Gompers responded with recrimination. Mitchell and Easley gave him a statement saying that Schaefer, while in Schwab's office by himself, had copied a letter from the steel master's desk. The president of the A.F. of L. thought so little of the effect of such a charge on the prestige of the labor movement that he aired it at a Federation convention. Gompers offered to prove his innocence before a court set up by the Federation, insisted on a trial, and was acquitted of any wrong-doing. Nevertheless, he was undoubtedly guilty of too great faith in the disinterestedness of Easley. That he was also taken in by the professed friendship of J. P. Morgan at the time was indicated by publication (in 1910) of a U. S. Steel board of directors' decision. This showed that while the Corporation wished in 1901 temporarily to stave off a finish fight with unionism, it had no intention of permitting the Amalgamated to make any advances. The board had decided: "We are unalterably opposed to any extension of union labor, and advise subsidiaries to take firm positions when these questions come up and say that they are not going to recognize it, that is, any extension of unions in mills where they do not now exist."

Wherever the responsibility lay, the American Federation of Labor was defeated by the dominant industry in the nation. Steel proceeded to set a pattern for all of heavy industry. It became an industrial oligarchy which created closed towns in place of closed shops, towns where free speech and assemblage were unknown, where men toiled at heavy labor in twelve-hour shifts and every fortnight for twenty-four continuous hours. Work was seasonable and wages miserable; and all around the smoking stacks of the steel industry's mills grew captive towns and cities. Soot-blackened frames housed workers whose poverty and fear belied every promise of a free America.

[35]

IV

There have been notable attempts to overcome the craft exclusiveness and timidity which Gompers and the Federation fastened on organized labor. The first and most far-reaching of these, before the advent of the Committee for Industrial Organization, came in the Pullman strike of 1894. Gompers has written that he could never find it within him to forgive Eugene V. Debs. The reason for this self-righteous superiority—or disguised inferiority—had to do with the American Railway Union and the Pullman strike. Cartoonists and editorial writers of the day called it "The Debs Rebellion."

The idealism of Debs and the political sagacity of Gompers fused in one man, or one movement, would have made the story of American labor a vastly different one. Debs came out of Terre Haute, a lanky, good-looking young man, with a style of oratory that gave hope and inspiration to the common man. His heart matched his voice and he was all sincerity in his burning devotion to the working people. Position and salary were no conditioning forces for him. In 1880 he took hold of the Brotherhood of Railway Firemen, a broken society, became its secretary-treasurer, and rebuilt it. Disillusionment in the railroad brotherhoods' super-exclusiveness brought a change in his ideas and in 1893 he quit his by now well-paying job to organize the American Railway Union, an industrial organization taking in all types of railroad workers on the trains and in the repair yards. Debs was by far the most popular labor leader of his day, which, perhaps, also helps to explain Gompers' stony heart. Members flocked into his organization, which competed successfully with the other popular movements of the day, Coxey's army and the People's Party. In April of 1894 the workers on James J. Hill's Great Northern walked out on strike, and sent for Debs to lead them to victory. Debs took a most inauspicious walkout and won many concessions. The rush into the American Railway Union was greater than ever.

George M. Pullman had established a model town in Illinois, and had modestly named it for himself. Those parts of Pullman visible to the casual visitor were pretty to behold—neat homes, churches, stores, school, and library. Having created such idyllic surroundings, Pullman was shocked beyond belief when the workers in 1893 objected to more than a 20-per-cent cut in wages. He became really mad when the workers engaged in making and repairing Pullman cars began to join the A.R.U. The company discharged some union members who requested restoration of the pay cut, and turned down a plea for arbitration. A convention of the American Railway Union decided that on June 26th its members would refuse to work on trains to which Pullmans were attached.

The railroads had watched the growth of the A.R.U. with misgivings and made the battle of the Pullman company their own. The strike spread through several states, and was a complete success in Chicago, greatest of all rail centers. The General Managers' Association, representing twenty-four railroads, hired an army of several thousand nondescripts and thugs and had them sworn in as Federal marshals. Some appeared at Blue Island, Illinois, and brought about violence which Richard B. Olney, Attorney General under President Cleveland, welcomed as an opportunity to use the Federal courts and troops to break the strike. Workers and military met in battle on July 7th and seven persons were killed. Debs was arrested for obstructing the mails; Federal indictments jailed seventy-one strike leaders.

Gompers, as we know, was opposed to the American Railway Union. He did not like the idea of the railroad brotherhoods staying aloof from the A.F. of L.; on the other hand, he disliked even more Debs' attempt to organize the railmen into an industrial union. He denounced the injunction and the use of Federal troops, but he resisted many urgent calls by strike leaders to come to Chicago and give some practical help. He betook himself to the city on July 12th, when the strike had been virtually broken. Debs told him the strike was lost and urged him to go to the General Managers' Association and seek a promise that the strikers would be rehired if the walkout was terminated. He felt his own plea would be worthless. Gompers later stated that Debs had asked him to call a general strike. We have it on the word of Dr. Norman H. Ware, painstaking student of American labor, that Gompers' explanation,

[37]

"was pure invention on his part. He had squirmed out of the simple task Debs asked him to perform and later gave his own version, which has been generally accepted."

While Debs was trying to reform the American labor movement by a practical demonstration of solidarity, the A.F. of L., and Gompers in particular, had another opponent. This was Daniel De Leon, one-time lecturer on international relations at Columbia and all-time believer in the single righteousness of Daniel De Leon. Lenin gave him posthumous honors as a giant of Marxism, but American workers, Socialist and non-Socialist, found him no asset. He was a most vituperative professor. Gompers, to him was a "labor faker" and a "leech," to which Gompers retorted "mountebank" and "professor without a professorship." Having created such an atmosphere of good will, De Leon, in 1895 called upon the American unions to bolt the A.F. of L. and join his Socialist Trades and Labor Alliance. De Leon believed passionately in industrial unionism. He envisioned and created, in insignificant miniature, a movement in which a federation of industrial unions was tied to the will and needs of a political party. Both were to work for the overthrow of capitalism.

The party, the Socialist Labor Party, never amounted to much and its Socialist Trades and Labor Alliance to less. A few thousand workers joined. De Leon soon split his followers and then turned to the task of purifying his own faction. In the end his party was cleansed of all wrong-thinkers and he was left alone. The Socialist Trades and Labor Alliance was dead. Even after De Leon had become only a bad dream of a bygone day, Gompers found him useful to ward off more intelligent attacks of trade unionists who believed in industrial unionism. To this day, Frey still draws upon the memory of De Leon and his travesty on industrial unionism to instill fear of change in the policies of the A.F. of L.

The Industrial Workers of the World brewed a more potent opposition to the Federation. Though the I.W.W. program of revolutionary Socialism, later syndicalism, militated against its successful advocacy of industrial unionism, the I.W.W. nevertheless did point to the serious shortcomings of the A.F. of L. Dissatisfied locals of

Federation unions, including miners, brewers, longshoremen, machinists, printers, hotel and restaurant workers, joined with the Socialist Party, the militant Western Federation of Miners, the American Labor Union (inheritor of the American Railway Union's remains) and De Leon in Chicago in 1905 to form the new opposition to the A.F. of L. (De Leon had fourteen delegates to speak for his 103 members, while the Western Federation of Miners were satisfied with a delegation of five for their 5,400 unionists.) The I.W.W. stressed the revolutionary attainment of Socialism through industrial unions. Later it split several ways. Socialists left when they would not accept its growing disbelief in political action. De Leon went his own way when he found he could not run the show. Meanwhile, the I.W.W. and its Western Federation of Miners engaged in bloody struggles in the mountain states of the West. By 1908, the I.W.W. had taken on new character. It attracted the casual workers, the "bindle stiffs" who worked the harvests and felled the trees of the northwest forests, dock workers and seamen. This was the day of the "wobblies." They gloried in their defiant parody "Halleluja, I'm a Bum," and caused the respectable craftsman of the A.F. of L. to draw away in stiff dignity. Nevertheless, many were the gallant free-speech and labor fights the "wobblies" staged. Persecution in one town would bring a concentration of foot-loose "wobs" filling jails and demonstrating stridently. In 1912 and 1913, the I.W.W. was led by William D. Haywood, Arturo Giovanitti, agitator and poet, and Elizabeth Gurley Flynn, as gentle-hearted a woman as ever preached war against an oppressing class. They stirred the foreign-born and native textile mill hands as no flannel-mouthed A.F. of L. organizers had ever done. Strikes were launched in Lawrence and in Paterson, bringing wage increases to men and women who sorely needed them. But the I.W.W. was much better at stirring things up than at organizing unions, and by the time the World War rolled around, the movement was on the downgrade. It played a fitting finale to its militancy when it opposed the participation of the United States in the war and paid the price for it in jail sentences, terror, ostracism, and eventually destruction.

[39]

V

The year 1912, when the Federation started on its greatest period of growth, is a convenient point from which to look back at what had happened inside the Federation and its craft unions since they had cut away from the Knights of Labor in 1886. The formative years brought no striking advances. By 1900, only 548,321 workers had been attracted. Meanwhile, the failure of the "Debs rebellion" and the bitter tirades of De Leon confirmed the Federation in its mold of craft unionism and economic "voluntarism." Gompers could talk of only one great achievement: that the depression of 1893 had not destroyed the labor movement, as previous depressions had done. In 1898 the fortunes of the Federation began to improve. A strike of soft-coal miners was successful that year, and the typographical union won a national agreement by which working hours were gradually to be reduced from ten to nine a day. The prosperity of the Spanish War years gave the building trades courage to fight, and they won many strikes. The union label was pushed as a religion. A group of vigorous young leaders, Gompers, McGuire, James Duncan, James O'Connell of the machinists, Frank Morrison of the printers, John Mitchell of the miners, and Andrew Furuseth, Norse leader of the seamen, worked tirelessly and began to win results. The membership by 1904 was raised to 1,676,000, and the number of affiliated international unions (each with a "jurisdiction" duly accorded) to 114. The great anthracite-coal strike of 1902 and its comparative gains compensated somewhat for the defeat in steel in 1901. Railroad maintenance workers began to join the Federation. The bulk of the membership came from railroaders, building tradesmen, and the miners, who had an industrial union too large for the craft unions to attack.

The problems of craft jurisdiction were already troublesome in this period, so casually had the executive council been handing out charters and demarking craft spheres of influence. In 1900, the historic Scranton Declaration was adopted. It was called a "compromise" and was to settle the problem of craft and industrial unionism into eternity. The declaration ascribed the "magnificent growth" of the Federation to craft lines and urged that the line be hewed to "as the recent great changes in the methods of production make practicable." A proposal to ally the crafts of a given industry in "departments" was approved, but the jurisdictions parceled out in past conventions were to remain intact. The declaration changed nothing except to lead to the formation of superficial structures, the Building Trades, the Metal Trades, Mining, and the Railway Employees departments. The Building Trades Department was rendered innocuous by the defiance of the large unions. The Metal Trades department and Mining Departments lingered on as ineffective frameworks. Only the Railway Employees Department emerged into something substantial: a "federation" system through which the already well-established unions banded together for joint collective bargaining.

Meanwhile, a new giant industry—automobiles—had risen in the country. The Federation never gained the smallest toehold in it. The craft unions refused to waive their jurisdictions, and on the other hand did nothing to organize these men themselves. Back in 1891 the Federation granted a somewhat vague charter to the International Union of Carriage and Wagon Workers. The union considered itself an industrial union. The manufacture of automobiles was still in the experimental stage. In 1900 there were 74,000 workers engaged in making carriages, coaches, and wagons, and 2,241 on the new-fangled horseless carriages. By 1909 the number of auto workers had increased to 76,000. The Federation had no auto union of any kind, officially, until 1913, when the Carriage and Wagon Workers' Union took it upon itself to add "automobiles" to its name. Craft union troubles early beset the union. It complained to the A.F. of L. in 1902 that the blacksmiths and painters were invading their industry. Each of the three following years, the carriage workers' union made new complaints against the painters. In 1908, it complained against the upholsterers' union grabbing some of its members. Three years later, the blacksmiths' union took the offensive and demanded that the carriage workers' union turn over all blacksmiths. The clashing unions got together in 1912 in a conference out of which emerged a proposed peace agreement. The carriage workers' union was told to go ahead and organize the auto factories "without interference from the craft unions." How-

[41]

ever, it was to "concede the right of the craft unionists (in the auto industry) to remain within their respective organizations if they so preferred." The painters' union refused to go along, but graciously agreed they would do nothing to "impede the efforts of the carriage workers to organize the trade."

A year later, the blacksmith's union was again dissatisfied and charged that the carriage workers' union was not honoring the agreement. Thereupon the 1913 convention of the Federation— by this time some workers were calling it "The American Separation of Labor"—ordered the struggling union in the automobile industry to surrender to the respective craft unions all blacksmiths, sheet-metal workers, metal-polishers, painters, pattern-makers, machinists, carpenters, electrical workers, and upholsterers. Those of the 4,000 members who remained might stay in the carriage workers' union. To emphasize its edict, the Federation instructed the union to drop the word "automobile" from its title and to cease taking in workers "properly coming under the jurisdictions of affiliated organizations." It was of no account that these jurisdictions had been handed out before there ever was any automobile industry. The decision represents the quintessence of the craft union's view of their "proprietary rights." On another occasion, Green called it their "vested interests." The carriage workers' union refused to change its name, and its membership voted 4,000 to 6 to inform the A.F. of L. of that decision. The Federation, in 1917, suspended the stubborn organization and a year later expelled it. The union decided to go it alone. In 1926 it had 3,000 members, who by 1929 had dwindled to 1,500 in an industry of half a million. At that it was doing better than the Federation.

The failure to get started in automobiles, the rout in steel and a bitter period of employer resistance, complicated by a serious panic and the attacks of the I.W.W., cut the membership of the Federation down to 1,482,870 in 1909. By 1912, partly because of the emergence of unions in the needle trades, it rose to 1,770,145. The years that followed to 1920 found American industry thriving, partly on Europe's travail and, starting in 1917, through our own entrance into the World War. Ships, food, munitions, clothing, machinery, coal, and lumber were needed in great quantities and for immediate, profitable delivery. Prices rose, as did wages. The war against American labor suddenly ceased. The workers were needed to prosecute the war. Gompers, abetted by Easley and chaperoned by Frey, became among the most ardent of the war-time patriots. Labor was taken into "partnership" and its membership boomed: 2,072,-702 in 1916; 2,726,478 in 1918; and 4,078,740 in 1920.

Gompers, to whom all doors of social conviviality had opened while he was engaged in his countless recruiting speeches, was invited, after the Armistice, to attend a Lafayette birthday dinner in Washington. General John J. Pershing was also an honored guest. The Old Man of Labor spoke with enthusiasm, but modestly, of the part his workers had played in the war. He did not say that labor had won the battle. An observer reported: "When General Pershing arose to speak . . . rage fairly consumed him, his words fell burning and blistering . . . on the assumption that Gompers had laid a claim to victory. . . . Pershing denied that organized labor had been loyal to the country. . . . Vituperative, vitriolic, he poured upon the head of the old man a torrent of passionate contradiction which fairly swept the audience off their feet." The Grand Old Man sat humbled before an audience that was "tense and antagonistic."

Pershing's tirade was the handwriting on the wall. American labor was in for deflation, in morale as well as economically. It met the first attacks on its positions with militancy, even taking the aggressive at times. The men's clothing workers demanded a forty-four-hour week and won it after a thirteen weeks' strike. Longshoremen and others on the New York waterfront struck and obtained a ten-hour day. Lawrence textile-mill hands walked out. Seattle labor staged a general strike in support of its shipyard workers. New England telephone girls answered no calls in twenty-one cities and towns. The actors took to the streets, picketed, danced, and sang for their new union. Unionism spread to policemen, and in Boston officers of the law staged an ill-fated strike that propelled Coolidge into the White House. The insurgency extended even against union officials. New York printers and longshoremen, and railroad switchmen the nation over, quit work despite their leaders' opposition. Miners joined the strikers' procession and registered substantial gains. American labor was riding high, taking literally the promise of industrial democracy which was to have been part of the reward of winning the World War.

But the greatest battle was lost and was to spread its virus of despair through the entire movement. Again it was the steel industry which stopped labor in its tracks, and again it was divisive craft unionism which played into the hands of the steel masters.

The Amalgamated Association had kept its promise of 1901 to make no organizing effort in the mills of U.S. Steel. It had 8,000 members in 1918. The strike which came in 1919 was not the doing of the Amalgamated or its president, Michael F. Tighe. Pressure came from a group of Chicago unionists, John Fitzpatrick, Edward Nockels, and their ace organizer, William Z. Foster, then in an interlude between syndicalism and Communism. They urged the hesitant Federation convention of 1918 to embark on a steel campaign. The craft unions hesitated, but promises of strict jurisdictional division and of dues from half a million new members won them. With great reluctance, Gompers became chairman of an organizing committee composed of representatives of twenty-four unions which claimed jurisdictions over steel workers. These included the unions of boilermakers, machinists, blacksmiths, switchmen, firemen, sheet-metal workers, carpenters, electricians. Foster was chosen director of the drive. The craft unions turned down his proposal for cheap dues, insisting on a $3 initiation fee. The bricklayers would not take less than $7.50, and the patternmakers compromised at $5. Foster urged a campaign to cover all steel centers simultaneously and proposed an initial fund of $50,000 to organize 500,000 men. The unions told him to start on a small scale and voted $100 each, or a total of $2,400. The treasury of any one of a number of the unions could have easily supplied $50,000.

Nevertheless, the steel workers flocked into the unions. U.S. Steel was led, on October 1, 1918, to announce a "basic" eight-hour day, actually a twelve-hour day with a small bonus for overtime. The concession failed to halt the tidal wave which swept men into the unions in the Calumet region, South Chicago, Gary, Indiana Harbor, and Joliet. Less, but substantial, progress was made in the Pittsburgh-Youngstown area. The workers rallied to eloquent appeals for a united drive, and were then divided up among twenty-four craft unions. Early in 1919 hundreds of union men were fired. It became evident that the period of organizing was over and a strike close at hand. At this point, Tighe shattered the ranks by offering Judge Gary a separate peace with the Amalgamated. Tighe urged the steel master that jointly, as patriotic citizens, they "use every effort to stem the tide of unrest, if possible." To which Gary replied: "As you know, we do not confer, negotiate with, or combat unions as such. . . . In our own way, and in accordance with our best judgment, we are rendering efficient patriotic service in the direction indicated by you." Gompers then asked Gary for a conference. He received no reply. The steel workers enrolled by the drive had reached 200,000. A strike was voted. The committee asked Gary for a conference. He refused to answer. A delegation called on him in New York but he would not see them. President Wilson asked Bernard Baruch to seek a joint meeting. Baruch failed. Now Gompers grew faint of heart. He wanted the strike put off. President Wilson appealed to both sides to suspend hostilities until the convening of an industrial congress he had called for October 6th. Gompers seized on the plea and wired virtual instructions that the strike was not to take place, thus placing the strike, when it did come, under the cloud of having had the disapproval even of its own sponsors.

The strike could not be halted, however, and started September 22nd, when 343,100 workers quit the mills. By October 1st the number had increased to 365,000. The strikers in Pennsylvania, the heart of the battle, were subjected to a campaign of terror and suppression. Meetings were broken up, union halls smashed. Strike-breakers and "guards" recruited from vicious elements poured into the towns. The Pennsylvania state police showed they deserved the title, "Pennsylvania's Cossacks." The press of the steel area dropped all pretense at impartiality and alternated between banner lines heralding "back to work" movements and the alleged revolutionary intent of the strike's leaders. It was the period of A. Mitchel Palmer's "white terror" and, some reporters possibly believed the stories they wrote about a revolution-in-the-making in Pittsburgh, Homestead, and Braddock. William Hard, then a liberal journalist, totaled the figures in the "back to work" stories and found that 4,800,000 had reëntered mills where only half a million had worked before.

The strike was lost by January, 1920. The craft unions lost interest. Friends had given $418,000—almost half of it from non-A.F. of L. sources—to succor the strikers, but they could not hold out. Eighteen had given their lives. On January 8th the strike committee admitted defeat. Foster and Jay G. Brown, his successor as secretary of the committee, went to the Amalgamated convention in Scranton to report on the battle, but they were refused admittance, so eager were Tighe and the other union elders to wash their hands of the entire affair. The union was anxious to go back to its safe 8,000 members and its few, precious contracts in small shops. The new locals of steel workers disappeared, their leaders blacklisted and deserted. Meanwhile the craft unions had profited financially. By the end of the strike, Foster had begged a total of $101,047 from them—in return for $500,000 in dues and initiation fees which he had turned over. The Amalgamated did most handsomely by itself. It gave the organizing committee $11,811.81, and received from it $150,000 in initiation fees. Foster estimates that it received twice as much directly from steel workers. These "dividends" of the strike, Tighe invested in a handsome Pittsburgh headquarters.

In 1921, there were demands for an effort to revive the drive. The A.F. of L., feeling the issue would stay buried if turned over to Tighe, gave the Amalgamated exclusive jurisdiction over the steel industry. It thus washed its hands of the problem. The twenty-four internationals and their leaders who had "coöperated" in the strike were also "cured." They wanted no more visions of hundreds of thousands of mill laborers, "hunkies" and "foreigners," eagerly offering themselves as recruits for unionism and demanding leadership.

VI

Judge Gary represented the "public" at President Wilson's industrial congress, and from then on organized labor became something apart from respectable patriotic Americans. To stigmatize the undesirability of unionism, the open shop was renamed the "American Plan" and committees of employers, bankers, and lawyers preached the "new" gospel in every state and city. Unions, smiled on during the war, were smashed. The International Seamen's Union was goaded by wage cuts into a strike and came out of it without its 100,000 members. Furuseth, grown a lonely, morose, and cantankerous leader, in addition to his craft pride mistrusted all landsmen, and would brook no effort at a defensive alliance with the longshoremen. The packing-house workers' new unions were also smashed in the process of restoring "normalcy." The building trades' craft unions were attacked, and they, too, took wage cuts. Coal felt the competition of electric power and cutthroat fighting within its own ranks, and the miners' union sank lower and lower. Factionalism prostrated the ladies garment workers' organization. Wage deflation forced 400,000 railway shopmen into a strike, and the railway unions lost 175,000 members. From 1920 to 1923 the Federation lost 1,052,000 members and remained with 2,926,468.

From 1923 to 1933 was the Federation's period of sterility. Goaded by its losses and even more by its left-wing critics, it made two gestures at recovery, one in autos and one in Southern textiles, a great wilderness of anti-unionism, low wages, stretch-out, long hours, and child labor. Both these "campaigns" were indicative of the Federation's new spirit of offering itself to employers as a bulwark against radicalism or as an "efficiency influence" in industry. Each was another exhibit of the aloofness of the craft unions, exhibits which gave rise to the belief that the Federation not only could not organize the unorganized, but that it did not want to.

Talk of an effort to unionize the automobile industry began to be heard in 1925. The industrial unionist views of the recently elected President Green raised hopes that some results might be attained. In 1926, talk reached the stage where it was proposed that there should be a moratorium, at least temporarily, on jurisdictional claims. Seventeen unions wanted to divide the auto workers among them, which was something of an improvement on the claims of twenty-four unions for the steel workers in 1919. Green proposed to the seventeen, in December of 1926, that they suspend their claims "at least in approaching the workers." He suggested that some of the manufacturers were in a "receptive" mood and might be led to consider "bargaining" if assured there would be no jurisdictional

[47]

squabbles. Most of the unions were unreceptive. A few weeks later, Green reported that General Motors Corporation would consider union coöperation in a few plants as an "experiment." There followed still another conference. Nine unions agreed to submit to the "experiment." There was more talk, and a plan was worked out whereby the auto workers would be enrolled in federal unions, directly affiliated to the Federation, and later parceled out to the crafts. During all this time there were many suggestions about seeing General Motors and Henry Ford, but the workers still remained to be consulted. Finally the campaign received a death blow. GM and Ford rejected all overtures, including inducements of union assistance as an instrument of efficiency.

The Southern workers were not the completely spiritless and resigned lot the craft leaders believed them to be. They had waged several struggles between 1925 and 1929 without A.F. of L. assistance, or much of it. Two thousand struck in 1929 at Elizabethton, Tennessee, led by a student of Brookwood Labor College which Matthew Woll was then putting on the Federation index as a radical institution. Communists went into Gastonia, North Carolina, and the response showed again that the mill hands were eager for unionism. At Marion, North Carolina, the "lint-heads" struck against a fifty-five-hour week. Sheriff's deputies killed five and wounded twenty-one workers in a battle. The executive council of the Federation began to ponder a "campaign," and in 1930, President Green betook himself to the South. There he made six addresses to business men, doing his best to sell the Federation as a conservative, anti-Communist and entirely reasonable organization. He returned to Washington and awaited the result, which was silence. The campaign was over.

By that time the depression had come and some union leaders of the old school were considering whether their positions were even "good jobs" any longer. The Federation was hopeless, defeated. In 1933, it reported a new drop in membership to 2,126,796.

3.

THE NRA—AN OPPORTUNITY LOST

I

WHEN Lewis threw himself into the fight for a resolution endorsing unemployment insurance at the Federation convention which met in Cincinnati in November, 1932, the long reign of unquestioned "voluntarism" was ended. During the post-war years, only a fringe of progressives and radicals had dared the futile gesture of challenging the intellectual leadership of Woll and Frey. None had risen to doubt the authority of the craft unionists.

Chagrined at inadequate government appropriations for relief of the jobless, the seniors of the executive council had been swayed early in 1932 to the point where they had suggested that the "principle" of systematic relief might lay within the province of the several states. When the Cincinnati convention opened, however, the subject was referred to the resolutions committee, of which Woll was chairman. The committee was prepared to recommend nonconcurrence. Lewis promptly warned that he would fight.

When the sessions of November 9th had ended, the corridors of the convention hotel held knots of unhappy old-timers, many of them wishing that "Old Sam" could have been with them again that day. Unemployment insurance under state auspices, with compulsory payments by employers and the state, had found sanction in the sacred halls of the Federation, last arena in modern America of Jeffersonian "voluntarism." Frey had remained resolute for the old faith, but Green and Woll had gone "radical." Green spoke for the proposal. Woll did not oppose it. Only five delegates out of three hundred raised their hands in opposition. Nevertheless, Louis Stark, the *New York Times* correspondent, later observed "unhappy" dele-

[49]

gates "who showed extreme concern" and expressed the opinion "that before long the Federation would possibly lean further toward social legislation and go on record for health and sickness insurance." The spirit of "voluntarism" had been twice outraged that day. With Lewis again forcing the issue, the delegates had been stampeded also for a campaign to seek a shorter working day by legislation! This, Stark wrote, was "especially regrettable to some of the older men" who saw a "complete break with the past."

If Lewis pushed the American labor movement a furlong at the 1932 convention, he shoved it ahead a mile with his next move. This came at a hearing before the Senate Committee on Finance on February 17, 1933. The committee had convened to hear various proponents of plans to end the depression. The suggestions which Lewis and Sidney Hillman set forth kicked labor's philosophy of "voluntarism" into the rubbish-bin and called for the widest government intercession in industrial matters the nation had yet seen. Eventually the Lewis program became embodied in the National Industrial Recovery Act.

Lewis had striven for years for national legislation which would substitute planned, controlled production for competition in the soft-coal industry. He had urged a moratorium on anti-trust laws and had advocated price and wage fixing as a method of aiding both owners and workers. His proposals were introduced in the Senate by Senator Thomas Watson in 1929 and 1930, but died in both sessions. They were revived in January, 1932, by Senator James J. Davis and Representative Clyde Kelly, both of Pennsylvania. The Davis-Kelly bill would have granted the producers new privileges in the direction of price-fixing. In exchange, the workers' right to organize and bargain collectively was to be written into law. Representative F. H. La Guardia had incorporated such a pious hope in an anti-injunction law which he fathered jointly with Senator George W. Norris. A similar declaration had become part of railroad labor legislation. The Davis-Kelly bill also provided that the federal government was to grant or withhold licenses to operate on the basis of fulfillment of the law, with its drastic labor provisions. This bill died, too.

Early in 1933 Lewis came to the conclusion "that instead of an-

[50]

other prolonged fight for special legislation for stabilization (of the soft-coal industry), the wiser and quicker course to pursue was to stimulate the existing tendencies towards general industrial stabilization, and to make a condition for their attainment the acceptance of labor's right to organize and bargain collectively through representatives of their own choosing." The "existing tendencies" were represented in some thirty recovery plans then before Congress. Reflecting the views of bankers and industrialists, these proposals aimed to arrest price deflation and restore a more or less orderly system of production by suspending the anti-trust laws and permitting manufacturers to get together, under government supervision, for stabilization of prices and production. This was what Lewis proposed to the Senate committee: that Congress declare a national emergency and call for a reorganization of industrial and financial activities; that an emergency board, composed of industry, labor, agriculture, and finance, acting under the President, be set up and given plenary powers; that the board be instructed to reduce the hours of labor to the point where the unemployed would be absorbed; that labor be accorded the right to organize and bargain collectively; that the board fix prices of commodities to assure a reasonable return to labor; and that the board further undertake fundamental economic planning, as Congress might decide was wise. Through various further conferences, the Lewis plan became the basis for the National Industrial Recovery Act. The labor proposals became the famous Section 7A and the less famous Section 7B of the act.

II

Despite the songs of joy, parades, and ballyhoo which greeted the NRA, Lewis was not one to deceive himself into the belief that he had made capital and labor lie down together. He knew there would be chiseling, not only on minor details of compliance, but on fundamentals. Section 7B imposed on the President the responsibility of encouraging collective bargaining and "mutual agreements" between workers and owners on "the maximum hours of labor, minimum rates of pay, and other conditions of employment." These agreements were to have become fixed parts of the NRA codes. But the code authorities, completely dominated by employers, assumed the function of fixing hours and wages, frequently—with the acquiescence of the federal government—without even consulting the employees. Section 7A suffered a similarly deadening, if less quiet, fate. The core of the NRA took on meaning only where labor assumed the task of enforcing it. Lewis, Hillman, and Dubinsky realized this would be the case. Immediately upon the enactment of the NRA, they set about rebuilding their unions until they were in a position to take full advantage of the novel legislation in which government, for the first time, gave lip service, at the least, to the principle of labor organization and collective bargaining. Within two months, from May 15th to July 15th, the United Mine Workers added 300,000 members to its ranks; the Ladies' Garment Union, more than 100,000, the Amalgamated Clothing Workers fully 50,000.

So swiftly had the drastic new policy been enacted, that the American Federation of Labor chieftains did not have time to question this intrusion of government on its hitherto isolated isle. The craft unionists still did not wish to organize the unorganized, but hundreds of thousands of workers clamored for admission to the unions. The Federation was led to institute a "campaign." It set up modest machinery which became the receiving end, rather than the initiator of the great impetus for unionism that swept through the mass production industries of the nation and reached down to the service trades.

"There was a virtual uprising of workers for union membership," the executive council reported to the convention of 1934. "Workers held mass meetings and sent word they wanted to be organized."

Between 60,000 and 70,000 joined unions in the Akron rubber plants and adjacent industries; almost 200 local unions with 100,000 members sprang up in autos; the membership of the Amalgamated Association of Iron, Steel and Tin Workers increased by 90,000; the metal miners climbed from less than 5,000 to 40,000; union recruits in aluminum totaled 15,000; the lumberjacks and sawmill workers of the Northwest came together, 90,000 strong, and organized 130 unions; in the cement industry, 20,000 workers joined; 385,000 workers in the South and North flocked to the standard of the textile union.

The groundswell turned Green into an enthusiast. He told the 1933 convention that he had nailed to the Federation's masthead the slogan, "Organize the Unorganized in the Mass Production Industries." The next objective of the Federation was to be a membership of 10,000,000, and after that 25,000,000, "which will bring the majority of Americans genuinely and actually within the trade-union family." Technical requirements of closing the membership reports a month before the October, 1933, convention did not afford an accurate picture of the Federation's gains, Green said. The membership then, he estimated, was almost 4,000,000 if one included the recent recruits.

It was neither a planned campaign nor a change of policy which brought about the great influx. Heads of the international unions convened in Washington early in June of 1933 and "authorized" a concerted drive for membership. A handful of special organizers, largely craft-union wheel-horses chosen for their regularity and infected with the years of mistrust of the unorganized, set to work independently of each other, and each in a score of industries at the same time. It was not until months had passed that it was thought advisable and possible to assign specific organizers to single large industries. But the machinery of organizing was brilliantly executed compared with the attack on the problem of organizational forms and structure. Here again the interests of the craft unions came to the fore. In the summer of 1933 Green had decided upon the strategy of organizing the new recruits into federal unions based on plant units. The federal unions had for years served to a great extent as a recruiting station for the craft unions. As in other years, those members of the federal unions which the craft unions cared to absorb were eventually to be divided among the respective holders of jurisdictions. The federal unions lent themselves to the execution of such a policy. Unlike the international and national unions, they had no autonomous charters. Their by-laws were written by the Federation; they could make no demands, call no strikes and reach no settlements without the approval of Federation organizers. Their charters could be revoked by the executive council. They offered the craft unionists an excellent stop-gap arrangement.

But by October of 1933, the craft unionists wanted the new federal unions dismantled without delay. At a convention of the Metal Trades Department, Frey joined with Arthur H. Wharton, jealous watchdog of the interests of his International Association of Machinists, to sponsor a bitter resolution, which was adopted, attacking the Federation for having chartered 584 federal unions. They insisted the new members "should have been placed in the proper existing organizations." The resolution declared that "this condition, if allowed to continue, will completely demoralize, if not actually destroy, the various international unions' charter rights." The delegates further, "vehemently as possible, protested the further continuance of this disregard of charter and jurisdictional rights." One of the delegates, sneering at the "low" dues asked of new members, called the organization drive "The Woolworth Plan." Green hastened to assure the metal trades convention that the Federation would "respect and observe" all jurisdictional rights.

Nevertheless, Frey presented the Metal Trades Department resolution to the October, 1933, convention of the Federation. From the other camp, Elizabeth Christman of the Women's Trade Union League offered a resolution looking toward industrial unionism for the newly organized workers. Before the issue was reached, a test vote came on ratifying an executive council decision which directed the industrial union of brewery workers to turn over its teamster members to Daniel Tobin's organization. This was approved, 13,877 to 5,859. The vote was accepted as an indication of the outcome of the Frey-Christman contest. Lewis thereupon agreed to refer the issue to a conference of Federation leaders to be convened subsequent to the convention.

Seventy-five national and international unions sent delegates to the special conference which met in Washington on January 24 and 25, 1934. A committee chaired by Woll, with Victor Olander of the International Seamen's Union as secretary, and Wharton and Tobin as members, submitted another of the many craft-industrial union compromises which have consistently failed to settle anything. The conference, on the report of the committee, stated that it was "without power and authority to alter or change the fundamental principles of trades autonomy upon which the American Federation of Labor was founded." Having thus sidestepped the problem for which it had been called together, the Federation leaders added that organization work was "imperative" and that the "paramount issue" was not the form of organization to be followed. They urged "organization in whatever form or method is best designed to rally the wage-earners to the cause of organized labor, bearing in mind that in the pursuit of organization the present structure, rights, and interests of affiliated national and international unions must be followed, observed, and safeguarded." Reference was made to the stratagem of the federal unions as evidence of the Federation's desire to meet the needs of the immediate situation. The executive council was given the "fullest possible latitude" in the granting of federal charters, with the understanding that the claims of the craft unions were eventually to be honored. Having thus again upheld the ideal of separatism, the declaration concluded by urging the workers "to get together, to organize."

Green carried the conference decision into action by instructing his organizers that all jurisdictional rights were to be rigorously respected and that the unorganized were to be given "special instructions and advice . . . regarding the jurisdiction of national and international unions."

III

Notwithstanding the watering down of the promises of the NRA and the A.F. of L.'s refusal to modernize its organizational set-up, 1933 and 1934 witnessed spectacular demonstrations of labor militancy. Fully 812,000 workers struck in 1933, as compared with 243,000 in 1932. The hosiery workers' union organized and called out 20,000 men and women in Pennsylvania; 50,000 silk workers struck to win higher wages than those fixed in the code; the Amalgamated Clothing Workers penetrated unorganized shirt factories. The United Mine Workers, for the first time, won agreements in 20 of 29 soft-coal mines owned by the steel corporations. New York dressmakers, with only 20,000 members in their union, called a strike and 60,000 responded. They returned to work victorious. Cloak and dressmakers followed suit, and before the end of the year the International Ladies Garment Workers' Union had organized and won better working conditions for 160,000 men and women. There were shoe strikes in Lynn; 5,000 workers quit at the Weirton Steel Company in West Virginia. Even autos felt the wave of militancy as the newly-organized Mechanics Educational Society called out tool and die makers in and near Detroit. All of these strikes, with the exception of that at Weirton, succeeded in translating some of the New Deal promise into reality.

The strike wave continued into 1934 and 1935. Toledo saw the bloody Electric Auto-Lite strike and, in 1935, the walkout of the Chevrolet workers which affected 30,000 General Motors employees. Striking Minneapolis truck-drivers waged street warfare against vigilantes, while the new-found solidarity of San Francisco water-front workers and seamen brought a general strike and eventually victory for the longshoremen. In New York City, hackmen stopped all cab service for days; hotel workers' picket lines harassed the diners at the Waldorf and other transient dwelling-places of the élite; humble elevator-operators and janitors turned skyscrapers and Park Avenue apartments into unheated monuments of stone. Alabama coal miners, Pennsylvania aluminum workers, New Jersey shipyard mechanics, caught the infection and took to picket lines for better pay, shorter hours, and union recognition. In the summer of 1934 came the uprising of the Southern lint-heads, the textile hands who marched from mill to mill calling men, women, and youths to the union banner and the strike. Streets of the model village of Kohler, Wisconsin, were stained with blood of strikers killed and wounded by the guns of deputies. Cigarmakers at Red Lion, Pennsylvania, also battled against guns for the twenty-seven cents an hour minimum promised them in an NRA code. Milwaukee street-car men and utility workers quit, and the entire city joined with them to bring victory. Six thousand Anaconda copper miners walked out in isolated Butte. Meek grocery clerks, cynical newspaper men, furriers, teamsters, shipping-clerks, lumberjacks, struck. Terre Haute, Indiana, had a general strike of two days' duration. Farm hands in the darkest South and in California left the fields to meet a terrorism equally vicious in enlightened California and benighted Arkansas. Fifteen strikers were slain in August, September, and October of 1933, but the violence did not stay the unrest. Guns of strike-breakers, police, and military killed forty more in 1934.

In the year and a half from the summer of 1933 to the winter of 1934 troops were called out in sixteen states.

Most of the strikes were led by rank-and-file leaders who had arisen to meet the need of the hour. Many of the walkouts were condemned by the Federation, which nevertheless offered no effective leadership of its own. The advance of the miners, the garment workers, the west coast maritime workers was most significant when compared with the débâcle of unionism in autos, steel, textile, rubber, and metal mining, where the Federation's influence prevailed.

IV

The automobile industry, with steel, was in 1933 the strongest barrier against the advance of trade unionism. General Motors, Ford, and Chrysler, dominating the industry, had kept trade unionism outside their gates by highly centralized ownership and direction, which contrasted with the separatism of the A.F. of L. crafts. Collective bargaining was short-circuited in General Motors and Chrysler through the medium of company unions. Ford's "service division," G.M.'s and Chrysler's spy and espionage forces, costing hundreds of thousands of dollars annually, kept the workers continuously in terror of discharge and blacklist. The speed of the belt lines and the conveyor system sapped them of their strength early in their manhood. Improvements in machinery increased the length of seasonal layoffs and created a reservoir of unemployed to fill the places of workers who "slowed down." In 1934, 45 per cent of the auto workers received less than $1,000 a year in wages.

The National Recovery Administration assigned the task of correcting this situation to the owners of the industry. The National Automobile Chamber of Commerce became the auto-code authority. All of the manufacturers belonged to this organization with the exception of Henry Ford, who refused throughout to have anything to do with the NRA. The code submitted by the manufacturers and signed by President Roosevelt called for a thirty-five-hour week, except during seasonal rushes, when forty-eight hours of operation was to be permitted. Wages were to range between forty-one and forty-three cents an hour. Labor's worst defeat in the code was in the labor-relations section, the "merit clause." The first version of the clause submitted by the industry promised to observe Section 7A and then proceeded to nullify it by declaring that the open-shop policies of the industry would continue. General Hugh S. Johnson, National Recovery Administrator, balked and declared, "there can't be any language that uses 'open shop' or 'closed shop' or any of that." The Code Authority took the hint and said the same thing without mentioning "open shop." The "merit clause," as finally signed by President Roosevelt on August 27, 1933, quoted Section 7A and then added: "Without in any way attempting to qualify or modify, by interpretation, the foregoing requirements of the NRA, employers in this industry may exercise their right to select, retain, or advance employees on the basis of individual merit, without regard to their membership or non-membership in any organization." The Labor Advisory Board of the NRA was led to urge approval of this clause on the condition that its qualifications on collective bargaining were not to be precedents for other codes. (Actually, almost ten other codes had already "interpreted" Section 7A nearer to the hearts of the employers.) Green and the new automobile unionists set up a great protest against the merit clause, arguing that the outright privilege of hiring and firing, without regard to seniority, was an instrument which would make possible the discharge of all active unionists and the consequent death of unionizing efforts. But the code prevailed. It was extended by President Roosevelt on December 18th, to run until September 4, 1934, without change. Discharge of unionists began in the fall of 1933. The hours limitation was also widely violated, the unionists complained. Over labor's bitter protests, the code was again extended on September 4, 1934, and once again on November 2, 1934. In an effort to meet some of the labor protests, the President in November ordered the research and planning division of the NRA to make a study of wages and unemployment in the industry.

The automobile code was getting to be the No. 1 scandal of the NRA as far as labor was concerned. Each time a protest had arisen against extension, the workers had been denied the hearing which, under the National Recovery Act, was to be accorded them before a code could be approved. The first labor protest had not brought the desired results; the second brought the appointment of a labor board headed by Leo Wolman; and the third brought the Presidential order for a survey. The code was to expire again on February 1, 1935, and this time labor swore it meant business. Nevertheless, it was again extended, although with some revisions. One amendment called for staggering the introduction of new auto models, thus lengthening the work season from five to eight months; a second change met the protests that the hours clause was being violated by providing for payment of overtime rates to 20 per cent of the workers for their labor in excess of forty-eight hours a week. The labor gains were offset by the President's action in making the by now hated Automobile Labor Board part of the code machinery. Labor had just denounced the board. Amid the protests of Green and the spokesmen of the auto workers, Donald Richberg, head of the National Economic Council, insisted that labor had been "consulted" before the code had been signed. Francis J. Dillon, then the A.F. of L. generalissimo in the auto industry, was so moved he talked of strikes. It devolved on Lewis to castigate Richberg in the most bitter terms heard in the many of the scathing NRA word battles.

The attitude of Donald Richberg and the President's willingness to devitalize Section 7A by the addition of the "merit clause" were only part of the difficulties in the path of the automobile workers. The other trouble was with the A.F. of L. Mr. Roosevelt is reported to have sighed frequently over the lack of acumen of William Green in the auto situation and his failure to back up his demands with a strongly entrenched, inclusive union of auto workers. After all, it was argued, it was not the President's job to organize labor.

By June, 1933, there was not a single large A.F. of L. union in autos, despite the eagerness of the workers for organization. Six thousand workers at the Briggs plant struck in January, forcing a shut-down at Ford's which depended on Briggs for its bodies. That month, 1,200 employees at the important Motor Products plant also organized and struck, without benefit of the Federation. In February, 3,000 Hudson body workers quit in support of a plea for a 20-per-cent wage rise. Still other groups beat the Federation to the draw when the NRA became law. The Mechanics Educational Society of America, the Associated Automobile Workers, the Automotive Industrial Workers Association, and the Auto Workers Union came to the front at once. The M.E.S.A. appealed to the skilled tool and die makers, enrolled 25,000 members in the summer of 1933 and won union conditions, including wage raises, for at least 9,000 of them by a spectacular strike in the fall. By that time the companies had begun to realize that unionism was to be a major problem. General Motors rushed through a series of company-union elections and announced that "collective bargaining" had become a completed fact. On August 27th the code with its virtual open-shop declaration was signed, with no popular movement of the auto workers to raise a protest strong enough to carry weight.

To the task of winning almost half a million workers and stemming the trend to independent unionism, the Federation assigned William Collins, its representative in New York State, and three others. Collins' attitude toward unorganized, unskilled workers was indicated by an experience of Norman Thomas, the Socialist leader. A group of Italian workers had come to Thomas, asking for guidance in forming a union. Thomas communicated with the A.F. of L., and shortly Bill Collins, heavy-set, flannel-mouthed organizer, appeared on the scene. Thomas and Collins spoke to the workers, and then the representative of labor turned to the Socialist. Said Collins: "My wife can always tell from the smell of my clothes what breed of foreigners I've been hanging out with." Collins took with him as an auto workers' organizer, Alexander Marks, an expert on small federal unions in New York City. The executive council of the Federation also generously donated the services of Francis J. Dillon, no less a regular than Collins and Marks. They set up shop in Detroit, Flint, and Pontiac. To their amazement, auto workers by the thousands joined the newly-created federal unions.

For months, from the summer of 1933 to March of 1934, the new unions of auto workers vainly tried to meet with company representatives. By March many leaders had been discharged under cover of the "merit clause." The entire movement was in danger of collapsing if it did not go forward. Fisher Body, Buick and Hudson workers were on the verge of a strike. They demanded reinstatement of their fired leaders, a 20-per-cent wage increase, a thirty-hour week, and union recognition. The federal government intervened; Collins agreed to refer the dispute to the recently appointed National Labor Board. A few days later Ford attempted to steal the unions' thunder by restoring a five-dollar-a-day minimum wage for 47,000 of his workers. The member companies of the National Automobile Chamber of Commerce increased wages by cutting the working week from forty to thirty-six hours without reducing the daily pay rate. These concessions failed to satisfy the auto unionists and they renewed their threat to strike unless discriminatory discharges ended, union leaders were rehired, and the union recognized.

Sixty union heads went to Washington on March 13th to charge wholesale violations of Section 7A in the auto plants. Again strikes threatened, but Collins prevailed. He won a postponement of five days while General Johnson went into session with the National Automobile Chamber of Commerce. In vain did Collins plead for the auto owners to at least "sit down" with him so that he might be able to face the heads of the federal unions who were waiting in Washington, impatient to return to the auto centers for a strike which, they felt, could alone bring the companies into line. The Automobile Chamber of Commerce withdrew to New York, General Johnson on their trail, and announced that "the industry does not intend to recognize the A.F. of L. as such" nor to enter into any contract with it. Meanwhile, auto workers assembled in mass meetings renewed their strike threats. Johnson having had no success with the manufacturers, the President, on March 20th, called both A.F. of L. and owners to the White House, urging Collins, in the meantime, to again put off striking. The magnates came, polite but firm in their refusal to alter their stand against dealing with the unions. Nor would they agree to employee polls on collective bargaining. The President then met with the auto workers' delegation. Outside the White House, General Johnson, having failed to budge the owners, was "putting the heat" on the workers. He called the discharge of 200 active union men "nothing at all," and said they should have taken their protests to the Code Authority. Collins again wired the auto centers cautioning them against striking.

On March 25th the White House announced a peace agreement. The settlement, the President said, was based on these principles: Employers to agree to bargain collectively with freely chosen representatives of groups of workers; no discrimination; "if there be more than one group, each bargaining committee shall have a total membership pro rata to the number of men each member represents"; NRA to set up a board to pass on alleged discriminations; "the government makes it clear that it favors no particular union or particular form of employee organization or representation." The proportional representation of company unions, independent unions, and other employee groups was a novel idea. It was completely at variance with successful union procedure in that it provided an arena in which workers of a given plant could be divided and set against each other. The President's refusal to endorse "any particular form of organization" gave the company unions a standing they had been denied under Section 7A. Nevertheless, the President was enthusiastic about the probable success of his peace agreement. He called it "one of the most encouraging incidents of the recovery program" and "the framework for a new structure of industrial relations." He felt he had "charted a new course in social engineering in the United States," and "set forth a basis on which, for the first time, in any large industry, a more comprehensive, a more adequate and more equitable system of industrial relations may be built than ever before."

Green and Collins concurred. The President of the A.F. of L. called it "a great step forward for the automobile workers. . . . For the first time in the history of the automobile industry the right to organize has been conceded and collective bargaining assured through representatives chosen by the employees." Green was particularly pleased with a substitute which had been evolved for the workers' demands for employee elections. The new board was to compare lists of union members with payrolls furnished by the companies, and thus determine the bargaining rights of the unions. This would save much time, said Green. Collins wired the auto union in Flint: "Tell the men to go to work. It's the biggest victory they have ever won." The New York *Times* correspondent thought differently. He wrote that "organized labor's drive for a greater equality of bargaining power with industry has been nullified." Alfred P. Sloan, president of General Motors, said, "All's well that ends well."

[62]

Within a month President Roosevelt's enthusiasm for the peace plan proved to be unfounded. The core of the plan lay in the work of the board, of which Wolman became chairman, Richard E. Byrd, the labor member, and Nicholas H. Kelley, the employer member. Wolman had come into the labor movement as the adviser of Sidney Hillman. He went out amid bitter accusations hurled at him by thousands of auto workers. The board had been appointed in the midst of the 1934 production season and the auto workers felt that they had to win redress of their grievances at once or an entire year would be lost. Strikes broke out at the Nash plants in Wisconsin, and once again at Motor Products in Detroit. The board tried settlements in both. The Nash workers rejected one Wolman proposal, and the leaders of the Motor Products walkout tore up the other. Mistrust of the board was soon succeeded by open opposition. The Flint unionists had sent forty-one complaints of discriminatory discharge to Wolman for investigation. He had forwarded them to General Motors, which rehired only eighteen men. The auto workers wanted action on employee representation which would make possible immediate collective bargaining on wages, hours, and speed-up. Wolman, backed by Kelley, urged "a statesman-like approach," which, he said, would consist of postponing collective bargaining until discrimination cases had been adjusted. Leaders of the Cleveland Fisher body workers presented a list of 5,400 members, 64 per cent of the working force, and asked the board to certify the union as a bargaining agency. The Hudson Motor Company workers gave the board a list of 8,000 members and asked an immediate check and certification. By April 12th, the board had lists of 50,000 union members and still had made no check on them.

Three hundred union leaders from Detroit, Toledo, Lansing, Flint, Pontiac, and Buffalo met in Detroit on April 8th and denounced the delay. A strike vote was demanded and was blocked only by the pleadings and threats of Collins. The St. Louis local, in a rage, turned back its A.F. of L. charter. Refusing to wait any longer, 7,000 Cleveland workers struck on April 22nd, defying Collins' orders. St. Louis Fisher body and Chevrolet workers also quit. The Cleveland union had twice appealed to the board to certify its representatives and had spent $1,000 sending emissaries to plead with Wolman. The Cleveland plant made bodies for all Chevrolet cars and stamped doors for Buicks and Pontiacs. Continuance of the strike there would have brought most of General Motors production to a standstill. William F. Knudsen, for G.M., agreed to meet with the union heads and the Wolman board, whereupon Collins prevailed on the Cleveland strikers to return to work.

Knudsen, Collins, the Wolman board and local auto leaders met on May 1st. Renewed threats of an industry-wide strike brought an agreement from Knudsen that plant managers would meet with union "committees in their representative capacities and not as individuals representing individuals." This was to be tried in Pontiac and Cleveland, and possibly later in other plants. So tense was the situation that 5,000 men struck at the Fisher Body No. 1 plant in Flint, in protest against the discharge of twenty-five union members. In Tarrytown, N. Y., 2,000 more workers quit. Meanwhile the conferences at Pontiac and Cleveland had started, and, as many of the unionists had feared, company unionists walked into the conference room. The "experiment" collapsed. The Flint strikers returned to work on a promise of reinstatement of the discharged men, and the Tarrytown strikers also went back. By that time, seasonal layoffs had begun. The A.F. of L. campaign had been a complete failure, except in the Toledo sector, where the rank and file ignored both the Wolman board and the A.F. of L., struck against the Electric Auto-Lite Company, refused to permit the smashing of their ranks by injunction and the militia, and finally won a 5-per-cent wage increase, a six months' contract, and the death of a company union.

When 157 representatives of seventy-seven federal unions of auto workers met in Detroit on June 23, 1934, they listened to Green tell of the Federation's services to the auto workers, and then voted that all A.F. of L. organizers be kept off the convention floor. With great difficulty Green dissuaded the delegates from demanding immediate chartering of an autonomous industrial union of auto workers. They wanted no more Federation guidance. Green tried to placate with talk of a new campaign, a "grand campaign," to organize the industry. He would set up a national council of the federal unions to act as "adviser" to officers which the executive council of the

Federation would appoint. Meanwhile, the Workers Education Bureau would start study classes. As a sample of these classes, the handsome Spencer Miller, Jr., director of W.E.B., delivered in his resonant baritone and impeccable English a lecture on the beauties of industrial democracy, when and if established. Green said he would not divulge his "full plan" at that moment (it would have been a rather difficult feat, considering that he had no plan worthy of the name), but urged the unionists to believe that he had "well-laid plans that will accelerate collective bargaining in the automobile industry." Collins, by now generally unpopular and soon to be replaced by Dillon, argued against "hasty" denunciation of the Wolman board. Byrd spoke and pronounced the board a "great success"! Wolman was "unable to attend." Ten resolutions for immediate formation of an autonomous union having been defeated, the national council was set up.

The Green plan was not visible to the naked eye in the year that followed. On November 6th, Dillon did indite a long letter to Sloan asking for a conference. President Roosevelt had just pleaded for a "breathing spell," and Dillon assured Sloan that the A.F. of L. was eager to coöperate. The verbose communication indicated the approach of Collins' successor.

"I think I may with propriety assume," Dillon wrote, in part, "that you have definite knowledge of the fact that many thousands of your employees are now organized into independent unions affiliated with the A.F. of L. They are capable employees, honorable citizens and want to share in the responsibilities and benefits of the industry. . . . For the purpose of emulating the philosophy of industrial peace as enunciated by the President of the United States . . . a conference is respectfully requested."

Sloan and General Motors were already enjoying peace, so completely discredited was the A.F. of L. among the auto workers. Dillon received no reply. By February, 1935, the membership of the auto unions had dwindled from 100,000 to 20,000, and a series of addresses by Green and Dillon in a few auto centers failed to improve matters. On March 1 the national council of auto unions initiated a strike vote, the result of which was never made public, probably because of the poor response.

[65]

The Federation had one more opportunity to reinstate itself with the auto workers. Again it failed. In April, 1935, the Wolman board, over the protests of the unions, completed a series of plant elections which were to establish the proportional representation plan enunciated in the President's peace plan of March, 1934. Largely boycotted by the Federation, the results nevertheless revealed its weakness. The board announced that 163,150 workers had been polled, that 88.7 per cent had voted for representatives unaffiliated with any organization, and that 14,057, or 8.6 per cent, had voted for leaders of the federal locals.

In the Chevrolet plant at Toledo, however, the workers had voted 1,327 to 813 for Fred Schwake, local unionist. The Toledo auto union leaders, Schwake, James Roland, and George Addes, were the same who had fought through the Auto-Lite strike to victory. The Chevrolet workers struck on April 22, 1935, demanding a signed contract, seniority rights, a five-day week, minimum pay of seventy cents an hour, and the end of the speed-up. They would not deal with the Wolman board. Green, informed of the strike, said he had not ordered it but would give his support. Dillon did not arrive in Toledo until the walkout was four days old. He felt that the strike was "unauthorized," and acted accordingly. Meanwhile, Fisher Body and Chevrolet workers quit in Norwood, Ohio, and in Cleveland. Before long, G.M. plants employing 30,000 men were forced to close in Atlanta, Janesville (Wis.), Kansas City, Fort Smith (Ark.), and Tarrytown (N. Y.). The Toledo plant supplied Buick and Chevrolet transmissions and its continued shut-down could play havoc with G.M. production. A compromise settlement was turned down by the strikers, 1,251 to 605, in a poll supervised by Edward F. McGrady, Assistant Secretary of Labor. Several days before the vote, a "back to work" leader had announced that 1,400 wished to end the strike.

The eyes of all auto workers were on Toledo. The strike leaders proposed widening their demands to win collective bargaining in all closed G.M. plants. To further this aim, they asked all other auto union locals to send delegates to a conference in Toledo. Dillon promptly vetoed the invitations. The A.F. of L. organizer, seconded by James Wilson, personal representative of Green, then urged the strike committee to drop its demand for sole recognition. He came out in the open on May 12th, while the strikers' ranks were solid and the plant completely at a standstill, and announced that he favored a peace plan in which the Toledo strikers would settle for themselves and abandon their hope for an agreement covering the other plants. When Dillon appeared at the strikers' meeting the evening of May 13th, he was so roundly booed he could not speak. Shouting that the union was from that time on "out of the A.F. of L.," he left the hall, pausing in the midst of his rage to pose for news photographers. Then Roland made his misplay. In a burst of generosity he pleaded with the men to hear Dillon. Grudgingly, they agreed. The A.F. of L.'s old hand returned. He spoke for an hour, pleading, promising, threatening. He was an orator, as Roland was not. A vote was taken amid great confusion. It stood 732 to 385 for returning to work.

The settlement which Dillon had prevailed upon the strikers to accept provided for no signed agreement, but for a memorandum which was to be posted on the plant bulletin board. The management agreed to meet with a shop committee of nine, the workers to decide the basis of electing the committee; minimum-wages were to be raised from 50 to 54 cents an hour. The Toledo strikers had dealt the Wolman board a bad blow, but had fallen far short of establishing the auto union and the A.F. of L. as a force in the industry. The day after the settlement was voted, the strikers declared they had been betrayed and wanted to walk out again. But the spirit had been broken. Dillon ordered the Cleveland and Atlanta strikers back to work. At Norwood, Ohio, the returning strikers were barred until they removed the union buttons from their overalls. Dillon advised them to comply. Thus Green's "grand campaign" to "accelerate collective bargaining" in the automobile industry came to an end. By the winter of 1935, the A.F. of L. auto unions had 10,000 members.

v

The NRA code for the steel industry was, like the automobile code, a one-way bargain. Steel won legal sanction for its disregard of the anti-trust laws, and labor was given a reiteration of the industry's open-shop policy. By arrangement with Richberg, the American Iron and Steel Institute presented an open-shop "clarification" of Section 7A and then withdrew it on the understanding that the "omission does not imply any change in the attitude of the industry."

If Section 7A was to mean anything more than the old regime, it was obvious that the steel workers would have to force the issue. On June 17th, President Tighe, now tolerantly known as "Grandmother" Tighe, was pecking away at his Oliver typewriter in the headquarters of the Amalgamated Association of Iron, Steel, and Tin Workers in Pittsburgh. He was busy preparing for negotiations for the bulk of his 6,000 members, puddlers, rollers, and other skilled men employed in the small mills of the Western Bar Iron Association. Tighe looked up from his typewriter to read a letter from Green which informed the seventy-six-year-old steel union head that the National Recovery Act had become law the day before and that a drive to organize the steel workers was in order. Tighe returned to his ancient Oliver and wrote a reply. The Amalgamated had no money. He was busy with the bar iron negotiations. Couldn't Green undertake the campaign? Grandmother Tighe was a benevolent gentleman. He had no malice, only pity and contempt for the steel workers because they had not joined his union. Yet he could be pettish when questioned too pointedly. He was proud of the fact that Elbert H. Gary had spoken of him as "one of the few labor leaders for whom he had any respect." His reply to Green disposed of the matter, Tighe thought. But when the Grandmother returned from the bar iron negotiations with a 5 to 10 per cent wage cut for his members, the problem was still around. Company union elections had been held. Green wanted "action." Surprisingly enough, steel workers were not waiting for invitations, but were flocking into the Amalgamated. They were organizing lodges and naming them "New Deal," "NRA," and "Blue Eagle" to show their faith and enthusiasm in the new era ushered in by President Roosevelt.

A 15-per-cent wage increase did not halt the rush into the union. Tighe was moved to seek advice. He wrote to Green for guidance in the "present anomalous situation." All he knew, said Tighe, he had gathered from the newspapers, and these did not make clear "where such organizations as ours come in." Meanwhile, steel workers had struck in Weirton and at the U.S. Steel coke by-products plant in Clairton. Tighe condemned both walkouts as unauthorized. The Weirton strikes forced the issue, however, and the National Labor Board ordered an employee election. Ernest T. Weir, amid the cheers of the steel magnates, went ahead with a poll of his own, as a result of which, he announced, the Amalgamated had been defeated. Mel Moore and William Long, Weirton strike leaders, were fired. The National Labor Board handed the case over to the Department of Justice, and the Department of Justice refused to act.

With this graphic illustration of how much they could count on the New Deal, the new steel unionists came to a convention of the Amalgamated on April 16, 1934. There were 250 delegates from fifty lodges, representing a rejuvenated organization. Most of them wanted to strike. Tighe tried to unseat half of the delegates because their lodges had not paid their dues in full. He backed down, however, and the convention elected a rank-and-file committee of ten to make preparations for a strike. In accordance with the strategy mapped at the convention, lodge leaders went to their respective mill managements to seek collective bargaining conferences. At one mill their letter seeking an appointment was returned unopened. At the Edgar Thomson mill in Braddock, the union committee was shown out. In all mills there were rebuffs.

The committee of ten thereupon summoned a conference of union district presidents which asked Tighe for $10,000 to organize strike machinery, and for the use of the Amalgamated's offices and printing-shop. Tighe replied that the committee was "illegal." When a delegation called, they found he was out. A letter on his desk told them that Clarence Irwin, Youngstown rank-and-file leader, was to be expelled. Meanwhile, Tighe was following his own policies. He had sent a letter to the American Iron and Steel Institute asking its members "to give ear to the plea of those who had joined their fellow workers and are asking for recognition." Tighe assured the steel-mill owners that he had "only one purpose, that of advancing the interests of both employer and employee." He asked for a conference. The Institute not only gave no "ear," but did not reply.

The A.F. of L. was almost completely uninterested. Tighe was hostile. The steel workers thereupon decided that the only thing left to do was to go to Washington and lay their demands for fulfillment of the New Deal on the White House steps. The President sought to meet the situation by a promise of plant elections. Recalling the Weirton experience, the rank-and-file leaders retorted, "bunk!" Tighe raged that the steel workers had "insulted" the President. He again said the committee had no "legal" standing and declared its members Communists and "vipers." He broadcast a message to the steel workers: "'Keep away from the committee' is not only our advice, but our command." The rank-and-filers thereupon left Washington, saying that there was no alternative but to strike. Meanwhile some steel companies laid in supplies of tear gas, bullets, revolvers and Thompson sub-machine guns. General Johnson now stepped into the breach. He proposed a board to hear the workers' grievances, and added that the rank-and-filers could "take it or leave it." The proposal was submitted to them, "not for their acceptance or rejection, but for their information," the General thundered. He added that he had worn enough skin off his hide "to make half a dozen such critics as they." The determined militancy of the rank-and-filers rankled deeply. Their leaders came to Washington again to see the President. He was away on a week-end cruise. Expressing their regret they could not join him, what with pressing business at hand in the steel towns and cities, they rejected the Johnson offer. They wrote the President that they thought it "useless to waste any more time in Washington on the National Run Around."

Meanwhile, Johnson, Richberg, and the President were at work. They had gained the assent of the steel industry to the appointment of a steel labor board which would hear grievances and hold elections. The problem now was to sell the plan to the steel workers. Who would bell the cat? Who but Green? The president of the A.F. of L. readily agreed. Tighe summoned a special convention of the Amalgamated, and Green appeared. He begged the delegates to forget that he was president of the Federation, and to think of him only as a simple coal-miner talking to steel workers. He urged that the time was not ripe to right the wrongs of long hours, inadequate pay, espionage, and terrorism under which the steel workers were living. The moment called for "strategy," Green declared. He promised money and men for an intensive organization campaign. Meanwhile, he urged, the best thing to do was to accept appointment of a steel labor board. His plea carried. *Steel,* organ of the industry, commented, "Organized labor in the steel industry has lost the offensive."

The growth of unionism in steel was arrested as the workers awaited the results of the board's labors. It was a more sympathetic commission than the Wolman auto board and its subsequent failure to budge the steel industry in the direction of collective bargaining was the more disillusioning. Carnegie Steel promptly challenged the right of the board to order elections, whereupon the board gave U.S. Steel's largest affiliate seven days in which to turn over its payroll sheets for checking purposes. The Corporation ran to the Federal courts for protection, and there the matter ended.

Tighe reported to the A.F. of L. convention of 1934 that out of 100,000 recruits who had signed Amalgamated applications in 1933 and 1934, only 5,300 remained in the union as dues-paying members. This was too much even for Green to defend, and a proposal by Lewis that the Federation take the task of organizing steel out of the hands of the Grandmother was approved. Ignoring the decision, Tighe announced that he would institute a campaign "immediately." He asserted that the main problem was to allay the industry's "fear" that it would be surrendering any of its rights if it accorded the steel workers the privilege of unionizing and bargaining collectively. The patriarch had just been reëlected to the presidency of the Amalgamated by the simple device of disfranchising a large bloc of voters. He credited himself with a majority of 259 out of a total of 5,319 votes.

The rank-and-file leaders continued their efforts. Two hundred met in Pittsburgh on December 30, 1934, and drew up demands for recognition, a five-day week, a six-hour day, and a minimum wage of one dollar an hour. They decided that a second conference would be held February 3rd after a campaign to revive the dwindling union spirit. Tighe denounced the conference and its program as "treason." He threatened to expel all lodges that attended the February meeting. The Amalgamated building in Pittsburgh, purchased

[71]

with the fees collected from the 1919 strikers, was barred to the 400 delegates who assembled despite Tighe's warnings. Driven to desperation, they proclaimed themselves the true spokesmen of the majority of Amalgamated members.

Tighe quickly demonstrated he could be a man of action. Before a week had passed he expelled 75 per cent of his members. A committee of the rank-and-file convention went to headquarters to remonstrate. They found a wall of policemen. Encouraged by support from Lewis and David Dubinsky, the rank-and-filers sent a delegation to Washington to see Green. Tighe bustled into a train and arrived in time to argue that the steel workers were secessionists and agents of the Communist International. Angered, Lewis demanded to know whether the Grandmother had any plans of his own to unionize the industry. The reply was more denunciation of the "reds" and a plaint that the opposition of the steel barons was a formidable one. The executive council thereupon appointed a committee of three to tackle the problem. The committee promptly split on the issue of the craft unions' "rights" to some of the steel workers. This problem was thought to have been settled after the 1919 strike, when the executive council had washed its hands of a troublesome situation by giving the Amalgamated an industrial charter covering all iron, steel, and tin workers. Now that the possibility of enrolling steel workers had reappeared, however, the craft union demands came to the front again.

The final scene of the Green-Tighe satire, entitled "Organizing the Steel Workers," was played at the sixtieth annual convention of the Amalgamated. Having faith in the Pittsburgh police, Tighe had arbitrarily shifted a convention scheduled for Canton to the general headquarters of the Amalgamated. When sixty-three delegates from twenty-six expelled lodges appeared, they were met by the same array of police who had barred the rank-and-file committee several months before. They withdrew to a meeting of their own, amid the scorn of Tighe, who charged them with having failed to pay dues in exchange for the benefits of Amalgamated membership. The rank-and-file movement by this time was itself demoralized. In the summer of 1935 the A.F. of L. effected a reconciliation between the remnants of the new unions and the Tighe machine. The

[72]

Grandmother was too exhausted to attend the Federation convention that year. He sent his able understudy, Louis (Shorty) Leonard, secretary-treasurer, to report a total membership of 8,600 in an industry of half a million workers.

VI

The influx of textile workers into the Federation's United Textile Workers of America was fully as sensational as the growths of the steel and auto unions, and even more remarkable. The textile workers suffered from low wages, periodic unemployment, and a "stretch-out" system which constantly increased the number of looms tended by a single worker. In addition they included hundreds of thousands of Southern workers who had never before heard trade-union appeals. Nevertheless, the textile union's membership jumped from 50,000 early in 1933 to 300,000 by the summer of 1934.

The textile code was the first to be adopted and General Johnson had termed it a "model." It fixed a forty-hour week, and wages of thirteen dollars a week in the North and twelve dollars in the South. Nevertheless, the Department of Labor found that the average wage in June, 1934, was $10.86 a week. The union produced figures showing that the stretch-out had increased the work load from 33 to 100 per cent, depending on the machinery and the driving ability of the mill management. Despite the vaunted protection of Section 7A, 4,000 unionists had been fired by the summer of 1934 and the Cotton Textile Industrial Relations Board had dismissed 2,000 of the complaints placed before it. In May, General Johnson had complicated the situation by sanctioning a 25-per-cent curtailment in production, with proportionate wage cuts, which brought pay for a full week's work down to seven dollars and nine dollars. A strike threatened, and Johnson offered to have the research and planning division of the NRA make a survey. The textile union and the A.F. of L. accepted the proposal. The survey was to report on hours, wages, stretch-out, and wage differentials. The planning board came back after several months of study and reported that a "normal" supply of cotton textile for the country would take ninety machine hours of work weekly to produce. Thus, by direct implication, shorter hours were not advisable. It could find "no factual or

[73]

statistical basis" for wage increases. Having been afforded a sample of the survey's final results, the union decided not to await its researches on stretch-out and wage differentials.

Five hundred leaders of the union came together in convention in New York's Town Hall on August 31, 1934, and voted for a general textile strike. Southern delegates mingled their "amens" with the vigorous "ayes" of Italian silk workers from the Passaic Valley, and Portuguese and French weavers from New England. The strike was to seek a thirty-hour week with no reduction in the twelve dollars and thirteen dollars minimum wages; establishment of a maximum work load and the end of the stretch-out; reinstatement of all workers fired because of their union activity; and recognition of the United Textile Workers of America. The growth of the union, as in steel and autos, had not been the result of any plan by the A.F. of L. Nevertheless, the response to the strike call assumed the proportions of a human tidal wave. On September 6th the Associated Press tallied 364,795 men and women on strike. Sixty thousand had quit in Georgia, as many in South Carolina, 11,000 in North Carolina, 110,000 in Massachusetts, 38,000 in Alabama, 25,000 in Tennessee, and 50,000 in Rhode Island. The spirit of the strikers reached a religious fervor. "Flying squadrons" marched from one Southern mill town to another, and at their approach, men, women, and youths flocked from the mills to join the walkout. The opposition brought violence into play. Ten strikers were slain, six when sheriff's deputies clashed with a "flying squadron" at Honea Path, South Carolina. In Woonsocket and Saylesville, Rhode Island, strikers fought troops in the streets. Eleven thousand national guardsmen were arrayed against the strikers in eight states. The army of local police, private guards, sheriffs' deputies, and vigilantes numbered at least three times eleven thousand. Governor Eugene Talmadge of Georgia played a conspicuous part, declaring martial law in strike centers and setting up a concentration camp for pickets charged with disorderly conduct.

Peace came on September 22nd, and for the strikers it was the peace of defeat. Responding to an appeal from President Roosevelt, the A.F. of L. called off the strike. There were indications that the Federation leaders had asked the President to provide a plausible pretext for ending the walkout which had developed into a battle far more serious than the old Federation leaders had bargained for. The President's plan proposed merely a new Textile Labor Relations Board. There was no agreement that the strikers would be rehired, only a request that the mills do so. George F. Sloan, head of the Cotton Textile Institute, gave no indication he assented to the settlement. He was not asked to, for if he had said "no" the task of calling off the strike would have been made more difficult. Boiled down, the settlement provided for a new board which would take over the job of enforcing the labor provisions of the code and a second board to study and regulate the work load. There was to be no decrease of the work load, but there could be no increases, except upon approval of the "work assignment control board."

The Federation and textile union leaders interpreted the settlement through rose-colored glasses: "We have secured these definite things: 1. An end to the stretch-out. 2. A method of determining hours on a basis of fact. 3. A method of determining wages on a basis of fact. 4. Practical recognition of our union. 5. Reform in the whole administration of the labor provisions of the code, on a scale so sweeping that we must confess ourselves surprised at the sweeping character of the victory we have won." The signers of the statement admitted "it is necessary to study the board's report with some care to see how far-reaching it is." The textile union leaders were very good on rhetoric, if rather weak on analysis.

The surprise of the union heads and the A.F. of L. at the "sweeping" character of their victory was not nearly so great as the amazement of the strikers when they sought to return to work. Publicly, Sloan maintained his silence. Privately, word went out that when and if the strikers returned it was to be as beaten dogs, grateful for being taken back. "Despite the calling off of the strike, peace did not return to the South," the New York *Times* reported on September 25th. Troops barred 80,000 mill hands from 200 plants in Georgia and the Carolinas alone. Some were told to come back later. At least 10,000, the more active union spirits, were told they could seek work elsewhere. At Lyman, South Carolina, 400 national guardsmen with drawn bayonets drove the "victorious" strikers from plant gates. At Concord, North Carolina, 2,500 former strikers in eight mills, told their services were no longer required, stormed into the county courthouse, demanding food for their families. At Roanoke, N. C., 4,000 were turned away wholesale. In some mills former strikers were readmitted, but were forced to sign pledges renouncing the union. Governor Talmadge closed his concentration camp in Georgia, but maintained martial law. In Washington, Francis J. Gorman, strike leader, said that the discriminations would not affect the order terminating the strike. Subsequently, it was reported that 15,000 local strike leaders had been refused reëmployment, each to stand in his mill town as a symbol of the impotency of the American Federation of Labor and the danger involved in joining a union. The textile union in August, 1935, claimed 79,200 members, a drop of more than 220,000 from its high point in the summer of 1934.

VII

The defeat in autos, steel, and textile was duplicated among the rubber workers. From its inception, the rubber industry had never known any effective unionism. Almost a thousand Akron workers joined the A.F. of L.'s Association of Allied Metal and Rubber Workers back in 1902, but one day the office was broken into and the membership list stolen. Systematic discharges followed. A strike in Trenton early in 1903 failed, and unionism was not heard of again in the industry until 1912 and 1913, when the I.W.W. invaded Akron and succeeded in bringing 5,000 workers out on strike. This strike, too, was lost. The A.F. of L. sent an organizer to propose the advantages of craft unionism. The organizer was John L. Lewis, but even his persuasiveness failed to revive the rubber workers' interest. For twenty years after that, neither Akron nor any other rubber-center factories were visited by labor organizers. In 1933, under the impetus of Section 7A, Goodyear, Firestone, and Goodrich rank and file organizers mobilized more than 30,000 Akron workers into independent unions.

Faced by a threat of company unions, the workers accepted A.F. of L. federal union charters. Green, in 1934, reported that between 60,000 and 70,000 workers, most of them in rubber, had been organized in Akron. By March of 1935, Coleman Claherty, the Federation's overseer in the industry, estimated the rubber unionists at 22,000, which was an overstatement. The true figure was near 3,000. A combination of craft-union rapaciousness and Green timidity were responsible for the decline. Rejecting the demands of the rubber workers for an industrial-union charter, the Federation parceled them among seven craft unions. A national council, which included craft and federal workers' unions, was set up to "advise" the A.F. of L. Two organizers were assigned to the industry of 90,000 workers.

By the spring of 1935 the rubber unions were completely demoralized. Company unionism flourished, while the companies engaged in bitter price wars made possible by driving down labor costs and speeding up the workers. Spies multiplied. Efforts of the bona-fide unions to win National Labor Relations Board elections were blocked by company appeals to the courts. Early in 1935 the union rallied sympathy for a strike. Claherty steered the conflict to Washington, where Green worked out an agreement which surrendered the workers' demands for employee elections and signed contracts. Understandings reached in conference between union delegates were to be posted on bulletin boards of the plants, but were not to be signed. There was to be no strike pending a ruling of the Supreme Court on the legality of Section 7A. Thus the unions had their hands tied for at least a year. The Akron leaders objected, but Claherty forced acceptance. Those of the unionists who remained turned in rebellion from A.F. of L. leadership.

VIII

Meanwhile, in the mountainous mining camps of Montana and Utah the craft unionists were short-circuiting a growth which had brought 49,000 recruits into the International Union of Mine, Mill and Smelter Workers. Here the crafts' insistence on charter rights was honored in the breach.

The mine, mill and smelter workers' union, inheritor of the fighting traditions of the old Western Federation of Miners, reapplied for admission to the A.F. of L. in 1910. They asked for renewal of their industrial union jurisdiction, which covered all men

[77]

working in and about metaliferous mines. Some of the craft unions objected and the issue reached the point where a convention of the United Mine Workers of America, with William Green voting approval, threatened to secede from the Federation unless its sister union in the metal mines was granted an inclusive jurisdiction. Gompers and the executive council of the Federation yielded and the industrial-union charter was granted with the single exception that machinists working at the Butte and Bingham, Utah, mines were to remain in the machinists' union.

During a period of violence and blacklists notorious in industrial history, the organization maintained a precarious existence until the advent of the NRA. With no craft-union organizers in sight, a new, young leadership succeeded in bringing most of the workers into the fold of the union. A strike was called in May, of 1934, and 6,600 employees of the Anaconda Copper Company at Butte and Great Falls, Montana, responded. Operations were completely suspended. As the strike entered its second month, spokesmen of the Federation's Building and Metal Trades Departments, shepherded by Frey, met in New York and Washington with company executives. Without informing the strikers, Frey made an agreement covering 600 of them who were craftsmen. These were to be divided among fifteen craft unions. The strikers first learned of the settlement when representatives of the crafts arrived in Butte to inform the craftsmen that an agreement had been reached. Frey appeared, equipped with a briefcase full of reports to show that craft unions had chartered Montana locals 'way back in the 'nineties. The strikers' ranks were demoralized, and the walkout dragged along to an inconclusive settlement in the fall of the year. The metal miners union lost most of its membership in Utah as well as in Montana. Eight thousand recruits in Alabama iron mines refused to continue paying dues. Meanwhile seven newly formed craft unions in Utah died. The union in the summer of 1935 could report a membership of only 14,600.

4.

COMPROMISE AND REBELLION

GREEN, in October, 1933, had spoken of a membership of 10,000,000 as "the next step" and 25,000,000 as "the ultimate goal" of the A.F. of L. He had given as a "true" picture of the membership of the Federation on that day the total of 3,926,796. It was perhaps too much to have expected the "ultimate goal" to have been reached within a year; but by October, 1934, the "next step" had not even been approached. On the basis of the membership tabulation as of August 31, 1934, the Federation had 2,608,011 men and women in its ranks. This was a gain over the paid-up membership of 2,126,796 reported on August 31, 1933, but a drop of 1,318,795 from the "true" picture which Green had given to the press on October 12, 1933. In other words, the Federation had failed to hold more than 1,300,000 workers who had paid initiation fees, some amount of dues, and had indicated their desire to remain within the Federation. Green had reported 350,000 "recruits" in new and old federal unions, which offered the best index of growth in the mass-production industries. The Federation reported on August 1, 1934, that it had a total of 89,093 in federal unions, and, on August 31, 1935, that it had only 111,489 in federal unions. In 1936, the membership in these unions fell to 83,153. Only a fraction of the loss was represented by members turned over to international unions. Even the international unions, most of them crafts, had failed to hold the gains which Green had announced with enthusiasm in October, 1933. He had said then that new and old locals affiliated with internationals had added 950,000 members, yet the entire membership gain in 1934, federal and international unions, proved to be only 481,215. The paid-up membership reported August 31, 1935, showed an advance for the Federation, which brought the membership to 3,045,347, or a gain of 918,551 since August, 1933. Out of this, nine industrial or semi-industrial unions, those of men's clothing workers, women's garment makers, textile hands, oil-field workers, brewers, hatters, glass workers, coal-miners and metal-miners, contributed 484,000.

The figures for the federal unions in 1935, showed the failure of the Federation most eloquently. The Federation had 1,708 directly affiliated federal and local unions in 1934; a year later it had only 1,354, and in 1936, 914. Only 340 had been handed over to international unions, which meant that 454 new unions had perished. In the year ending August 31, 1935, 306 new directly affiliated locals were added to the rolls; in the same year 620 were disbanded or suspended. A year later, the council reported that 245 new unions had been added, and that 584 had been dropped from the rolls.

Whatever regrets the Federation executive council may have experienced over the decline of the federal and local trade-union membership, they had consolation in the fact that the charters they had issued were good business. The members of these unions had for years been good milk cows. A loan from a "defense fund" created by the federal unions and earmarked for their exclusive use made possible financing the construction of the Federation's building in Washington in 1917. In 1933 the executive council, taking advantage of a new Constitutional provision, transferred $15,000 from this fund for general Federation purposes. Three years later, when many of the federal unions had broken away and formed affiliations nearer their own interests, the council took $50,000 more from the "defense fund" to help finance the Federation's fight against the C.I.O. Thus the dollars of the auto and rubber unionists came to be used against them. *The American Federationist,* which constantly exalted the interests of the large craft unions over the desires of the federal unions, was supported in the main by the tax on the federal unions. Had it not been for the dues and initiation fees of these unions, the executive council would have ended each year from 1933 to 1936 with a large deficit.

[80]

While the international unions paid the Federation one cent a month per member, the members of the federal and local trade unions paid an initiation fee of one dollar and per capita dues of thirty-five cents monthly. Of the per capita, twelve and one-half cents was turned over to the "defense fund," fifteen cents to the *American Federationist*, and seven and one-half cents to the general fund of the Federation.

This arrangement not only saved the Federation from annual deficits, but it changed the *American Federationist* from a money-losing affair to a profitable enterprise. In 1934 the magazine had a surplus of $104,288, in 1935 of $128,694, and in 1936 of $93,047. Part of these surpluses remained in the magazine's fund; the remainder went into the general fund as a further contribution of the small federal unions to the service of the large internationals and the upkeep of President Green and his staff. The federal locals' financial support of the Federation thus came from several sources: from the one dollar initiation fees, from the seven and one-half cents monthly taken directly from the thirty-five cents per capita tax, from the surplus accumulated by the *American Federationist*; and, as the council decreed, "transferrals" of large sums from the "defense fund" to the "general fund."

The annual reports of Secretary-Treasurer Morrison indicate that the "defense fund" has been used sparingly for its avowed purpose. The fund received $133,615 in 1934 and expended $1,575; its receipts in 1935 were $167,186 and its expenditures $45,650. In 1936, one of the few years when the executive council gave more for defense purposes than it collected, the receipts were $124,701 and the expenditures $151,656. This unusual generosity was induced by an effort to win the strike against the Remington-Rand Corporation in which the craft International Association of Machinists, as well as several federal unions, was involved. By the end of the Federation's fiscal year 1936, the "defense fund" had been so zealously guarded by the executive council that it had the tidy total of $510,623.

The entire story of the A.F. of L.'s exploitation of its directly affiliated locals during the good pickings of 1934 to 1936—pickings which were only proportionately smaller in previous years—may be seen from a simple table:

	1933	1934	1935	1936
Average membership of A.F. of L............	2,126,796	2,608,011	3,045,347	3,422,398(A)
Membership of directly affiliated locals........	19,396	89,083	111,489	83,153
Total A.F. of L. income..	$422,923	$1,070,432	$1,032,475	$924,390
Receipts from directly affiliated locals..........	$88,172	$628,017	$563,363	$464,719
Proportion of members in directly affiliated locals.	.09	.03	.03	.02
Proportion of income from directly affiliated locals.	22%	60%	55%	50%

(A) Includes members of suspended C.I.O. unions.

II

Those delegates to the Federation's San Francisco convention in 1934 who bothered to read the report of the executive council received no inkling of either the failures of the 1933-1934 efforts, nor the great dissatisfaction which was being voiced in the troubled ranks of the new unions. Nor were they given any impression that any great problems lay in the path of the Federation. The executive council profoundly urged more "planning" for organization, and the inauguration of educational work. Concerning the problem of union structure, the council felt that the decision of the international unions conference in January, 1934, had worked satisfactorily. Major difficulties had arisen, it was admitted. These were listed: 1. fear of workers that they would be discharged if they joined a union; 2. the extension of company unions; and 3. the difficulty of "adaptation to mass production industries." Under this pregnant heading it was held that "the problem of establishing the organization to be responsible for organizing the industry has been worked out in various ways, depending on the industry, the jobs and the number employed for various jobs." In promising fashion, the next subject was captioned "Organization Carried into New Fields," but here indications of progress were as elusive as helpful suggestions in "Adaptation to Mass Production Industries." Glowing language told of the rubber unions' joint council. "Considerable progress" was

[82]

claimed among auto workers. Continuing with the recital of its exploits in "new fields," the council told of the aluminum workers' council which had been "provisionally" set up. No gains could be reported, but a strike had been averted. Lumber and sawmill workers had organized 130 federal unions, but "only a beginning has been accomplished in negotiating union contracts." The "ultimate goal" was to organize 400,000 lumber workers. "Fine gains" were reported by radio workers in Philadelphia (where, it was not reported, a federal union had resisted efforts of the crafts to divide it up). In the coke and gas, the cement, the flour, feed, and cereal, the electrical appliance, the cleaning and dyeing, the canning industries no progress toward collective bargaining was reported. "No real attempt has been made to organize agricultural workers," it was admitted, although forty federal farm laborers' unions had spontaneously come into existence.

Part of the reason for the general failure was the workers' "cruel disillusionment," in the promise of Section 7A, the report concluded, evidencing a complete turn about from the "voluntarism" of the old days to a feeling that the government and the law ought somehow to be an agency for promoting trade unionism. In contrast with the rest of the report, the council conceded that the United Mine Workers and the International Ladies' Garment Workers had made great progress in their industries.

The San Francisco convention received fourteen resolutions dealing with the problem of organization policy. One, by Frey, proposed that all Federation organizers be instructed "that under the laws and policies of the A.F. of L. wage-earners cannot be organized except into the respective national and international unions whose jurisdiction has been established by the charters which have been issued by the A.F. of L., or in federal unions whose membership shall not include those over whom jurisdiction has been given to national or international unions." The boilermakers' union went further and wanted an end of the policy of federal unions through which "industrial unionism has been somewhat carried on." In another resolution the boilermakers' delegates wanted the oil-field, gas-well, and refinery workers to surrender its craftsmen or face expulsion. The teamsters' union renewed its fight to have the pugnacious industrial brewery workers' union surrender all truck drivers.

Demands for extension of industrial unionism came in resolutions from auto and rubber locals, from radio workers, from the mine, mill, and smelter workers, and from the Pennsylvania State Federation of Labor, which represented the views of John L. Lewis and the mine workers' delegation. The brewers-teamsters fight again provided a test vote, the delegates going 15,558 to 9,306 for the teamsters. It was during this debate that Tobin spoke what was on the mind of many of the impatient craft unionists, resentful of the upstart notions of the "new recruits."

"We have to use force in our organizations," said Tobin, speaking of the refusal of the brewers to accept the decision of a previous convention. "If we didn't use force and enforce the decisions, we would not have an international union of 135,000 members—and they are not the rubbish that have lately come into other organizations."

Shouts of protest and demands for retraction came from all parts of the floor, but Tobin remained adamant.

"I will take nothing back," he shouted. "I am not in the habit of taking things back. I know what I am speaking about."

With this warning that the craft unionists were prepared to stand at the bridge, the convention's key committee on resolutions went into session to tackle the fundamental aspects of the craft versus industrial union issue. Woll, as in times immemorial, was chairman of the committee, and Frey its secretary. They were bolstered by a Green-appointed majority. Huddled around Lewis were Howard, Dubinsky, and J. C. Lewis, miner president of the Iowa State Federation of Labor. For six days and five nights the committee wrangled. Lewis wanted a clear-cut promise of industrial charters for auto, rubber, cement, radio, and aluminum workers. He insisted that the task of organizing the steel industry be taken from the aged hands of the Amalgamated Association of Iron, Steel, and Tin Workers and entrusted to competent directors who were to operate free of craft interference. Frey and his building-trades men, contrariwise, wanted an end to the "encroachments" of the federal unions, and insisted that they surrender all craftsmen then in their ranks. As the days dragged along, Woll deviated somewhat and took over the task of "softening up" his bitter-enders, while Howard undertook a similar mission with Lewis. A compromise, written by Howard, resulted. Charters were to be issued for mass production workers in auto, cement, aluminum "and other mass production and miscellaneous industries" as the executive council might decide was necessary. The craft unions' rights were to be safeguarded. Exact definitions of jurisdiction of the new unions were to be entrusted to the executive council, which was to be enlarged by the addition of several new members, among them a few industrial unionists. The council, it was also recommended, "shall at the earliest possible date inaugurate, manage, promote and conduct a campaign of organization in the steel industry," Lewis was leaving no loopholes, he thought. The newly chartered international unions were for "a provisional period," to have their policies formulated and their officers appointed by the council.

Lewis took the floor, upon submission of the committee's report, to help smooth out some of the feelings which had been badly ruffled in the week-long series of hotel-room battles, strategy conferences, caucusses, persuasions, and threats. He was, necessarily, in view of the compromise, chary on detail, but emphasized the "specific instructions" given the executive council, and the discretionary power which it would be granted. Immediately Wharton was on his feet to voice his suspicions. He wanted to know what was meant by the "automotive industry." He was opposed to giving the projected auto union jurisdiction over workers in accessories or parts factories, or over garage employees. Lewis replied that he was in no position to give the requested definition, and added that the executive council would be the final arbiter. Wharton was not satisfied. Would the rights of the crafts be protected?, he demanded. Lewis replied in the affirmative. The machinists' chief was still not satisfied. He wanted an answer from Green or Frey. Frey replied that automobile repair work, auto reconditioning, and work on automobile accessories would not come under the heading of mass production-industries.

Now it was Hutcheson's turn to seek qualifications. He wanted to know whether plant maintenance men would be included in the

[85]

jurisdictions of the new unions. Woll replied in the negative, but pleaded that "these perplexing questions" be left to the executive council. Thereupon, Franklin of the boilermakers, and Joseph V. Moreschi, padrone-president of the International Union of Hod Carriers and Common Laborers, demanded assurances for the record that the "rights" of their unions would not be molested. Lewis felt the thing was going far enough, and took the floor again, this time to insist that the committee's recommendation "means what it says." That brought an end to the efforts at "defining" the report.

Before the vote was taken Andrew Furuseth rose for his last talk in a Federation debate. The old president of the International Seamen's Union spoke for the new idea in the old terms of Gompersian "voluntarism." Many times in his declining years the ancient mariner had taken the side of conservatism, for old-style individualism as against accepting the "favors" of government, for splendid isolation, craft labor independent of the rest of the world. Now he was revealing a capacity and a willingness to grapple with a problem which men younger by decades, all with soft berths to compare with his cheerless boarding-house room in Washington, would not bring themselves to face. He spoke words of praise for the skilled craftsmen, the proud old ironmongers, toolmakers and carpenters of the days before machinery had made their art a less useful one.

"The things they have done for civilization," he said, "cannot be done by anybody else. . . . But that does not mean that new things will not come into the world and that men will not have to learn how to make them. It is not the work that one does in one hour or another hour that counts here, it is the work that accomplishes a specific purpose. . . . As a certain tool is made, or certain appliances are made, many men will work upon them, and sometimes several crafts will work upon them. . . . And for the labor movement to oppose in any way the kind of organization necessary for these men who manufacture these new appliances would be nothing short of suicidal for the labor movement."

Let the men in the new industries decide on their own form of organization, Fureseth urged, for, "if we should commit the damnable crime of robbing them of their self-determination and freedom we are nothing better than a new tyranny taking the place of the old. . . . The corner stone of the American Federation of Labor is voluntary association." The old man then turned to the craft unionists, the traders in jurisdictions, "contracts" and craft-union "rights."

"I have heard many times in the labor movement the term, 'these are my men,'" he said. "A delegate or a labor council or a man who is sent out to organize says, 'you are my men.' Who the devil is he? That is the way the master talked for centuries of the slaves. . . . And along comes the industrial employer and says, 'he belongs to me; he is my employee. You mustn't interfere with him, he is mine.' Is he? If he is, then our whole civilization is a lie, our religion is a lie, our American system of government is a lie. Let the American Federation of Labor always remember that fundamentally this is a voluntary association that is pledged to respect the rights of every man affiliated, and work by conciliation and not by force."

Delegate Gainor, with a thick, grinding voice that seemed to start somewhere in his entrails, rose to demand, "Is there no way of bringing this debate to a close?" The vote was taken, the report unanimously adopted, and the troublesome issue disposed of for another year.

There remained before the convention the task of enlarging the executive council. To the end a group of craft-union delegates strove to keep Lewis off the council. Most of the craft-union leaders kept their part of the bargain, however, and Lewis and Dubinsky were elected as new members. Tobin, Hutcheson, George L. Berry of the printing pressmen, H. C. Bates of the bricklayers, and Edward J. Gainor of the letter carriers were also added. Berry was a sometimes supporter of industrial unionism. For Lewis and Dubinsky, then, the crafts had added four of their own men. The old council had included representatives of but 1,052,600 of the Federation's 2,608,011 members; the new one had members who spoke for unions with a total membership of 1,475,400. Howard had been offered one of the new places, but he insisted he would not take advantage of a reform he had fought to inaugurate. There was some weak suggestion that Frey might logically be one of the crafts' designees, but it came to nothing. Despite his lifelong service to the craft unionists,

[87]

they have never yet found it within their generosity to honor him with a place on the council.

The executive council of the Federation can be a most deliberative body when it chooses, and the presence of Lewis and Dubinsky at the sessions which followed the October, 1934, convention, did not avail to hasten its leisurely attack on pressing problems. Thus it was seven months before the council decided to grant the automobile federal unions the promised international union charter, and ten months before the unions received this blessing. Meanwhile another production season had come and gone and another opportunity to organize the industry had been lost. The rubber unions did not receive an international charter until eleven months after the San Francisco decision.

To the first constitutional convention of the International Union, United Automobile Workers of America, which convened August 26th, "by authority of the American Federation of Labor," Green spoke of 135 federal auto unions which had been organized by the Federation. Dillon spoke of 147, but only eighty-three were alive enough to send delegates. The Toledo delegation was the largest, and least in the favor of Dillon and Green. Together with the large South Bend, Kenosha, Cleveland, and Norwood, Ohio, representations they constituted themselves a large thorn in the sides of the A.F. of L. representatives. Dillon's report on his stewardship of the federal locals was lengthy. He told of having called the auto locals' national council together three times, listed twenty-two communications he had addressed to the Federation's executive council, each consultation with local unionists, the meetings he had addressed, the telephone calls he had made, and the exact amount of "interviews with the press." He told how he had gone to Toledo during the Chevrolet strike and "assumed charge of the situation and directed the officers and members of the union as to the proper procedure in the handling of the strike in conformity with the policies of the A.F. of L." He resented criticism of his conduct in Toledo, called it "malicious and unjust," and insisted he had no apologies to make. Despite his criticism of the Toledo leaders, the list of six-

[88]

teen signed contracts enjoyed by the entire union, which he presented, showed that nine of them were obtained by the Toledo local. Not one agreement was listed with a General Motors, Chrysler, or Ford plant.

Following an address by President Green, Delegate Mayberry of Toledo moved "that all general organizers who are paid by the A.F. of L. be instructed and compelled to remain away from the hotel and the convention during the time of this convention." Dillon, presiding by designation of Green, felt embarrassed, he said, but thought, nevertheless, that it "developed" upon him to make a ruling. The convention had been "convened by the authority of the Federation," therefore Delegate Mayberry's motion was out of order. In the days that followed, many motions were ruled out of order as the delegates continued to rebel against the "authority." In the end Green and Dillon prevailed, but their victory was a Pyrrhic one.

With the stuffy formality he had observed at Federation conclaves, Chairman Dillon "charged a committee with the honor and responsibility of proceeding to Suite 1863 of the Fort Shelby Hotel and there conveying to the president of the American Federation of Labor your desire to usher him to this convention hall." This message was duly conveyed, the minutes record, and "as President Green entered the convention hall, the chorus sang, 'How Do You Do, Mr. Green?'" Green responded, but not until Dillon, by way of an introductory address, had reminisced about his childhood, his loyalty to labor, and President Green's peerless qualities as a labor statesman. Green graciously accepted the tribute and then dwelt in generalities on the responsibility of the hour.

"And now, my friends, the dramatic moment has arrived," he finally said.

The "dramatic moment" brought the announcement of the executive council's decision of May 9th. The automobile workers were to have the privilege of a charter "to embrace all employees directly and indirectly engaged in the manufacture of parts (not including tools, dies, and machinery) and assembling of those parts into completed automobiles, but not including job or contract shops manufacturing parts or any other employee engaged in said automobile production plants." Green did not elaborate on the exceptions, but they eliminated fully 15 per cent of the auto workers from the proposed jurisdiction. Continuing with his "dramatic message," Green announced that he would temporarily designate the president of the new union, and that he was to "direct" an "organizing campaign," to be launched at a time not specified. Conflicts with the crafts on jurisdiction, he said, were to be decided by the executive council "at such time as the council may elect to give these questions consideration." Green termed the charter a "broad one," but begged the delegates "to observe that it does demand and insist that the jurisdictional authority of other organizations, particularly over skilled mechanics employed in tool and die shops, must be respected and observed." The President of the Federation concluded with his philosophy that life demands "adjustments to a large degree of the circumstances and conditions which exist." He used his favorite and characteristic phrase, "we must find a basis of accommodation," and then sat down amid slight applause from some delegates and silence from the others.

The mechanics of the convention, as managed by Dillon, permitted no immediate response to Green's presentation of the charter, but a few days later the storm broke. Forest G. Woods of South Bend charged that the charter granted would lead to disintegration. He argued that the craft unions had made no effort for years to organize in the automobile industry, and pleaded for the right of the auto workers to fix their charter rights within the industry. He moved that a protest be sent to the next Federation convention, and that if satisfaction was not obtained, "the officers of the union be and are hereby instructed to formulate such plans and take such action as in their opinion may seem desirable." The committee on jurisdiction, which had been appointed by Dillon, recommended acceptance of the charter. Dillon refused to consider amendments, and after hours of vigorous debating, both the committee's report and Woods' resolution were adopted. Acceptance of the limited charter was obviously nominal. The Woods resolution indicated ultimate defiance. The majority of the delegates had decided to make their principal fight on the election of officers, feeling that the

[90]

future of their union would lie largely in their hands no matter what the Federation executive council decreed.

The resolutions committee, which had also been picked by Dillon, brought in a statement praising Dillon's efforts in behalf of the auto workers and pleading earnestly with President Green to appoint Dillon president of the new union. Immediately, Carl Shipley of South Bend was on his feet to move that the convention select its own officers. By this time, Green had replaced Dillon as presiding officer. The Federation president directed his warmest smiles at the delegates. He addressed them as "my dear boys," and assured them "you will go a long way before you will find a man who will serve you more faithfully than Francis J. Dillon."

"Where can you find a man more capable, more trained . . . whole-hearted and sincere, than honest Frank Dillon?" Green pleaded. "We cannot be young men in a hurry. . . . It will be several months before you will have enough money in your treasury to pay the expense of this international. . . . We will pay your new president's salary and defray his expenses. . . . My God! Is it possible that we cannot extend to you the help we are craving to give you while you are passing through this most important change?"

To facilitate matters, Green ruled the Shipley amendment out of order. Nevertheless, the convention's answer to his question was "no." The vote was 112.8 in favor of the appointment of Dillon, and 164.2 opposed. Green, Dillon, and spokesmen of the minority thereupon retired to behind-doors councils on strategy. Emissaries were sent here and there among the rebels to seek votes, by trades, by promises of minor appointments and jobs, and by warnings of reprisals. The prestige of the executive council was at stake. But no amount of persuasion had any effect. The South Bend, Toledo, Cleveland, Kenosha, Racine, and Norwood delegates were not amenable to "reason." The situation grew worse on the floor of the convention as delegates denounced Dillon, one declaring he took his convictions from the same source which paid his salary. Dillon protested, "I have feelings, too," and demanded apologies. Mayberry, his accuser, was unmoved.

Three days of futile bargaining had failed to bring results and on August 29th Green assumed the chair once more. He found he could stay in Detroit no longer, and felt compelled "to advise you and render a very important decision."

"I have sought to find a way by which I could arrange for this convention . . . to select in democratic fashion its officers," Green declared. "After giving it thought, I have found too much division. . . . I have therefore decided literally to follow the instructions of the executive council."

Green had earlier indicated his willingness to permit the convention to name its executive board and other officers, if they would but accept his choice for the president. Now, however, he named Dillon as president, Homer Martin, of Kansas City as vice-president, and Ed Hall of Milwaukee as secretary-treasurer. He proceeded to name an executive board of nine. Seven of the appointed officers had voted in favor of Dillon, the four others were either absent or had refrained from indicating their wishes. The majority of the convention received no representation. The South Bend and Toledo mainstays of the union were ignored. Martin, vice-president by appointment, represented a small local, but he had stuck by Dillon throughout the convention.

"Naturally," Green continued amid sullen silence, "naturally, I have made this decision, my friends, courageously. Now, there is no necessity of any vote of approval or disapproval. It is the decision of the executive council. It is the president of the American Federation of Labor carrying the decision of the executive council. . . . I thank you."

Delegates Ellsworth Kramer and Robert Travis of Toledo promptly moved to return the charter. Dillon as promptly declared the motion out of order. He ruled that the charter had been granted and that Green, "after due deliberation, has rendered a momentous decision."

"As the president of your union," the A.F. of L. organizer declared, "I must now say that if there be those here who cannot conform to the terms and provisions of this document, then they must leave."

Kramer appealed to the delegates to overrule the decision of the new president, but Dillon was not to be trapped by a too literal

[92]

interpretation of rules of parliamentary procedure as raised by raw, inexperienced workers just off the belt-line.

"It does not make any difference what the decision is with reference to your appeal," Dillon postulated. "That is final, and we are only wasting time. Now the issue is settled and that is all there is to it."

Delegate Johnson of Flint was on his feet. Out of a sense of desperate frustration or in sublime faith, he moved that an appeal be taken to the executive council of the Federation. Green seized the opening and gave his assent.

The president of the Federation reiterated Dillon's advice that the majority of the delegates could bolt the union if they would not submit to discipline. He added, however, that an appeal to the executive council would be the proper course, and promised the council would give "sympathetic consideration." He closed on a firmer note, likening the executive council to the Almighty:

"You can't bargain with the executive council because that is the higher tribunal. The creator issued the charter and said, 'This is the charter. These are the stipulations.'"

The president of the Federation then pronounced the auto union "a happy family." Dillon felt that "propriety" called upon him to "indulge in a few remarks," and thereupon launched into a speech of acceptance. He ended on a Biblical note, "Forgive them, Father, for they know not what they do." Martin concluded obsequies with praise for Green and for Dillon, who, he said, had "faced trials and tribulations such as no man has ever been faced with." The American Federation of Labor, after forty years, had finally launched a union of automobile workers.

IV

President Green had but twelve days to recuperate from the auto convention before he went into an encounter with the brawny tiremolders from the acrid pits of Firestone, Goodrich, and Goodyear. The delegates from twenty-seven rubber workers' locals had observed the mechanics of the auto convention and were not slow to draw certain lessons. They had also sought legal advice and had been

[93]

informed that the prerogatives of Green and the executive council were not really rooted as firmly as the Ten Commandments, nor even the Constitution of the federal government. Therefore when A.F. of L. Organizer Coleman Claherty charged a committee at the rubber workers' convention in Akron with the duty of fetching President Green to the hall so that he might bestow a charter, Delegate W. W. Thompson rose in his place and asked why it was necessary to have Green present the charter in person.

"I believe Mr. Green will be able to speak for himself," Claherty curtly replied. He warded off a suggestion by Thompson that the convention choose its own chairman, and then presented the gentleman from Coshocton bearing the scroll of the executive council. Green spoke, again extensively, saying that "it is difficult to make clear to every rubber worker as to why the A.F. of L. pursued a policy of such sound discretion, of caution and care." Nevertheless, the council had at length arrived at the view where it felt the rubber workers could be chartered as an international union, not yet autonomous, like the other 109 internationals, but nevertheless an approach toward that goal. He stumbled a bit, linguistically, as he came to the "dramatic moment":

"Now, my friends, at this solemn moment, solemn to you and those you represent, significant beyond your comprehension and your appreciation, because in the days to come when you and I have passed into the great beyond, your children and your children's children will refer to this historic event when the international union, of which they will be proud, and the obligation rests upon us to protect it, to safeguard it and to preserve it at any cost and to transmit it unimpaired as a common heritage to those who will follow.

"Now, my friends, on this solemn occasion, I repeat, significant beyond your comprehension, in dramatic fashion, I present this charter. . . ."

Green emphasized that the charter was a "contract" between the United Rubber Workers of America and the Federation. He then proceeded to inform the delegates of the terms of the contract to which they were, whether they willed it or not, becoming a party.

It was to cover "all those in the rubber industry who are engaged in the mass production of rubber products, same not to cover or include such workers who construct buildings, manufacture or install machinery, or engage in maintenance work or in work outside the plants or factories." The machinists and other mechanical craft unions, and the building trades crafts had cut themselves slices of the rubber workers, as in the charter accorded the United Automobile Workers of America. Upon completion of Green's address, Salvatore Camelio, of Cambridge, Massachusetts, took the floor. Camelio subsequently proved to be the most querulous member of the convention, though he had able seconds.

"I would like to ask," said Camelio, "if we accept this charter, does this give the president the right to appoint its officers?"

"First of all," the president responded, "it is not up to you to decide as to whether or not you will accept the charter. That has been decided by the executive council. . . . It cannot be amended and it cannot be accepted and it cannot be rejected. . . . This confers upon me the right to designate or appoint your officers."

Claherty thought the entire subject was out of order, but Camelio was persistent and to the point:

SALVATORE CAMELIO: "In the granting of the charter, take these members such as machinists and steamfitters; does it mean after they have been formed into a union that the international machinists and electricians [unions] cannot come into the plant?"

PRESIDENT GREEN: "You are raising a question not covered in here. That is easy enough to settle at the conference table. I cannot tell you what can be done or shall be done. I think we can trust each other and we will settle those things. This is plenty broad. Everybody, surely, understands the English language."

Claherty could not muster enough delegates to organize a resolutions committee favorable to him, so he arranged by a simple inversion of parliamentary law, that a minority of the committee bring in its report first. It petitioned President Green to appoint Claherty as president, "because of his ability to handle our problems." Green, terming himself a "good soldier," assumed the chair. Delegate Thompson thereupon proceeded to tear the resolution

[95]

apart. He submitted that the rubber workers also had men of experience who would make capable officers. He called the report "completely nonsensible" and suggested that the A.F. of L., in presuming to dictate who were to be the officers of labor unions, was operating contrary to the freedom of choice provided organized labor in Section 7A of the NRA. How was the rubber union to train its own leaders, if it were not to be permitted democratic rights? he asked. Green replied with a homily on the relationship of sons to fathers, and on the foolhardiness of a new union throwing away an offer by the Federation to defray the salary of its president. Camelio thought otherwise and brushed aside the consideration of a generosity which demanded a *quid pro quo*.

DELEGATE CAMELIO: "You just said that we must appeal to our daddy for help in the appropriation of funds to establish this international union. It makes no difference. You will have to help our president, whether it be Burns, myself, or anybody else. You must help him, and all we ask for is the democratic right to vote for that man who we feel confident will lead the rubber workers to conquer. . . ."

PRESIDENT GREEN: "If you were called upon to employ some one, wouldn't you want to have the say about the selection?"

DELEGATE CAMELIO: "We feel just as confident as the A.F. of L. that we know who that man might be."

The debate raged for hours, one rubber worker after another pitting his humble opinion against the worldly-wiseness of President Green. The Federation head was not in a position, considering the overwhelming opposition he would arouse, to repeat the Detroit performance. In addition, Claherty had inadvertently included in the agenda for the convention an item dealing with the "election of officers." A vote was taken, and it tallied 45 to 9 against accepting the appointment of Claherty. The election of Sherman H. Dalrymple, of Akron, to the presidency followed. With less decorum than he ordinarily attains, Green departed from the convention and from Akron after informing the delegates and the press that the new rubber union could expect no financial assistance from the American Federation of Labor.

[96]

V

The stage for the historic 1935 convention of the Federation held at Atlantic City in October was set by the executive council's handling of the auto and rubber conventions and the events that followed. An attempt to disrupt the new radio workers' unions, disillusionment in textile and continued inaction in steel, brought issues to the boiling point.

In the automobile industry, craft raids were attempted, and the workers again formed independent unions, one of them with the blessing of the radio priest from Royal Oak. Auto unionists again tore up their A.F. of L. cards. They would not pay dues, refusing to throw more money after the $125,000 they had paid into the Federation treasury in a single year. The machinists' union demanded and received hundreds of auto workers, and then could not hold them. In a Cleveland plant of 2,400 men, the crafts took over hundreds of workers and succeeded in holding but six of them. One Toledo auto union, well organized, had its members parceled among seven craft organizations, until none but sweepers remained. Another Cleveland local of 600 workers was assigned to six craft unions, whereupon all left the A.F. of L. and joined an independent movement. At the Budd Manufacturing Company, the members of the auto local struck and the pattern-makers union members remained at work. A movement in the Mechanics Educational Society of America to merge with the new United Automobile Workers Union was held up because the M.E.S.A. members were demanded by the machinists' union.

The new rubber union was beset by similar sabotage. A Barberton local turned over 100 members to craft unions which failed to hold any of them. In an Akron plant, 432 workers were given to the machinists' union; only five chose to continue their membership.

Several locals of radio workers were refused charters because the electricians' union claimed jurisdiction; nevertheless, the Philco radio local helped organize a number of craftsmen for the building unions. In Cincinnati, a radio local organized 200 men and was then forced to turn over forty-five to the machinists. In one radio factory, five craft unions claimed jurisdiction over a single worker.

[97]

A machinists' union member became head of a company union formed in opposition to a federal radio local. During a Cincinnati radio workers' strike, members of the machinists' union "scabbed."

The report of the executive council to the Atlantic City convention presented further discouraging news. It had not seemed "opportune" for the Federation to initiate the steel organization campaign which had been directed by the San Francisco convention. It had also been deemed inadvisable to charter international unions in the cement, aluminum, and the gas, coke, and by-product industries. In textile, the "great victory" had proved illusory. The new Textile Labor Relations Board had certified the Good Will Adjustment Club, a company union, as the collective bargaining agency for the Standard Kossa Thacher Company; former strikers of the Ninety-Six Cotton Mill had been denied reinstatement, because, the board ruled, "the complainants' strike was unsuccessful and for that reason it is not incumbent upon the employer to reinstate the strikers."

After recounting these facts under the heading of "Progress of Organization in Mass Production Industries," the council's report for 1935 urged a "liberal, broad, and flexible policy in mass production industries . . .," and "calm, intelligent, dispassionate discussion, education and the pursuit of progressive policies." Central labor bodies in various cities were urged to take over the burden of organization, and the Federation, it was suggested, would "coördinate and help in every way possible."

5.

STORM OVER ATLANTIC CITY

I

THE peaceful calm over Atlantic City's broad sea walk found no counterpart in the breasts of the 500 delegates who descended upon it for the Federation's fifty-fifth annual convention in mid-October of 1935. Trouble was in the air from the outset. There was the feeling that the old Federation was at the parting of the ways. It was, perhaps, the last united convention for years to come of American organized labor, the first indications of the passing of an old institution, not the first futilely to pit tradition against the necessity for modernization. A convention of the old Federation was an opportunity to observe labor leadership and it would be particularly profitable to pause and note the constituent parts of the 1935 version, differing as it did from its predecessors.

Foremost and more numerous than any other definable group, there were the building-trades leaders, "the lords of labor": Hutcheson of the carpenters, Daniel W. Tracy of the electricians, John Possehl of the hoisting engineers, John Coefield of the plumbers, Joseph V. Moreschi of the common laborers, Lawrence P. Lindeloff of the painters, and lesser spokesmen of the aristocracy. Each was virtually a law unto himself in his organization. Each had builded a union, as men in other walks of life had builded a business, and each felt that the dividends —— the well-paid jobs, the patronage, the prestige, were by rights his own. Most of them Irish, all of them resembling municipal machine politicians, which, in fact, most of them were. Their organizations held conventions at intervals of five and seven and eight years, perfunctory affairs at which their re-election was as predictable as the sessions of the Daughters of the

American Revolution. Most of the charges of labor racketeering, substantial, if greatly exaggerated, had been leveled against these unions.

Possehl shares his influence with stubby, round-faced Joseph Fay of Jersey City, sometime close pal of Mayor Frank Hague, and renter of appliances which employers who want to hire engineers find it wise to lease. Norman Redwood, a bitter foe of Fay's in the New York labor movement, was murdered in the course of a labor feud. During the Redwood scandal serious charges were made against Moreschi's union, but this was not enough to bestir the Federation to investigate. Moreschi's union, in fact, has an aura of paternalism with its president a benevolent despot. For Moreschi's social gifts there is perhaps more to be said. At the Atlantic City convention he sat nightly at the head of a large raised table, weighted down with choice, spiced Italian foods and good wines. Around him was grouped a selection of Italian and other building-trades leaders from New York and Chicago, dining and drinking into the night, unconcerned with the headaches in the committee rooms of the convention upstairs. They would be on hand for the important voting. At Tampa, in 1936, Moreschi visited Ybor City, the Spanish settlement, and picked up an accordion-player who thenceforth became his nightly attendant at dinner and in the convivial midnight set-tos where he and Gainor, the aged but sturdy head of the letter carriers' union, would far outdo the others in absorption of potent liquids. It was at these nocturnal sessions that the veneer of trade-union solidarity came off, and one could hear the new unionists and the federal unions spoken of as parasites, reds, garbage and crackpots who were in the A.F. of L. on sufferance and had shown base ingratitude for the privilege accorded them.

Hard by the stalwarts of the building-trades men stood the leaders of the railroad unions, and those unions, like machinists, boiler-makers and blacksmiths, whose members work both in railroad repair shops and in machine shops. The rail union heads are several grades higher in trade-union standards than the building-trades lords. Wharton, the suspicious, mistrustful and uncompromising in his advocacy of craft unionism, belongs in this group. It includes

[100]

also Felix H. Knight of the Brotherhood of Railway Carmen; George H. Harrison of the Brotherhood of Railway Clerks, most progressive of the railroad organizations, and Fred H. Fljozdal, ruler of the Brotherhood of Maintenance of Way Employees. They have, because of the essential nature of the railroad industry, won a large measure of recognition by law, partly as a result of which they have evolved a chain of "system federations" in which the various unions join for collective bargaining with a given railroad. Since most of these unions were going concerns before they came together for' joint efforts, the "system federations" have worked well,˙and the union leaders in this group can, therefore, see no need for industrial unionism for the unorganized. In addition to their craft bias, their opposition is explained also by the fact that, in alliance with the building-trades unions, they control the executive council and the affairs of the Federation. Wharton imparts most of the fear of industrial unionism. His organization, he is afraid, together with Tobin's teamsters, stands to lose most by the possible extension of industrial unionism beyond the unorganized industries.

Ranged with the point of view of these two groups were a host of individuals who escape general classification. There was George J. Scalise, the swarthy, sleek Brooklyn undertaker, who tried a succession of unions before he came to roost as the president of the Building Service Employees' International Union, grounded most firmly in the notorious flat janitors' local built during the Capone reign in Chicago. The 1934 convention harbored at least one of the Capone luminaries, Louis (Two Gun) Altiere, then a vice-president of this International. It was Altiere who gained immortality in the gangster world when he avenged a fellow-gangster who had been thrown from a horse and killed. Two-gun Louis bought the horse and took him to a Chicago park for a "ride" which was terminated by shooting the animal in the head. Federation leaders recall the other Chicago labor leader who was sent as fraternal delegate to the British Trade Union Congress and took with him four armed bodyguards whom he introduced to his puzzled British hosts as "secretaries." In the undefinable groupings at the conventions there must also be placed Edward Flore, bald-pated president of the

Hotel and Restaurant Employees International Alliance and Bartenders League of America, who in 1936 aspired to and won a place on the executive council while the leaders of two large New York local unions were being indicted and convicted as racketeers.

Also a power to himself is Joseph P. Ryan, president of the International Longshoremen's Association, bulky and bellicose, with a weakness for tony silk pajamas and a handy predilection for blaming the "reds" for every difficulty that hinders his overlordship of the dock-wallopers who toil on the piers of the Atlantic coast. By the side of pier-boss Ryan should be placed the strange breed of seamen's leaders—beefy, verbose Olander; David G. (The Emperor Jones) Grange, story-teller-extraordinary, with a constant attendant who wears a hat labeled "personal valet" and a turbaned Negro chauffeur; and that pince-nezed labor leader, Gus Brown. It was they who took advantage of the illness and aloofness of Andy Furuseth to reduce the International Seamens Union to a position where even the executive council of the A.F. of L. was forced to abandon it.

We have treated of Woll and Frey, both of them, supposedly, men of superior intellect, who have nevertheless found a "basis of accommodation" over a period of years with the strangest assortment of leaders who ever claimed the common man's loyalty. Also among the stand-patters at the 1935 convention were the several veteran job-holders who clung to puny organizations which stood astride the path of progress for new, large organizations. Grandmother Tighe and Shorty Leonard, W. G. Desepte and C. C. Coulter of the Retail Clerks International Protective Association; the octogenarian, W. E. Bryan of the International Union of United Leather Workers; Walter C. Brooks, of the Laundry Workers International Union, were among these. Only the secrets within the recesses of the innermost circle of the Federation hierarchy can explain the tremendous importance of Thomas A. Rickert, president of the United Garment Workers. It was Rickert who drove the men's clothing workers from the Federation fold in 1914 and agreed to readmit them 20 years later only on the basis of a promise to purchase annually a large quantity of United Garment Workers' labels. This sale to a fellow union gave the Rickert organization a profit of about $20,000 a year.

The opposing array of Federation leaders appeared in 1934, and came into clear focus in 1935. There was, of course, Lewis and his group of miners, the calm, wise, and kindly Thomas J. Kennedy, Lieutenant-Governor of Pennsylvania; Philip Murray, erect Scotch-burred Pittsburghian, a clear-voiced and insinuating speaker and master of intricate negotiating; Van A. Bittner, the bitter-tongued old mine-union hand from West Virginia; P. T. Fagan, regular who had withstood many revolts in the coal mines near Pittsburgh. Lewis came to Atlantic City like a general. He brought a headquarters staff, Murray, Kennedy, Bittner, and John Brophy, who was enjoying a large measure of vindication for the principles he had vainly urged on the miners a decade ago. There were others, too: a full complement of orators, tacticians, researchers, and pulse-feelers, eyes and ears. They immediately set themselves up, a half-mile from the seething convention hotel, apart from the rest of the delegates, creating at once resentment and respect. At the few between-session recesses when Lewis paid visits to the convention hotel, he was the object of all eyes and tongues. Reporters and delegates elbowed one another for a word with him. One evening, Green bided his time for forty-five minutes in a hotel lobby to engage Lewis as soon as he was free. In his rush to get to the mine-union president's side, the president of the Federation forcibly shoved a newspaperman aside. Oratorical and dramatic on the platform, Lewis in his board-walk and hotel chats was informal, mellow, and satirical, presenting a telling comparison with the tedious, unending ramblings of Colonel Frey or the stand-offish, cautious phrases of Woll.

Under the leadership of Lewis, the Federation progressives, disheartened and forced into compromises for years, blossomed again. Dubinsky, of the International Ladies' Garment Workers Union, tugged toward caution by politic Isadore Nagler and pulled to the left by the Socialist, Julius Hochman, joined the Lewis camp. Hillman, slated because of his two decades of dual unionism to be forever an outcast from the A.F. of L. ruling circle, was with Lewis from the start. The other progressive needle trade-unionists, leaders of the furriers' and hatmakers' unions, found Lewis also a natural leader, although their years of association with the Woll leadership made them somewhat chary of Lewis' great driving power. The brewers' leader, Joseph Obergfell; Reid Robinson of the metal miners; the meat cutters' president, Dennis Lane; and the bakers' spokesman, A. A. Myrup; all these had backgrounds of Socialism or their unions were of the industrial type, which led them naturally to the side of Lewis. Then there was the host of newcomers, making up for their lack of votes by their persistence; George Addes and Wyndham Mortimer of the auto workers, shepherded leech-like throughout by their "president," Mr. Dillon; James F. Carey, the stripling from Philadelphia who had become the advocate of an industrial union for his radio workers; S. H. Dalrymple, W. W. Thompson, and Thomas F. Burns, who had so shamefully ragged President Green at the rubber workers' convention.

For integrity and intelligent devotion to labor, under tremendous odds, most delegates gave the palm to A. Philip Randolph, the Negro Socialist who had spent ten years organizing the Brotherhood of Sleeping Car Porters as a symbol for the rest of his race of what unionism might mean to them. Year after year, Randolph had arisen at conventions, amid snarls of impatience, to speak courageously and effectively for racial tolerance in a movement where race lines ought to have been forgotten. He was as moving as any other labor leader, and far better equipped mentally than most. It remained for Frey, at one convention, to refer in resentment to the Negro's college training, a training, Frey added, which he had not been fortunate enough to have.

II

How hopeless was the possibility of dissuading the craft unions from the homicidal perseverance with which they were attacking and raiding the new unions could be seen in the number of jurisdictional wars which raged between the crafts themselves at Atlantic City. Every jurisdictional fight is, in its most important characteristics, an expression either of craft possessiveness or aggrandizement. The logical cure would be amalgamation of the warring unions. Of course this would lead to industrial unionism and, equally obvious, to opposition by the craft chiefs. How could nineteen presidents of nineteen building-trades unions, each with a host of paid business agents, contemplate an amalgamation which would require but one paid president and a single set of business agents? The building trades war, which had started almost with the birth of the Federation, was in an acute stage again when the Atlantic City convention opened. The Federation had been led to recognize the larger building unions—those of the carpenters, electricians, teamsters, bricklayers, engineers, hod-carriers, and common laborers, and the International Association of Marble, Slate, and Stone Polishers, Rubbers, Sawyers, Tile and Marble Setters, Helpers and Terrazo Helpers—as constituting the Building Trades Department. On the outside remained twelve other unions, including those of elevator constructors, boilermakers, bridge and structural iron workers, granite-cutters, lathers, painters, plasterers, plumbers, and stonecutters. The latter, stating that the unions in the official Building Trades Department, had paid per capita dues on inflated memberships so that they might dominate jurisdictional disputes, had set up a rump department. The former was headed by J. W. Williams of the carpenters' union, the "rebels" by Michael J. McDonough of the plasterers. In addition, Frey's molders were having a private fight with the International Brotherhood of Foundry Employees; the Masters, Mates, and Pilots of America were at odds with the seamens' union; all the building-trades unions had ganged up to devour the new oil-field workers' organization; and the Mine, Mill, and Smelter Workers' Union was seeking redress for the craft unions' raid in Butte.

The strategy of Lewis, devised single-handedly, was to dent the prestige of the dominant forces, the building-trades men, and of Woll and Green, the crafts' spokesmen. This accomplished in the early days of the two-week convention, there might be a possibility of winning the fight for industrial unionism; even if this failed to result, a temporary defeat would demonstrate to the country that Green and Woll and their executive council were no longer the martinets they had been. This was something to be desired, since Lewis looked forward to a contest which would not end with the adjournment of the convention. He accomplished his purpose with several unexpected strokes.

Green had asked the convention to bless the Williams Building Trades Council. He had made it a matter of prestige, both his own and the executive council's. When the issue came to the floor, on a question of sustaining the council's stand, Lewis sent Murray to the rostrum. The appearance of the miner was a complete surprise. What had the miners to do with a building trades family fight? In a few well-turned phrases Murray presented the issue as one in which the council was attempting to intrude itself on the time-honored autonomy of the affiliated internationals. Each international is sovereign, Murray argued, citing precedent and policy. Murray proposed deferring action. The vote was taken. The Lewis bloc and the McDonough group of building-trades men joined hands, emerging at the winning end of an 18,092 to 10,603 vote. Green repudiated at an A.F. of L. convention! The press appreciated the story. Then came days of feverish secret bickering. Unless the two departments got together, Lewis would win on other issues. Green remonstrated bitterly far into the night with the hard-boiled craft unionists. On the third day he was relieved. With tired happiness he told the convention that "words are inadequate to express my feeling of happiness, satisfaction, and pleasure." The building unions had reached a compromise, thanks to the Lewis threat. Meanwhile Lewis had gained all he expected. Green, for the first time, had been at the short end of a vote.

"John, what have we got on the National Civic Federation?" Lewis inquired of Brophy that evening. "What kind of advertisements has the *American Federationist* been printing?"

Within a few hours the desired information was at hand. The following day Lewis rose in his seat in the rear of the convention hall.

"Mr. Chairman," Lewis said, and proceeded in measured deliberation, "I ask unanimous consent to present two resolutions."

There were objections. What were the resolutions? Lewis replied that they could be read after they had been accepted for consideration.

"Do I get unanimous consent?" Lewis repeated, taking in the delegations with a slowly executed arc of disdainful eyes.

"Not my consent. I want to hear them first." Wharton speaking.

Lewis read his resolutions, which were shorn of all "whereases":

"Resolved that no officer of the A.F. of L. shall act as an officer of the National Civic Federation or be a member thereof." And the other: "Resolved, that the *American Federationist* be prohibited from the acceptance of any advertisement or paid printing of any character from concerns which do not generally recognize and practice collective bargaining."

"Now is there any objection?" Lewis asked. There was none, and the proposals went to the resolutions committee.

Lewis was inviting Woll, the acting president of the National Civic Federation, to a pitched battle on the floor of the convention. The haste of the maneuver had not permitted Lewis to get the strongest possible case against the National Civic Federation. Woll did not know this, however, and feared the worst. He took council with the late William English Walling, Socialist gone conservative, and returned to the afternoon session with his resignation from the Civic Federation. In New York, Ralph Easley cried, "Sam Gompers would have put up a fight." But Woll apparently was not Gompers. He stated that he had been trying to resign from the Civic Federation for some time, and now that his membership had been objected to, he "would not continue an association that is disagreeable even to a minority of the A.F. of L."

"I am not acting under compulsion," Woll told the convention, "but under the spirit of voluntarism."

The resolution dealing with the *American Federationist* was a sharp criticism of the council which had been accepting funds in exchange for advertisements from General Motors, U.S. Steel, and other bitter foes of unionism. The resolution needed merely to be stated to make its point. It was passed without debate.

Lewis upset the smooth operation of the council's machine in one other respect. On the recommendation of Woll, the council had urged that the Federation constitution bar any union officered by Communists from representation at conventions. Lewis opposed the proposal for three reasons: he wanted again to humble the executive council; he was against the extension of red-baiting, which, he felt, was a cloak for attacks on most things progressive; and he did not wish to establish a policy whereby the council might circumscribe the rights of the international unions. He carried his point. As the council's report came from the committee on constitution, it was modified to apply only to representation in city and state councils of the Federation. As such it passed without opposition.

III

The debates on industrial unionism started on the eighth day of the convention. There were twenty-one resolutions on the subject, nine specifying single industries, the others dealing with the general principle. The resolutions committee made no effort to reach agreement on the subject, so obvious was the division. A majority, eight members of the committee, opposed industrial unionism; six, led by Lewis and Howard, were favorable. Frey reported for the majority, which held that the San Francisco resolution had been "misunderstood" and that the minority now sought to "set aside existing international unions" in favor of industrial organizations. The 1934 declaration had specified, the Frey report maintained, that only "mass production" workers were to be granted new charters. (Actually, the executive council had been "directed to issue charters for national or international unions in the automotive, cement, aluminum, and such other mass-production industries as in the judgment of the executive council may be necessary to meet the situation.") To support his interpretation, Frey quoted from the 1934 statement: "We consider it our duty . . . to protect the jurisdiction rights of all trade unions organized upon craft lines and afford them every opportunity for development of accession of those workers engaged upon work over which these organizations exercise jurisdiction." Thus, said the 1935 report read by Frey, the San Francisco statement had recognized "the contracts" entered into between the craft unions and the Federation during the latter decades of the last century.

"The American Federation of Labor could not have been organized upon any other basis of relationship," the report concluded. "It is recognized that where a contract is entered into between parties, it cannot be set aside or altered by one party without the consent and approval of the other. For these valid and vital reasons, your committee recommends . . . reaffirmation of the declaration of the San Francisco convention."

Howard then offered the minority report signed by six members

[108]

and approved by a seventh, who, he said, had not attached his signature "because of the pressure that was put upon him by well-known methods in this convention." The Howard report of 1935 was clear, where his 1934 proposal was vague. It held that after 55 years of effort, the Federation had failed to organize American labor and that it had approximately 3,500,000 out of 39,000,000 organizable workers in its unions. The statement continued:

"We declare the time has arrived when common sense demands that the organization policies of the A.F. of L. must be molded to meet present-day needs. In the great mass-production industries and those in which the workers are composite mechanics, specialized and engaged upon classes of work which do not qualify them for craft-union membership, industrial organization is the only solution. . . .

"In those industries where the work performed by a majority of the workers is of such nature that it might fall within the jurisdictional claim of more than one craft union, or no establjshed craft union, it is declared that industrial organization is the only form that will be acceptable to the workers or adequately meet their needs. Jurisdictional claims over small groups of workers in these industries prevent organization by breeding a fear that, when once organized, the workers in these plants will be separated, unity of action and their economic power destroyed by requiring various groups to transfer to national and international unions organized upon craft lines."

The American Federation of Labor, the minority report continued, "must recognize the right of these workers to organize into industrial unions and be granted unrestricted charters which guarantee the right to accept into membership all workers employed in the industry. . . . It is not the intention of this declaration of policy to permit the taking away from national or international craft unions any part of their present membership, or potential membership, in establishments where the dominant factor is skilled craftsmen. . . .

"The executive council is directed and instructed to issue unrestricted charters to organizations formed in accordance with the policy herein enunciated. The executive council is also instructed

[109]

to enter upon an aggressive organization campaign in those industries in which the great mass of the workers are not now organized, issue unrestricted charters to workers organized into independent unions, company-dominated unions, and those organizations now affiliated with associations not recognized by the A.F. of L. as bona fide organizations."

The Lewis proposal, in brief, was that the craft unions were not to have jurisdiction over any workers in predominantly mass production industries—autos, steel, rubber, aluminum, radio, electrical appliances, cement. It also urged a new approach to the company unions. It proposed an effort to win over and absorb these groups.

The principal debate came on the Frey and Howard reports. The issue was argued again on the fight of the Mine, Mill, and Smelter Workers Union against the craft-union raids; it had an airing a third time when delegates of the auto, rubber, and radio unions pleaded for a new policy with regard to their respective industries. For moments during the many hours of tense combat, the debate reached the high levels that had made noteworthy the conventions of three decades ago when Gompers led a young, aggressive, keen group of devoted craft unionists in defensive battles against the able attacks of Max Hayes, the Cleveland printer, and other Socialist trade unionists who aided Hayes' onslaughts on the policy of craft exclusiveness.

The addresses of Lewis, Howard, and Tobin at Atlantic City deserve to rank high. Howard was cool, analytical, and precise, establishing confidence at once by pointing out that he represented the typographical union, perhaps the most highly skilled collection of workers in the A.F. of L., but was nevertheless pleading for a new type of unionism. He referred to the fact that in some modern factories workers in a single day perform tasks which would bring them within the established jurisdictions of four or five craft unions. These workers, he pointed out, could not be induced to join Federal unions as long as there was the threat that eventually they would become the prey of conflicting crafts. Woll replied with legalistic citations, combining his attack on industrial unionism with a criticism of the Wagner National Labor Relations Act. Both, he insisted, would rob the Federation of its priceless "voluntarism," because both would take from the crafts and the executive council the power to determine proper collective bargaining units. The unions were in danger of being placed in a straitjacket. The answer to this threat, said the lawyer-labor leader, was to give the executive council discretion to meet such problems as those when they arose. He then gave way to Lewis. The miners' president combined humor, irony, and statistics, mingling with them prophetic warnings of division and decay unless the Federation was willing to grasp modern policies. He told of his years as an organizer for the Federation in the steel, rubber, glass, copper, and lumber industries.

"I have not gained my experience and knowledge through delving into economic treatises, or while sitting in a swivel chair pondering upon the manner in which those upon the firing-line should meet their daily problems," Lewis said.

"I have seen every attempt to organize these workers break upon the same rock that breaks them today—the rock of utter futility, the lack of reasonableness in a policy that failed to take into consideration the dreams and requirements of the workers themselves and the recognized power of the adversaries of labor to destroy these feeble organizations in the great modern industries."

He called the Federation's organizing efforts "twenty-five years of unbroken failure." He asked, where were the 25,000,000 members President Green had predicted would join the Federation? Quoting then from the executive council's report, he did some simple arithmetic with the federal union figures, showing how 1,650 paid and volunteer Federation organizers had failed to hold the gains of the NRA period. New unions were "dying like the grass withering before the autumn sun." Then he referred to Woll's plea for faith in the executive council.

"A year ago I was younger and naturally I had more faith in the executive council," he smiled. "I was beguiled into believing that the executive council would honestly interpret and administer this policy—the policy of issuing charters for industrial unions in the mass-production industries. Surely, Delegate Woll will not hold it against me that I was so trusting at that time. I know better now. At San Francisco they seduced me with fair words. Now, of course, having learned that I was seduced, I am enraged and I am ready to rend my seducers limb from limb, including Delegate Woll. In that sense, of course, I speak figuratively.

"At San Francisco, as I say, I was younger and more gullible, and I did not realize how much influence the National Civic Federation had with the A.F. of L. executive council—but I know now—perhaps not so much now, since the National Civic Federation is without a president, so I am informed."

The miners, Lewis continued, were anxious to have the steel industry organized, because until it was the mine union would not be safe from destruction. "Miners on strike in the captive mines of the Tennessee Coal & Iron Company," said Lewis, "are suffering tonight by the fact that the A.F. of L. has failed, after all these years, to organize the iron and steel workers." He turned then to the larger significance of the problem, holding that the feeble influence of the Federation was not enough to guarantee the future of democracy in the United States.

"What of the future of our country?" he asked. "Who among us that does not know the hazards of the present moment? The teachings of false prophets falling upon the ears of a population that is frightened and discouraged, depressed and disturbed, the attempts of interests to form a philosophy, the philosophy of the Communists on one hand and the philosophy of the Nazis on the other hand, equally repugnant and distasteful to the man of labor. . . . How much more security would we have for the future of our form of government if we had a virile labor movement that represented, not a mere cross section of skilled workers, but the men who work in our great industries, regardless of their trade and calling?"

Then Lewis turned advocate for the "under dogs."

"Why not make a contribution to the well-being of those who are not fortunate enough to be members of your organizations? The labor movement is organized upon the principle that the strong shall help the weak. Is it right, after all, that because some of us are capable of forging great and powerful organizations of skilled craftsmen in this country that we should lock ourselves up in our own domain and say, 'I am merely working for those who pay me?' Isn't it right that we should contribute something of our own strength, our own knowledge, our own influence toward those less fortunately situated, in the knowledge that if we help them and they grow strong, in turn we will be the beneficiaries of their changed status and their strength?

"The strength of a strong man is a prideful thing, but the unfortunate thing in life is that strong men do not remain strong. And that is just as true of unions and labor organizations. And whereas today the craft unions may be able to stand upon their own feet and, like mighty oaks before the gale, defy the lightning, the day may come when this changed scheme of things—and things are rapidly changing now—the day may come when these organizations will not be able to withstand the lightning and the gale.

"Prepare yourselves by making a contribution to your less fortunate brethren. Heed this cry from Macedonia that comes from the hearts of men. Organize the unorganized and in doing this make the A.F. of L. the greatest instrument that has ever been forged to befriend the cause of humanity and champion human rights."

The president of the miners' union, pleading for the scorned and exploited mill hands, the machine-tenders in steel, autos, and rubber, knew his plea would not be honored, and he closed on a note almost of despair.

"If we fail . . . the workers will believe and know that the A.F. of L. cannot and will not make a contribution toward the obvious need of our present economic conditions. . . . We will be compelled to carry on as best we can in the mining industry, knowing that our terrible adversary, the steel industry, having tasted blood, may at any time open up and attempt to destroy us. . . . We will accept that decision sadly, for despair will prevail where hope now exists. The enemies of labor will be encouraged and high wassail will prevail at the banquet tables of the mighty if the A.F. of L. refuses to grant the petition of these industries who are fighting for the objectives of labor and to defend the right of mankind."

The convention adjourned for a few hours after Lewis' appeal, and that evening the debate was resumed. Frey was peevish, taking time for inconsequential personal defenses, and ending with his version of the history of the labor movement. After that the debate sank to burlesque as Shorty Leonard told of the "great efforts" of his Amalgamated to organize the steel workers, and to punishing verbosity, as Olander, the sailor-politician, stated, at length, that he had nothing to say. Murray brought back reality as he told of the weakness of the craft unions in the great Pittsburgh industrial area. Wharton spoke of the railroad unions' success with the joint "system federations." The aged Thomas W. McMahon, president of the textile union, closed the debate with a plea for the older men to adjust themselves to new conditions. The roll was called and the vote stood 18,204 to 10,933 in favor of the craft unions.

The next day, October 17th, the resolutions committee brought in a report rejecting the petition of the metal miners, and the conflict was on again. The youthful, lanky Paul Peterson, hard rock miner and member of the Utah legislature, pleaded for the crafts to honor the jurisdiction which had been accorded his organization with the approval of both Gompers and Green. A succession of craft-union leaders, Franklin of the boilermakers, Horn of the blacksmiths, Tracy of the electricians, Frey of the molders, and Wharton of the machinists, rose to cite the dates, in the 'eighties and 'nineties, when the craft unions had chartered small locals in the mining camps and cities of Montana. Lewis spoke again, demanding to know whether the crafts would honor the "contract" made with the metal miners; and then the debate gave way to a barrage against the United Mine Workers. It had gobbled up craftsmen here and there; it was defiant and arrogant; it was unappreciative of the help given it by the crafts during coal strikes. Lewis tried to reply, but was rebuffed by cries from the craftsmen that they had heard enough from him. Van Bittner, the pointed-tongued miner, took over the defense of the miners' union and turned it into a piercingly satirical attack on the crafts and the executive council. If ever *lèse-majesté* was committed against the elders of the council, the widemouthed Van Bittner did it that day. He bade them not to take themselves too seriously, since nobody else did. He challenged the council members to deny that not a handful of the millions of Federation members knew their names. He told of the machinists' leaders' attempt to sabotage the mine union bill, the Guffey Coal Act, and challenged the crafts to try to pry loose so much as a single member of the miners' union. Kennedy followed with figures to show how the miners had repaid many times over the money donated to the U.M.W. in its hours of stress.

Finally, the sturdy Tobin thundered his defiance to the "gates of hell" to prevail against the "rock of crafts' autonomy, craft trades." The teamsters' president saw in the industrial unionism movement "an attempt to destroy the very foundations upon which this Federation has been builded and upon which it has succeeded for years." He called the roll—P. J. McGuire, James Duncan, and "Gompers the Jew, driven from London to become the greatest American citizen labor had ever produced"—men who had salvaged the crafts from the Knights of Labor; and asked the convention to contemplate how "these spirits must writhe in persecution and misery listening to the charges and counter-charges that this Federation of Labor has been twenty-five years of continuous failure."

Then an inebriated delegate gained the floor, relieved the tension somewhat, and that debate was over. The vote for the metal miners' claims stood at 10,897; opposed, 18,464.

The craft delegates were in no mood for the third installment of the debate, which came on the last day of the convention when delegates from the federal unions and the new auto and rubber internationals insisted on presenting their cases. The impatience boiled over at the carpenters' bench. Thompson of Akron was telling of the craft unions' failure to hold the rubber workers they had taken over, when Hutcheson reared his massive bulk to raise a point of order.

"My point," said the carpenters' president, "is that the industrial union question has been previously settled by this convention."

Thompson protested he was speaking on the peculiar problems of the rubber workers. Hutcheson persisted, and Green ruled his objection well taken. Howard protested, to no avail. Lewis then urged the right of the rubber union delegates to be heard on their own problems.

"This thing of raising points of order all the time on minor delegates is rather small potatoes," Lewis observed.

Hutcheson was on his feet again, his face florid with anger.

"I was raised on small potatoes. That is why I am so small," he challenged. "Had the delegate who has just spoken given more

[115]

consideration to the questions before this convention instead of attempting, in a dramatic way, to impress the delegates with his sincerity we would have had more time to devote to the questions before this convention."

There followed more points of order. Green was formalizing his ruling that Thompson could not continue to speak, but the attention of the delegates and visitors was elsewhere.

Lewis had stepped to the center of the floor to make his objection heard, and the way back to his seat took him beside the table at which Hutcheson and his delegation were seated. Hutcheson was on his feet, and Lewis had paused. There was low-toned conversation between them.

"Pretty small stuff," the miners' chief said.

"We could have made you small; could have kept you off the executive council, if we wanted to," Hutcheson retorted. Then he added something about a "bastard."

The mine leader's right fist shot straight out. There was no swing to the blow, just a swift jab with 225 pounds behind it. It caught the carpenters' president on the jaw. Instantly other carpenters' officials rushed at Lewis, and, as suddenly, the latter's colleagues sprang from their near-by seats. Hutcheson went crashing against his long table, which went over under the impact of ten or more delegates pushing, elbowing, punching. Other rushed to separate the fighters and in a few minutes the battle was over. Hutcheson was lifted to his feet. Blood streaked one side of his face from his forehead to his chin. Friends guided him to the washroom, where Lieutenant-Governor Kennedy, who had been an absentee during the mêlée, looked up in completely innocent solicitude.

"What's the matter, Hutch? Did you take a fall?" he asked.

Meanwhile, in the hall of the Chelsea Hotel the convention was trying to right itself. Frey was by the side of Green, clasping and unclasping his hand.

"This will wreck the labor movement," he cried.

Lewis casually adjusted his collar and tie, relit his cigar, and sauntered slowly through the crowded aisles to the rostrum. He mounted the platform.

"You shouldn't have done that, John," Green remonstrated.

"He called me a foul name."

"Oh, I didn't know that." William Green, ever the man to see both sides and usually end up on neither.

From then on, all was anti-climax. Addes, Mortimer and others of the auto workers, Carey of the radio workers, pleaded their cases, and there was none to halt them, though the Green ruling on the rubber workers' debate might have applied.

That night the convention, most fateful in the history of American organized labor, ended on a fitting note. In the absence of most of the delegates, as the session opened, the carpenters forced the tabling of a resolution calling for an amendment to the Federal Constitution. Later, Dubinsky drummed up enough support to countermand the snap vote. Randolph defeated an effort to choke off discussion of many of the craft unions' refusal to admit Negroes to membership, made his usual eloquent appeal to a largely bored audience, and was, as usual, voted down on his plea for erasure of color lines. The convention adjourned.

Lewis had lost the convention as far as the vote tallies showed, but he had risen to the position of organized labor's most important leader, a possible labor's man of destiny. The day after the convention adjourned, nine leaders of the Lewis bloc—Lewis, Murray, Brophy, Dubinsky, Kennedy, Hillman, Howard, Zaritsky, McMahon —met at the Hotel President in Atlantic City and planned the Committee for Industrial Organization.

6.

AMERICAN LABOR DIVIDES

I

"DEAR Sir and Brother," Lewis wrote to Green on November 23, 1935. "Effective this date, I resign as vice-president of the American Federation of Labor."

To a large audience of newspaper men who crowded the board room of the United Mine Workers headquarters in Washington, Lewis added that he had neither the inclination nor the time to "follow the council in its seasonal peregrinations from the Jersey beaches in the summer to the golden sands of Florida in the winter."

Lewis' desire after the Atlantic City convention was to plunge ahead with organizing campaigns in steel and autos, but it was fully a year before he had accomplished the task of casting aside Federation restraints without appearing to be intent on division. The latter was necessary if he was not to arouse cries of "splitter." He was spared this responsibility by the actions of the executive council, which took the initiative, first at discipline, then at suspension, and finally at organic, if not yet technical, expulsion.

The post-convention stock-taking of industrial union leaders in Atlantic City was followed by a session at the mine union offices in Washington on October 9th. Eight heads of international unions—Lewis, Howard, Hillman, Dubinsky, McMahon, Harvey Fremming of the Oil Field, Gas Well and Refinery Workers; Max Zaritsky, then head of the Cap and Millinery Department of the United Hatters; and Thomas H. Brown of the International Union of Mine, Mill, and Smelter Workers—attended and jointly announced formation of the Committee for Industrial Organization. They declared the committee would work in accordance with the principles and policies enunciated by their organizations at Atlantic City. The declared purpose of the committee was "to encourage and promote organization of the workers in the mass-production and unorganized industries of the nation, and affiliation with the American Federation of Labor." The functions of the committee were to be "educational and advisory." Lewis was named chairman, Howard secretary, and John Brophy executive director.

Two weeks after the C.I.O. proclaimed its purpose, Green informed its affiliates of his "apprehension and deep concern" over the turn of events. He warned that some within the Federation would consider the C.I.O. a dual organization. The leaders of the committee ought to continue the fight for their ideas at succeeding conventions of the Federation and, in the meantime, abide by the majority report adopted at Atlantic City, Green urged. The President of the Federation returned to his theme of "fighting the issue out within the Federation" many times later, insisting at times that "majority rule," rather than craft versus industrial unionism, was the basic issue. On other occasions he interpreted formation of the C.I.O. as a phase of Communist Moscow's plottings, but constantly he returned to the "duty" of a minority to accept the decision of a convention majority. It was Howard who undertook to challenge Green's view of proper democratic processes. The head of the typographical union argued that there were courts higher than the annual conventions—the membership of the Federation's unions and the workers in the industries.

"It is not unethical or improper," Howard insisted, "for a minority to endeavor to have its proposals adopted by the majority through proper discussion of the issues and by an effort to convert those whose interests are most affected—the rank and file of workers. To confine the effort to conventions . . . would be to presume that only the officers and delegates are to be considered, and that the members of the unions who support the Federation, as well as the millions of unorganized to whom we would make appeal, should have no direct interest or influence in making the fundamental policies of the Federation. My experience does not justify acceptance of such a restriction upon the rights of minorities.

"During the years I have been a delegate to the conventions of the

[119]

A.F. of L. I have observed the strongest cohesion in a controlling group for the purpose of determining every question. . . . Some of us have had the conclusion forced upon us that the merits of proposals are not the determining factor in rendering decisions. . . ."

Howard, in a letter to Green on December 2, 1935, declared that the C.I.O. contemplated no departure from the policies adopted by the majority of the Federation. He referred to the resolution approved unanimously at San Francisco, and insisted that the executive council had nullified it by "unsympathetic interpretation and administration." As the author of the report, he added, he felt he was in a fair position to know what was intended; and what was intended, he added, was what the C.I.O. was now setting out to do. He underscored declarations by Lewis that the C.I.O. did not intend to set up a new federation of labor nor "raid" the membership of established unions. The sole concern of the C.I.O., he said, was with the unorganized.

When the executive council of the Federation went into session in Miami, early in January, 1936, it had before it the refusal of the C.I.O. unions to heed Green's plea that they abandon their venture. To emphasize the Committee's determination to carry on, Brophy sent the council a new appeal for industrial union charters in automobiles and rubber, a campaign in steel, and an autonomous, industrial charter for the federal and independent unions affiliated in the National Radio and Allied Trades Council. The reply of the executive council was to declare the C.I.O. "a challenge to the supremacy of the Federation." The Committee, it was decreed, "should be immediately dissolved." To "achieve this purpose and to prevent division, discord, and confusion within the ranks of organized labor," the council appointed a committee of three to confer with the C.I.O. and inform it of the viewpoint of the council members.

The edict brought only further scorn from the leaders of the C.I.O. Brophy called it an attempt to "blackjack" the members of the Committee. He insisted the council could not command the support of a majority of American unionists for its course. The council did not have the power to enforce its decision, Brophy declared. He referred to Article IX, Section 12 of the Federation constitution, which provided that expulsion of international unions might only be carried through by the council acting on a two-thirds vote of a convention. Feeling secure in the protection of the Federation's basic law, Lewis announced that the work of the Committee would go forward without interruption. Meanwhile, he said, the C.I.O. would be glad to confer with the Federation's committee of three. Other decisions of the council served, however, to make remote the possibility of a peaceful adjustment. The Automobile Workers Union was granted the right to elect its own officers, but the council insisted that the machinists' union was to have jurisdiction over jobbing plants which made automobile parts. This would have meant dismemberment of several auto union locals. The radio unions' plea for an international charter was rejected and they were ordered to accept a class "b" (non-voting status) within the International Brotherhood of Electrical Workers.

The C.I.O.'s belief that the council could not master the two-thirds vote necessary to carry through its threats of expulsion, was based on the vote at Atlantic City, and seemed to be a safe enough assumption. But its self-assurance on this score failed to take into account the legal genius within the council. While issuing its "cease and desist" order, coupling it with the appointment of the peace committee, the council also prepared for the contingency that Lewis and his C.I.O. would be adamant. It did not become known until July that on May 18th the council had adopted a special rule which eliminated the restrictions intended by Article IX, Section 12 of the constitution. Section 8 of Article IX gives the council the power "to make rules to govern matters not in conflict with the constitution." This section, judging by its context, was intended to cover administrative problems that might arise between controversies. Under the assumed authority of the section, however, Woll drafted a drastic rule which gave the executive council the power to hear charges of alleged "breach of contract" by an affiliated international union, provided for the holding of "trials" on such charges, and gave the council the right, if the accused unions were found guilty, to order suspension.

That this rule, rather than the gesture of the peace committee, was the kernel of the council's policy became evident from the fact that the committee for more than four months made no effort to contact Lewis or any other C.I.O. leader. The supposed peacemakers, consisting of George H. Harrison, Joseph N. Weber of the American Federation of Musicians, and G. M. Bugniazet of the electricians' union, made its first and only effort toward peace when it informed the C.I.O. unions on May 26th that they had two weeks within which to announce acceptance of the council's "cease and desist" order. The United Mine Workers, followed by the other C.I.O. unions, promptly announced they would neither cease nor desist. Hutcheson and Wharton, supported by Frey, thereupon demanded immediate and drastic action in the shape of a "trial." Harrison and William D. Mahon, of the street carmen's union, urged further efforts at conciliation. The council's course was finally decided by the outcome of an important side-duel in which the C.I.O. and the A.F. of L. had been contesting for the leadership of a campaign in the steel industry.

II

Lewis, late in February, sent Green a C.I.O. offer to contribute $500,000 toward a fund of $1,500,000 for a steel drive. The C.I.O. proposal stipulated that the steel workers, once unionized, were not to be segregated among craft unions, and that "the leadership of the campaign be such as to inspire confidence of success." Green referred the offer to the executive council, which proceeded to outline a plan of its own. This declared that Green, subject to the decisions of the craft unions interested in steel, was to be in charge of the council drive, which was to be financed by a fund of $750,000. The council forwarded its proposal to its affiliated unions. A month elapsed and the only response came from Wharton, who flatly refused to give either financial aid or organizers. Wharton declared that the machinists' union would by itself seek to organize "the men eligible to join our organization in the steel industry." Howard, on behalf of the C.I.O. unions, meanwhile rejected the executive council plan because it failed to guarantee that the union to be organized in steel would be along industrial lines.

The Amalgamated Association was to meet in convention in Canonsburg, Pa., on April 28th. A week previous, Lewis and

Howard addressed a letter to Tighe proposing a joint C.I.O.-Amalgamated campaign. If the Amalgamated decided to accept the C.I.O. offer of funds and coöperation, Lewis and Howard stated, the Committee would expect the convention "to give the organizing committee a reasonably free hand in regard to taking in independent company unions as a body, and keeping initiations and dues low enough to meet requirements of a mass campaign." Green, meanwhile, forwarded the executive council's plan to the Amalgamated convention. The program was now revealed in detail for the first time. It proposed administration of the campaign by the council and the craft unions.

"The character of the campaign . . . shall and must be in accordance with the organization policy of the Federation as decided upon at the Atlantic City convention," Green wrote to Tighe. "While it is the purpose of the executive council to apply the broadest and most comprehensive industrial policy possible, due regard and proper respect for the jurisdictional rights of all national and international unions will be observed. . . ."

Funds would be accepted from all organizations who gave without conditions, said Green. In an interview with the press, he declared that the jurisdictions which would be honored in the steel industry would be those of the machinists, electrical workers, engineers, carpenters and "possibly others." He appeared skeptical about the readiness of the steel workers to respond.

"This business about steel workers clamoring to get into unions is all nonsense," Green declared.

Forty organizers would nevertheless be rushed into steel by the executive council, a headquarters would be opened in Pittsburgh, and a second, possibly, in Gary, Indiana, said Green.

The convention of the Amalgamated Association which secluded itself in Canonsburg for three weeks, locking doors against all reporters and visitors, was dominated by Tighe and Leonard. It nevertheless had a good proportion of new unionists, who were not slow to point out that the Green offer indicated the intention of the executive council to cut away at the jurisdiction which had been accorded the Amalgamated. Telegrams from Lewis and Green bombarded the delegates. Lewis termed the executive council offer "inadequate, futile, and conceived in a mood of humiliated desperation. . . . A rehash of the ancient and futile resolutions adopted from time to time by the A.F. of L. and which have resulted in frittering away years of valuable time." He warned that the executive council offer "would fill your industry with hordes of organizers fiercely competing with each other for the new members . . . and for the few dollars which might be taken in as initiation fees, dues, and collections." Green's telegram, which followed, was a general disclaimer of Lewis' charges. Its weakness, however, was its failure to give assurances that the Amalgamated's jurisdiction would not be invaded, and its omission of a definite pledge of financial support. The Amalgamated convention, torn between Tighe's ancient loyalty to the executive council and the superior offer of the C.I.O., elected a committee of five which journeyed to Washington to seek further light on the proposals. Finally, on May 14th, the Canonsburg delegates emerged to announce their decision. The offers of all unions which waived jurisdictions over steel workers would be accepted. These unions were to form a joint committee which, with the Amalgamated, would direct the drive.

The decision leaned toward the C.I.O. proposal, and Lewis immediately dispatched Murray and Brophy to consult with the officers of the Amalgamated. By May 22nd, however, no word had come from Tighe and Leonard. Lewis demanded an immediate response. A week later, Leonard replied with a request for a conference. The rank and file of the Amalgamated, meanwhile, had been judiciously and effectively approached by C.I.O. representatives, and Lewis' answer to Leonard was written with the confidence of an ultimatum. The C.I.O. chairman agreed to a conference with the Amalgamated officials, but suggested "that it will be a complete waste of time for your committee to attend this meeting unless you are definitely prepared to carry out the instructions imposed by the recent convention." Lewis told Leonard that he was "fully advised concerning your secret conference with Green in Coshocton." The ultimatum concluded: "Hundreds of thousands of men in the iron and steel industry . . . are going to be given the opportunity to be organized either with or without the benefit of the Amalgamated. . . . Your executive board must decide whether it will coöperate or obstruct.

If you do not yet know your own mind, please stay at home. If you are prepared to accept the help of the C.I.O. you will be made welcome."

Leonard immediately came to Washington, bringing a committee of the Amalgamated with him. Tighe, too ill to make the journey, gave Leonard full authority to act for him. On June 3rd, Lewis announced a compact between the C.I.O. and the Amalgamated by which the former was given virtually exclusive direction of a steel campaign. The agreement provided that the Amalgamated was to join the C.I.O. and that a Steel Workers Organizing Committee, which was to include two members of the Amalgamated, was to be appointed by Lewis. The committee was to have power to "handle all matters relative to the organizing campaign"; the C.I.O. unions were to contribute $500,000; the S.W.O.C., the organizing committee, was to have the power to waive payment of initiation fees; dues were to be fixed at one dollar a month; the termination of the campaign was to be on a date and in such manner as the C.I.O. and the S.W.O.C. were to decide.

The terms of the agreement were a complete victory for the C.I.O. Green announced bitterly that the executive council's intention "has now been thwarted." He added that all would "await with interest the final outcome . . . of the adventure."

III

The charges which Green forwarded to the C.I.O. unions on July 16, 1936, accused them of forming a dual organization "clearly competing as a rival organization with the A.F. of L. . . . and engaged in an effort to determine questions of jurisdiction which are in direct conflict with those of the executive council and the conventions of the Federation"; of "fomenting insurrection" within the Federation; of having "violated the contract" which each of them entered into with the A.F. of L. when they were granted certificates of affiliation; and of acts constituting "rebellion against the administrative organization policies adopted by majority vote. . . ."

The C.I.O. had grown to twelve affiliates since its formation in November. The United Automobile Workers, the United Rubber Workers, the Federation of Flat Glass Workers and the Amalgamated

Association of Iron, Steel and Tin Workers had joined in the meantime. All refused to honor the executive council's summons to appear for trial on August 3rd. Howard stated that he was a member of the C.I.O. in his individual capacity and that his union had not affiliated. Zaritsky informed the council that he had acted only for the Cap and Milinery Department of the United Hatters in his affiliation with the Committee. They joined, however, in denouncing the prospective proceedings as "wholly unwarranted by the constitution of the Federation." The trial, the C.I.O. maintained, was intended to circumvent the constitution and was being held because the craft unionists felt they could not muster a two-thirds vote for expulsion at a convention. The special rule which had been adopted was declared to be in express violation of the constitution. The executive council had prejudged the issues and could not sit as a fair tribunal, the C.I.O. unions declared.

The trial proceeded in the executive council room at the Federation's Washington headquarters on August 3rd. Green was in the chair. The judges were the council members, Hutcheson and Frank Duffy of the carpenters, Woll, Coefield, Wharton, Bugniazet, Tobin; Bates of the bricklayers, Gainor, Mahon, and Knight of the Railway Carmen's Union. Frey, who had framed the charges in behalf of the Metal Trades Department, was the prosecutor. For three days, he spoke, reading letters, telegrams, and press releases into the record. Most of the evidence came from the C.I.O.'s weekly clipsheet, the Union News Service. It dealt with Green's initial warning to the C.I.O. unions, and the "cease and desist" order adopted by the council in Miami; with personal references to Adolph Germer and John Brophy, as one-time expelled members of the United Mine Workers; resolutions adopted at San Francisco and Atlantic City; Lewis', Howard's and Green's correspondence with the steel union; and the agreement between the Amalgamated Association and the C.I.O. The agreement showed conclusively that the C.I.O. had "usurped the authority of the A.F. of L.," Frey argued.

Turning to the charges of "dual unionism," Frey read statements in which C.I.O. unions had urged the radio workers' locals to seek an autonomous industrial international charter. Lewis' aid to the radio union in obtaining a settlement of a strike against the Radio

Corporation of America was cited as further encouragement of "dualism." As proof of the "rebellion" against the Federation, Frey cited a newspaper interviewer's conclusions from a talk with Lewis in the summer of 1935, and a threat of a convention of the United Mine Workers to withhold dues payments from the Federation.

Prosecutor Frey then turned to alleged violations of craft-union jurisdictions by C.I.O. affiliates. He accused the rubber and auto workers' unions of appropriating machinists; the Mine, Mill, and Smelter Workers of enrolling hoisting engineers; the Industrial Union of Marine and Shipbuilding Workers, not then an affiliate of the C.I.O., of taking in boilermakers and hod-carriers; and the quarry workers' union of seizing others of Moreschi's dues-paying hod-carriers and common laborers. The quarry workers' union was also unaffiliated with the C.I.O., but Brophy was accused of having advised both it and the shipbuilders' organization to ignore the craft unions' jurisdictions. As a highlight of his case, Frey presented a letter signed by one William E. Siefke, which urged Toledo unions to set up a C.I.O. central labor council. This, said Frey, showed clearly the dual intentions of the C.I.O. He made no effort to link the letter with any responsible C.I.O. official. (As a matter of fact, the C.I.O. was not yet at that time forming central or state councils.) The prosecution concluded with the testimony of E. D. Bieretz, assistant president of the International Brotherhood of Electrical Workers. He told of the radio unions' refusal to accept a class "b" membership in his international, and charged that the C.I.O. had abetted this stand. He dealt in detail with Lewis' assistance during the R.C.A. strike at Camden and summoned one of his local organizers, William C. Beedie, who a few years before had fought the I.B.E.W. as a reactionary union, to identify Powers Hapgood, Socialist and C.I.O. organizer, as having been active in the Camden strike.

Neither members of the A.F. of L. union, nor those of the C.I.O., nor other interested persons may know, at this writing, the actual proceeding of the trial, a most momentous incident in labor history. The pamphlet printed by the A.F. of L., which purports to be a complete record, gives only the Frey presentation. Where important points appear to have been reached, the record reads, "Discussion Off the Record." At one point in the printed proceedings Frey deals with the Mine, Mill, and Smelter Workers' Union absorption of Butte members of the International Union of Operating Engineers. The record proceeds:

" (Discussion off the record.)

"President Green: How do you connect the Committee for Industrial Organization with that situation?

"President Frey: Because these developments in Butte are the direct result of visits of members of the C.I.O. with officers of the Mine, Mill, and Smelter men, and the avowed intention of the Mine, Mill, and Smelter Workers, who are affiliated with the C.I.O., to put its organizing policies into effect."

" (Further discussion off the record.")

Frey's deductions from other bits of "evidence" which he presented were equally esoteric. Speaking of Lee Pressman, who had been appointed general counsel to the C.I.O., he observed: "This fails to say who Lee Pressman was, and so the information will be added that he was formerly counsel for the Resettlement Administration; that he was very close to Tugwell, who, we are informed by the press, very recently, is very close to Mr. John L. Lewis. So the connection, so far as he is concerned, is not difficult to see."

In view of the obvious purpose of the "trial," which was to disfranchise the C.I.O. unions before the next convention of the Federation, it would be rather fruitless to attempt to weigh the "evidence" which Frey read into the record during three hot summer days in Washington. But even a cursory reading indicates that he failed to make out the case of dualism, insurrection, and rebellion of which the C.I.O. unions stood accused. Mutual aid between unions of the Federation had been an accepted policy for years, and the extending of a helping hand by the C.I.O. unions to the Amalgamated Association was nothing more than that. The agreement by which the Amalgamated turned over direction of its campaign to the C.I.O. was also proper when one remembers the autonomous nature of the international unions' charters. No infringement on jurisdiction was possible, since the Federation had years before accorded an industrial charter to the Amalgamated. The charges of C.I.O. unions' "raids" on craft-union memberships were hardly more serious or numerous than the usual number of jurisdictional conflicts within the Federation during a period of industrial expansion. These disputes had not, on most other occasions, merited suspension. As for the C.I.O.'s aid to the radio unions, its defense could properly have been that the executive council was never authorized to turn these unions over to the International Brotherhood of Electrical Workers.

How the "court" which heard Frey's charges against the twelve C.I.O. unions reacted to these considerations, if they reacted at all, cannot be known. The printed record of the proceedings merely states that for most of one day the members of the council discussed the issue "off the record" and in "executive session." Dubinsky, who arrived from a European trip in time to attend the last session of the trial, was heckled by Coefield, who questioned his right to be present, since the International Ladies' Garment Workers' Union was one of the accused. To which Dubinsky responded that Green was in the same position and that Coefield had taken part in executive council deliberations while his plumbers' union was a member of an "outlawed" Building Trades Department. Green finally ruled that Dubinsky was entitled to attend the meeting. The garment union's leader thereupon denounced the entire proceeding as illegal and conceived in an effort to forestall the appearance of the C.I.O. unions, with their more than one-third of the total Federation vote, at the forthcoming Tampa convention. Dubinsky counseled caution and said his union would waive the two-thirds rule and abide by a majority vote if the issue was referred to the Tampa sessions. Hutcheson insisted that his members were demanding "action" and proposed a verdict of guilty. The vote was taken, and it stood thirteen to one for suspension of ten unions with 1,026,200 members. Dubinsky alone voted in the negative. Harrison and Weber were absent. Action on the Typographical Union and the United Hatters was postponed. The decision gave the ten unions a month in which to repent and abandon the C.I.O., or stand suspended.

Lewis termed the suspension "an act of incredible and crass stupidity" and promply announced, on behalf of all twelve unions affiliated with the C.I.O., that they would continue their program with "no change of policy whatsoever because of the unwarranted and illegal action of the executive council." Appropriations were made and organizers assigned for work in the steel, automobile, and rubber industries. The United Mine Workers declared they would no longer pay their per capita tax to the Federation, and a few days later Dubinsky resigned his seat on the council. September 5th came with no indication of repentance, and at the end of the day Green announced that the ten C.I.O. unions had made "their own decision to leave the Federation. The official Federation news service announced: "Industrial Organization Committee Unions Withdraw from the A.F. of L."

Taking advantage of its new status, the C.I.O. admitted two non-affiliates of the Federation to its ranks. These were the United Electrical and Radio Workers Union, and the Industrial Union of Marine and Shipbuilding Workers of America. Confused peace efforts initiated meanwhile by the United Hatters union became bogged as the executive council refused to lift the suspensions and the C.I.O. declined to confer with the Federation until the "illegal" act was rescinded. Upon the request of the hatters' and ladies' garment workers' unions, Lewis at one point agreed to meet with Green. The latter accepted with the reservation that he lacked authority to change the executive council policies; to which Lewis replied he had no desire for social chats at the moment and canceled the meeting. Previous to the suspension, Lewis and Green had met briefly to explore the possibilities of a peaceful settlement. Green insisted there was room in the Federation for both industrial and craft unions, whereupon Lewis asked the Federation president to state a single unorganized industry in which industrial unionism would be tried. Green failed to respond, Lewis later told a convention of the garment workers' union, and the conference ended.

IV

The delegates who gathered for the Federation's fifty-sixth annual convention at Tampa, Florida, in November of 1936 overwhelmingly approved the action of the executive council. The C.I.O. unions registered their opposition by their absence. The report of the convention's resolutions committee, written by Woll, had as its main theme the "ingratitude" of the C.I.O. unions. Chief of the ingrates, said the reports, were the United Mine Workers, who had been "aided and fed" during strikes and had survived, it appeared, only through the rescue work of the Federation. The United Textile Workers were next on the list of ingrates. "Time and again we have given of our effort to bring a little more sunshine into the lives of these underpaid and undernourished workers," said the report. The ungratefulness of the International Ladies' Garment Workers was described with a suggestion of racial superiority that at once aroused a protest. "As for the organizations composed largely of Jewish workers, it can only be said," the report declared, "that we took them by the hand when there were few hands willing to greet them. . . . Let them think it over in their hearts and in their homes." The report went on to list further thankless unions who had been "nurtured" at the breast of the Federation only to desert to the C.I.O. These were the oil workers' union, which had been given "help and prestige"; the United Rubber Workers, whose existence was "the outcome of the sole activities of the A.F. of L."; the gas and by-product coke workers; the radio workers; and the automobile workers, who, "after years of insecurity and exploitation" sought the protection of the Federation, which had responded by expending $250,000 and establishing a "functioning organization." Having called the roll of the ungrateful ones—later the federal unions were added—the Woll report then touched on the alleged efforts of the C.I.O., a minority, to defy the dictates of the Federation's majority. He insisted, that the Federation was not bound to a single formula or organization, but welcomed industrial as well as craft unions.

The writing of the report had been entrusted to Woll, apparently because it required a lawyer to explain the legality of the suspension order. This problem Woll touched on briefly in his report. He returned to it in an address which received the general approval of the delegates, though it obviously left most of them in a haze. His brief was a devious one. He granted that autonomy of the affiliated international and national unions had been a basic law of the Federation. However, he argued, to the surprise of many of his own supporters, this had been changed at the San Francisco convention when the executive council was accorded the duty and privilege of supervising the policies and finances, and appointing the officers of

[131]

newly chartered unions. The new policy, which Woll was now offering as part of the executive council's defense, was nevertheless, he said, the possible "kernel and seed for a destruction of the Federation." He then reverted to the thesis that the acceptance of a charter from the Federation implied the signing of a "contract." From that point he elaborated on the difference between "suspension" and "revocation" of charters, thumbing the dictionary to support his distinctions. The executive council had "suspended," but not "revoked," he continued, and had thus acted within the powers intended by the constitution, if not specifically stated in it. Then he came to his tallest hurdle.

"Yes, it is true," Woll declared, "that nowhere specifically is the executive council authorized to suspend. . . . Necessarily in the absence of any specific provision . . . we must fall back to the doctrines adopted in all organizations, in all voluntary movements, accepted by courts, accepted universally as the practice; and that is the doctrine of assumed and implied considerations. And what is meant by that? . . ."

Finally, through tortuous readings and explanations of several sections of the constitution, Woll arrived at his conclusion. He referred to Section 8 of Article 12, which stated that the council "shall only have power to revoke the charter . . . when the revocation has been ordered by a two-thirds majority of the regular convention," and concluded: "This does not say the convention shall have the power to revoke, either by majority or by two-thirds vote, and still the question is open whether the convention may not, of its own accord, revoke a charter by a majority vote, because there is no restriction placed upon the convention itself. . . . Section 8 is but a limitation, a restriction, not a grant, a limitation upon its powers, and it can only exercise the power of revocation when the convention authorizes it to do so by a two-thirds vote. Now, the executive council, having been vested with this greater power of revocation, specifically limited by the convention, it necessarily follows that it has the power to suspend without further recommendation or limitation, because the constitution is completely silent on that point."

Woll suffered a breakdown after this effort and was confined to his bed for most of three days. Meanwhile, William R. Trotter, delegate from the Typographical Union, nominated him as "an admirable candidate for the Supreme Court as now constituted"; and J. C. Lewis, of Iowa, said he had "made everything as clear as mud." The fight on the Woll report was, of course, a lost one from the start. The only concession the craft unions made was an announcement by Frey withdrawing the reference to the Jewish trade unionists. This was being done, he explained, "so that the newspaper accounts of this session will not find it possible to twist and distort." All through the period of the break with the C.I.O. unions, Green and Frey maintained that the press was in cahoots with the C.I.O. Green closed the debate at Tampa. He was amazed, he said, at the abuse which had been directed at him, but he was "consoled by the fact that when the mighty Lincoln gave his life to save the Union, there were many who denounced him." Thereupon, by a vote of 21,679 to 2,043, the craft-dominated convention approved the action of the craft-dominated executive council.

The suspensions, it was decided, were to remain in effect until the "present breach be healed and adjusted under such terms and conditions as the executive council may deem best." Meanwhile, the special committee appointed to seek peace was to be continued. Finally, the convention empowered the executive council to call a special convention of the Federation "to take such further steps and actions as the emergency of the situation may then demand."

v

The full effect of the suspensions was not felt until March of 1937, when Green, by decision of the executive council, instructed city and state central bodies of the Federation to expel all delegates from the ten suspended C.I.O. unions. The C.I.O. responded with an announcement that C.I.O. central labor bodies would be formed in cities and states "where the A.F. of L. officials acted to split the movement." Judging from the reactions of the state and city bodies, probably the most representative of A.F. of L. forums, the suspension of the C.I.O. unions was in complete disfavor with the membership of craft as well as industrial organizations. While the suspensions were being considered in 1936 resolutions of protest poured into Federation headquarters from hundreds of local unions and city bodies, the latter including those in Louisville, Chicago, Los Angeles, Denver, New Orleans, Philadelphia, Pittsburgh, Detroit, Youngstown, Jersey City, New Haven, Chattanooga, Columbus, and Milwaukee. Local unions of Frey's molders, Hutcheson's carpenters, and Wharton's machinists joined in denunciation of the executive council's course. In the summer and fall of 1936, twenty-two state federations of labor conventions spoke out in defense of the C.I.O. The remaining two state conventions adopted pleas for the re-establishment of unity.

The executive council, where it could, compelled expulsion of the C.I.O. unions from city and state bodies. In most cases the industrial unionists were thrown out not by votes of delegates, but by fiat of executive committees. The Arizona federation first endorsed the C.I.O.; at a subsequent meeting it was compelled to expel the miners' locals, but added an expression of sympathy and "best wishes." The 1936 convention of the California federation enthusiastically endorsed the C.I.O.; the 1937 convention expelled its representatives. In Connecticut, the 1936 convention had only two dissenters from C.I.O. support; when the 1937 convention convened, the C.I.O. delegates were barred. The Georgia Federation voted for the C.I.O. in 1936 and again in 1937, whereupon Green sent Dillon to Atlanta to organize a new Georgia council. The tactful Dillon announced to his Southern supporters that "the A.F. of L. will truly march through Georgia with our banners high." The executive board of the Massachusetts Federation expelled forty-nine locals of C.I.O. unions without chancing a convention vote. The 1936 convention in Ohio had urged unity; the executive board, on the eve of the 1937 sessions, suspended sixty-seven C.I.O. locals. A "unanimous" endorsement of the suspension was obtained in Washington by the same process. When the West Virginia federation refused to decapitate itself by expelling the miners' locals, the executive council organized a new federation. In New York City, President Joseph P. Ryan of the Central Trades and Labor Council refused to entertain a motion criticizing the suspensions. Later both the city and state federations in New York, through their executive committees, barred all C.I.O. affiliates. At a Texas convention, the delegates were required to take an oath of allegiance to the A.F. of L. at the opening of each session.

Pursuing its announced policy, the C.I.O., in May, 1937, started to charter directly affiliated local industrial unions, and city and state bodies. At that time, some 300 applications for local charters had been received by the Committee. Forty-two local industrial unions and eight local industrial councils were chartered by the C.I.O. on May 13th, and each week that followed saw the total raised. The split was becoming organic division.

The trend was accentuated when the executive council of the Federation, on May 24th, convened a special conference of its national and international unions in Cincinnati. Following bitter attacks on the C.I.O., the conference voted to request the international unions still loyal to the Federation to increase their per capita tax from one to two cents a month. Howard, who was present for the I.T.U., fought the proposal and was subjected to vigorous heckling from Green in the chair, as well as from the floor. An address by Green concluded two days of vitriolic attack on Lewis and his associates. Like others, he raised the cry of Communism as a C.I.O. factor. Mixing his biblical characters somewhat, the Coshocton lay preacher compared Lewis with Michael the Archangel.

"The first dual movement occurred in heaven itself, a place where harmony and peace prevailed," Green cried. "Yet a dual movement began, when as a committee of one, Michael the Archangel rebelled against God and His authority. The executive council in heaven did not hesitate to act. After examining the facts, it expelled his Satanic Majesty and his dual movement from heaven."

The leaders of the Federation unions, thus compared with a council of angels, voted with enthusiasm to contribute an additional penny a member per month to combat the C.I.O. and extend the A.F. of L. influence. They resolved also to strengthen the barriers against C.I.O. unions in the thus far unpurged state and city bodies. Ryan pledged to keep "Communism" from the waterfronts, and hinted he might step on a few craft union jurisdictions in the process. Frey reverted to the theme of "red" influence, drawing his data from the columns of the *Chicago Tribune*, and Roy Horn, head of the blacksmiths union, contributed an attack on the National

[135]

Labor Relations Board, which he accused of a C.I.O. bias. Hutcheson, moved to one of his few oratorical efforts, congratulated Green on his declaration of war and promised to be a soldier in the crusade.

"A council of desperation," was Lewis' comment. The Cincinnati conference met in May. The following month, the C.I.O. announced it had set up a system of per capita payments. Hitherto the Committee's work had been financed by voluntary contributions of the miners' and the needle trades workers' unions.

The division of American organized labor was now an accomplished fact. In the steps by which this separation had come about, the executive council had each time been the aggressor, and the C.I.O. had struck back in self-defense. The C.I.O., launched to bring newly organized unions into the Federation, had limited its membership to Federation unions. Then came the suspension, whereupon two independent unions had been accorded Committee membership. After the Tampa convention had come the purge of the city and state bodies; the C.I.O. retaliated by chartering C.I.O. councils and local unions. Finally, there was the Cincinnati council of war and the raising of an A.F. of L. war chest, which was answered by the C.I.O.'s creation of a dues-paying organization completely independent of the old Federation.

VI

There was no move to reunite the two wings of American labor until October, 1937, when the C.I.O. sent the A.F. of L. an offer to enter negotiations. By that time the Committee had grown in numbers to a point where it felt it could demand peace on the basis of acceptance of industrial unionism. The difficulties in the path of peace were many. Some could only be removed by complete surrender on the part of the C.I.O. or A.F. of L. The conferences which followed the C.I.O. offer came about largely because neither side wished to appear to be in the position of continuing the breach. The sentiment for peace within the C.I.O. was built up by Hillman and Dubinsky. Their organizations have the task of organizing factories in outlying towns and cities, where support of A.F. of L. labor councils has always seemed a requisite of success. Added to Hillman's motives was a desire to re-unite a labor movement in support of President Roosevelt. Internecine warfare in Cleveland had cost Dubinsky's union $150,000 and the loss of jobs of 1,500 members. Compared with these C.I.O. peace advocates, the unions of miners, steel, and automobile workers were only lukewarm. Given the absence of a new depression, these unions could stand on their own feet. They still feared craft-union raids.

Within the A.F. of L. the peace-seekers were George Harrison, whose railway clerks' organization had nothing to lose either in a compromise or in a surrender settlement, and Woll, vice-president of the photo engravers' union, but more actively president of the highly profitable Union Labor Life Insurance Company, which, prior to the split, enjoyed unquestioned favor in both camps. Against Woll and Harrison were Hutcheson, Tracy, Wharton, etc. They were ready for peace any time the C.I.O. was ready to surrender.

The peace conferences dragged along for two months, breaking down completely in December. The A.F. of L. proposal, put forward by Woll as head of the Federation's negotiators, was that the ten unions which had been suspended from the A.F. of L. were to be admitted with no questions asked on jurisdiction. The remaining 22 C.I.O. unions, it was proposed, were to negotiate mergers with A.F. of L. organizations in their respective industries. When all points at issue had been cleared up, all of the remaining C.I.O. unions were to be admitted in a body and to take seats in a reunited convention of the A.F. of L.

Lewis and the C.I.O.'s peace committee of ten, with one dissenting voice, rejected the offer. They argued, first, that the Federation committee did not have authority to make any agreement which the Federation's executive council or any of its affiliated unions would be obligated to honor. Murray, chairman of the C.I.O. negotiators, pointed to the "autonomous" character of international and national unions affiliated with the Federation. (Tobin later indicated that the A.F. of L. peace committee had exceeded its authority.) The C.I.O. objected vigorously to the proposal that the 22 more recent affiliates of the C.I.O. should bargain with A.F. of L. internationals on terms for amalgamation. On the basis of numerical strength, this would have meant that the C.I.O.'s United Electrical and Radio

Workers Union, with a membership of 130,000 would have been turned over to the A.F. of L.'s International Brotherhood of Electricians, which has 200,000 members; and that the C.I.O.'s International Woodworkers Union, with 100,000 members, would have been turned back to the Brotherhood of Carpenters, with its 300,000. Both the electrical workers and carpenters unions were willing to assign the C.I.O. members only a class "b," non-voting status. To agree to such terms would have meant desertion of some of their unions, the C.I.O. chiefs felt.

The C.I.O. felt also that peace on the terms proposed by the A.F. of L. would have given the craft unionists a majority in the proposed reunited convention. The carpenters' union having "swallowed" 100,000 former C.I.O. members, would have had the votes of 400,000 members to cast in a bloc against industrial unionism; the A.F. of L. electricians' union would have the votes of 130,000 erstwhile C.I.O. members at its disposal. Under the circumstances, the C.I.O. felt that it could have no assurance that any peace agreement would not be emasculated after the C.I.O. had disbanded. Only Dubinsky, among the C.I.O. unionists, favored acceptance of the A.F. of L. proposal. He argued that A.F. of L. absorption of some of the new C.I.O. unions would be counter-balanced by the C.I.O. taking over smaller A.F. of L. unions and by the votes of industrial union elements who had remained in the A.F. of L. Even should the C.I.O. be outvoted, Dubinsky argued, there would be the compensation of a reunited labor movement in which industrial unionism for the mass production industries would be safe. In this respect, he placed greater faith in the A.F. of L. promises than did Lewis and Murray.

The C.I.O.'s counter proposal was that all of its 32 unions be admitted into the A.F. of L. with full voting privileges based on their membership. Jurisdictional problems and proposals for mergers could then be taken up, the C.I.O. said. Since this would have given the C.I.O. a majority it was rejected by the Federation chiefs.

PART TWO

THE GREAT UPHEAVAL

7.

AKRON AND FLINT

I

THE fate of the C.I.O. was not to be decided by executive council edicts handed down from a Miami beach resort nor from secret tribunals in Washington. While the press of the nation reported the war in labor's household as a duel between Lewis and Green, with the issues of craft and industrial unionism as the background, the masses in rubber, auto, and steel centers were beginning to react in a manner that soon brought the greatest upheaval in American industrial history.

Two streams of events fused to make the C.I.O. the rallying-ground of millions of American working people. One came from the political developments since 1933, intertwined as they were with the economic needs and aspirations of the workers. The other came from the shattering of the barriers of tradition and vested interests that had enveloped the official labor movement and made it the instrument of labor's upper crust. One was personified, perhaps unwillingly, frequently with hesitation and back-tracking, by the Roosevelt administration; the other was represented by the dynamic leadership of John L. Lewis.

The original inspiration of the New Deal was in 1936 still strong in the minds of American labor. Short-circuiting of the promise in steel, autos, and textiles had caused millions of workers to term the NRA "The National Run Around." The first National Labor Relations Board epitomized its own unpopularity and failure when it reported to the President, in February, 1935, that it was unable to enforce its own decisions. Formal nullification of the NRA, with its Section 7A, was an accomplishment after the fact. A new board

[141]

which the President temporarily established by executive decree after the Supreme Courts' ruling did not have even a pretense to the limited powers of its predecessor. Labor saw greater possibilities in the third board, which was created by the Senate in June, 1935, on motion of Wagner of New York. The board was clothed with apparently adequate powers of enforcement. The rights accorded labor in Section 7A were enlarged and reinforced. Employers were forbidden to engage in a specified list of unfair practices. These included interference with, restraint or coercion, of employees in organizations or during collective bargaining; the formation or encouragement of company unions; discrimination against union members by discharge or otherwise; and refusal to bargain collectively with representatives of a majority of the employees. The board was granted the power to invoke the aid of the courts to enforce its decisions, violation of which were to be punished by fine or imprisonment or both. The personnel of the Wagner board, J. Warren Madden, chairman, J. M. Carmody and Edwin S. Smith also gave promise that the new law would be carried out.

The employing interests were not, however, ready to submit. A committee of 'American Liberty League lawyers offered an opinion that the Wagner Act was unconstitutional. Most of them were on retainer for large industries. Industry thereupon acted on the theory that the law, although passed by the Congress and signed by the President, need not be obeyed until the Supreme Court had given its sanction. U.S. Steel, General Motors, Goodyear Tire & Rubber, joined by the Associated Press, rushed to the Federal courts for injunctions to tie the hands of the labor board. The courts obliged. In the factories and mills of the nation, labor's revived hope proved another mirage.

The hopes gave way to cynicism of the power and authority of the government to bring labor the new deal which had been promised it. By the side of the cynicism, however, there developed a saving sense of determination. If the government could not sweep away the barriers, labor would have to do the job itself. Lewis, Hillman, and Dubinsky realized that, as in their own industries, self-organization would have to be the basis for any effective assertion of unorganized labor's hopes. They understood also that unless they extended the influence of labor, their miners' and clothing workers' organizations might soon be isolated in a sea of anti-unionism. Affirmatively, they wanted to organize the unorganized for their own sakes. They still believed in the first maxim of the labor movement, that the strong shall help the weak. But astride the path of their determination lay a smug and self-satisfied labor hierarchy, satisfied to ignore the needs of the unorganized as long as they could and, as they imagined was possible, preserve their own organizations, prestige, and jobs. Coincidentally with the ambitions of Lewis, Hillman, and Dubinsky, there was the undiminished unrest of the men who labored in the mass-production industries. The spokesmen of the workers in the mills, mines, and factories, on the ships and at the piers, were willing to carry on the battle, but they required a seasoned leadership which would not stand in awe of the oligarchs of the Federation's executive council. This leadership was at hand, and the C.I.O. came into being.

Politically, America's future was obscured when the C.I.O. prepared its attack. The election of 1936 was at hand, and the forces of conservatism and big business were bending all their energies to rid themselves forever of the New Deal. The C.I.O.'s first battle was in the campaign to reëlect President Roosevelt. An auxiliary weapon, Labor's Non-Partisan League, was forged. While Roosevelt and Landon waged their campaigns, the momentum of the C.I.O.'s drive was comparatively slow. A Roosevelt defeat would probably have ended the campaign or deflected it into channels of widespread violence. President Roosevelt's reëlection and the endorsement of the New Deal with which the American people associated him created the atmosphere for C.I.O. success. When the results of the landslide became known, the framework for the new labor movement had been set up. Labor had defeated reaction; it now faced its second task: to implement its political victory with economic power, and through both win economic security.

II

The mercury dropped to nine below when thousands of Akron rubber workers on the night of February 17, 1936, initiated the first skirmish in the great upheaval. Threadbare overcoats and belted mackinaws gave the only protection against the blizzard which enveloped the Goodyear rubber plants and the determined pickets who patrolled eleven miles of fence and gates. Akron's rubber workers had been restless since the summer of 1933. By the winter of 1935 and 1936, although the union ranks had dwindled, the bitterness against speed-ups and discharges had mounted. Sit-down strikes at Goodrich, Firestone, and Goodyear brought inconclusive settlements and uncertain peace. In January, Lewis came to Akron and an audience of thousands of rubber workers and their wives listened again to the message of unionism, this time to a plea for the new-type industrial organizations. Then the C.I.O. sent Adolph Germer, one-time Illinois mine-union leader and foe of Lewis, now enlisted under his banner in the new crusade. Germer held large meetings at which hundreds of workers rejoined the United Rubber Workers.

Disregarding protests, Goodyear Tire & Rubber cut wages in November, 1935, and again the following January. The final straw came on February 15th, when the company without warning discharged 137 workers. All had been fired from the third shift, and while a delegation remonstrated with the management, other shifts which reported for work sat down at their machines. A meeting of all employees held on February 17th was told that the management would make no concessions. The workers went from the meeting to form picket lines. Through a night when the wind roared down the bleak streets at forty-five miles an hour, swirling heavy snow around the pickets, the lines grew. Daybreak found the eleven-mile front completely covered. Most of the pickets and the overwhelming majority of the 14,000 Goodyear employees were not members of the union when the strike started, but the second day of the strike found the largest rubber factory in the world at a standstill and more than 10,000 in the strikers' ranks.

All six common pleas judges in Summit County joined in signing an injunction to restrain the mass picketing. But there were none to enforce the writ. The Akron Central Labor Union, led by Wilmer Tate, a machinist, and dominated by craft unionists, declared there would be a general strike if force was attempted against the strikers. The C.I.O. sent $3,000 and four more organizers, Powers Hapgood of the miners, Rose Pesota, New York dressmaker, Leo Krzycki of the men's clothing workers, and John Schafer of the oil workers. A check for $1,000 followed from the A.F. of L. Local leaders, Tate, and Sherman Dalrymple, John House and William Carney, soon brought order and discipline into the ranks of the strikers. McAlister Coleman was brought from New York to direct publicity. Akron's two newspapers lined up with the strikers against threats of vigilante force to smash the picket lines. Public support was largely with the strikers. Merchants, most of them owners of neighborhood stores, donated $25,000 worth of foodstuffs, clothing and other supplies. The strikers' wives organized a commissary which served as many as 5,000 meals a day.

The picket line, longest in the history of American strikes, soon developed a housing program, and before long sixty-eight shanties of corrugated paper, plaster board, and wood arose to shelter pickets from the biting winds. Many of the huts had stoves made from old tar barrels and cans. The picket posts became the pickets' homes for five weeks, and many of them came to boast of radios, cushions, cots, and pot-bellied stoves. American flags flew from the shanties and union slogans plastered the outer walls. Each had a meaningful name—"Camp Roosevelt," "Camp Senator Wagner," "Camp John L. Lewis," among them. Once the police threatened to demolish their shanties, but a swiftly gathered concentration of strikers led them to abandon their plan.

The Goodyear management pleaded with Governor Davey of Ohio for troops, but a state election was approaching and the Governor agreed with the emphatic contentions of the Ohio labor movement that there had been no violence which would justify the use of the militia. A "Law and Order League" then appeared, under the leadership of a recently defeated candidate for mayor. One day there were reports that his followers would attack the picket lines. The union immediately leased the facilities of a local radio station. Strikers were instructed to keep tuned in on the station all night. Starting at 11 P.M., then, Coleman, Germer, and other leaders, singing pickets and strikers, poured news bulletins, pleas for solidarity, improvised strike plays and union songs into the microphone. In thousands of homes and in the pickets' huts Akron's rubber workers sat at their radios that night. Many whittled handles on crude clubs.

[145]

Weapons of every conceivable kind, from stove pokers to clothes trees, stood near at hand ready to be taken up by an army of defense. The radio program did not end until eight the following morning, when all danger of the threatened vigilante raid had disappeared. The "Law and Order League," an inspiration sold to the rubber industrialists by Pearl L. Bergoff, one-time "strike-breaker king," made one more threat before the strike was over. Again a union S.O.S. went out and within two hours ex-service men among the strikers were drilling at the several union headquarters. Union and C.I.O. organizers were given protective escorts. Tate went on the radio and in an impassioned, eloquent address appealed to the people of the city against efforts to bring bloodshed into a hitherto peaceful strike. The local papers denounced the "Law and Order League" and again the threat of violence passed.

Goodyear Tire & Rubber, adamant when the strike broke out, agreed in the fourth week of the strike to meet a union delegation. Negotiations proceeded for a week. The strikers' position was meanwhile reinforced by word to the company from Lewis that should any violence against the strikers be attempted, the millions of C.I.O. members and followers throughout the country would forever refuse to purchase Goodyear products. On March 22nd, the strike leaders felt they had an offer which they could present to the rank and file. A meeting of 5,000 workers heard the terms and voted approval. The strike was ended. A great concourse of strikers paraded through Akron's main streets, thousands on the sidewalks shouting congratulations. The strikers won reinstatement of all discharged employees with no loss of seniority rights, recognition of the union as spokesman for its members, a promise to notify workers of wage-rate changes before they were put into effect, reduction of working-hours to thirty-six in some departments and to forty in others, and recognition of union shop committees. The company still held its right to deal with a company union, but the tide had been turned again in favor of the United Rubber Workers Union. Akron was set on the road to becoming a fortress of the C.I.O.

III

The fate of the C.I.O. in its first stages lay in the hands of the workers of Akron, rubber capital of the world, and Flint, Michigan, General Motors' queen city. Akron had met the test. Flint labor's task was even more difficult.

The executive council of the A.F. of L. informed the convention of the United Automobile Workers in May, 1936, that it might elect its own officers. The concession was superfluous, since the union had already indicated it would assume self-rule. More important to the delegates at the South Bend convention than the appearance of Green, were addresses by Howard, in behalf of the C.I.O., and messages of greeting delivered by Miss Pesota, Hapgood, and Krzycki, for their respective organizations. Lewis had already stirred the auto workers in an address before a huge meeting in Cleveland. Dillon was relieved of the presidency and Homer Martin, who now opposed A.F. of L. domination as vigorously as he had defended it a year before, was elected president. A former Baptist minister, his principal asset was an extremely effective style of oratory. It was evident from the spirit of the convention that the C.I.O. had become the guiding influence of the union. Renewed interest in the United Automobile Workers began to sweep the auto centers and several independent organizations took steps to affiliate. The largest of these was the Automotive Industrial Workers Association, composed largely of Chrysler employees, and led by Richard T. Frankensteen. The A.I.W.A. and Frankensteen had for a time enjoyed the blessing of Father Coughlin, who now in May suddenly appeared at a U.A.W. meeting and, on the urging of Frankensteen, delivered an address approving the merger of independents into the United. The locals of the Associated Automobile Workers in the Hudson motor plants, as well as several of those in the Mechanics Educational Society, also merged with the U.A.W.

The ferment in the ranks of the auto workers showed its first effects in June, when the Bendix local at South Bend won a blanket wage increase, union recognition, and seniority rules. The summer lay-off season brought a lull in union activity which was utilized by the C.I.O. and the auto union leaders for planning. In October a crisis arose in Chrysler's Dodge plants which ended in a significant material and psychological victory for the union. The union charged that the management had violated seniority rules in rehiring workers laid off at the end of the 1936 spring season. Several union members found themselves slated for permanent loss of work in the industry. Strike votes were taken and were almost unanimous for walkouts. The C.I.O. sent Allan S. Haywood, Illinois miner, Germer, and Krzycki to Detroit. Together with Frankensteen and the local leaders they rallied the workers for a walkout. By the middle of October, however, Chrysler, third largest automobile producer in the nation, capitulated. The union won a promise of strict observance of seniority in rehiring; three men discharged after they had boasted that the union was responsible for wage increases, were reinstated; workers whose operations in the plants had been discontinued were to be offered other work while they awaited the resumption of their old tasks.

With Philip Murray and John Brophy as close advisors, and with Lewis directing strategy, an organization drive now proceeded with what the union's newspaper called "the tempo of the early NRA days." C.I.O. and auto union leaders addressed scores of meetings in thirty-four automobile manufacturing centers. General Motors plants were the principal target, and Flint, General Motors' key center, was among those where the workers responded by the thousands. A sudden sit-down strike on November 13th, in Fisher Body Plant No. 1, Flint, ended in the union's favor and the U.A.W. again came out into the open. A local paper, the *Flint Auto Worker*, appeared. Robert Travis, militant Toledo leader, and Wyndham Mortimer of Cleveland, a one-time coal miner, were assigned to the task of consolidating the Flint drive.

A seven-day sit-down strike at the Bendix Corporation plant in South Bend in November brought concessions substantial enough to be called a victory. The U.A.W. had all but 70 of 2,600 Bendix workers in its ranks. An employee poll had been ordered by the National Labor Relations Board, only to be halted by the company's appeal to the courts. Thereupon more than 1,500 started their victorious occupation of the plant. The union scored next in the heart of Detroit, at the Midland Steel Products plant, winning union recognition, seniority rules, and wage increases, after a fourteen-day sit-down. The Bendix settlement provided that the company was to make no agreement with any employees before it had

[148]

first bargained with the union; in Midland Steel Products, the peace agreement gave the union shop delegates the exclusive right to present grievances. The Midland strike showed the resurgence of solidarity among the auto workers. Chrysler and Dodge locals informed their managements that they would not work on steel frames that did not come from the Detroit Midland plant, thus bringing added pressure for a settlement. Plymouth workers refused to touch auto frames that came from Midland's Cleveland plant. Successful termination of a five-day sit-down at the Kelsey-Hayes wheel plant in Detroit followed in December, and placed the union in a spirited and confident mood for the approaching showdown with General Motors, which was scheduled, in the C.I.O. and auto-union strategy, for January, when the production season would be near its peak.

IV

The strike of General Motors workers in January and February of 1937 was the most significant industrial battle since labor's defeat at Homestead. It held in its hands the future of the C.I.O. and the new labor movement which was soon to sweep millions of American breadwinners into its ranks. It aroused bitterness equal to that which accompanied the brief heyday of the Knights of Labor. It was more than a strike. It was a momentous struggle between the aroused forces of labor and the third largest corporation in the country, typifying years of unchallenged anti-unionism. It involved seizure of industrial plants worth more than $50,000,000 and the failure of the owners, vigilantes, courts, police, and military to recapture them.

Automobiles and steel-manufacturing form the backbone of American capitalism, and in the realm of autos General Motors was second to none in financial importance and in the 250,000 workers it employed. Its control lay in the hands of the Du Ponts and J. P. Morgan. The Corporation recovered strikingly from the depression years. Its net profit in 1934 was $167,000,000, while 1936 brought a profit of $227,940,000. Its average wage to its workers in 1935 was $1,150, which meant that many workers received far less. The auto workers were not comforted at all to know that the Corporation paid Alfred P. Sloan, its president, $374,505 in 1935, vice-president

William F. Knudsen $325,868, and a total of $3,779,730 to seventeen top officials. General Motors employees felt the speed-up more keenly than low wages. Belt-line production and the conveyor system were based on speed, and in the quest for ever-quicker, uninterrupted production the limbs and eyes and strength of the workers were geared to meet the pace of the machines. The workers had to meet competition between corporations, between plants and even sections of plants. Foremen, driven to bring up production, in turn drove the workers under them. The mere twist of a dial determined the speed of the line, and those workers who could not meet it faced the scrapheap. Automobile manufacturing yearly consigned men who had given their best years to the horror of being "old" at forty years or less. Over and over again, the strikers of 1937 summarized their chief complaints.

"We don't want to be driven," they said; and "We don't want to be spied on."

The espionage activities financed and promoted by General Motors sought several general objectives: to keep men from evading the demands of the speeded belt-line; to keep their unions, when they joined them, weak and ineffective; and eventually to destroy the unions. Without union grievance committees to speak up for them, many workers conspired in simple manner to keep down production. Word would pass through a section of a plant: "Only ten crank-shafts to be turned this hour; let's not burn ourselves up." To workers deprived of recognized spokesmen this was one way out of an intolerable situation. Here the work of the plant stool pigeon came in. General Motors accumulated weekly sheafs of reports on workers who had joined to keep down production. These "ears" also reported friendly references to unionism. It became so that no man could tell whether his neighbor was a friend or a company spy. In the ranks of the unionists, the General Motors espionage system had another function: to ferret out the leaders, to turn them in for discharge or discrimination and to watch the "outside agitators," i.e., the organizers. The La Follette committee which investigated violations of labor and civil rights discovered that General Motors spent $994,855 on private detective services from January 1, 1934, to July 31, 1936. As the probe got under way, most of the files of the company were stripped of spy reports. Knudsen sought to explain the use of Pinkerton men and detectives of the Railway Audit and Inspection Company as the maintenance of a force to police and protect G.M.'s vast properties. But that did not explain how shadowing Adolph Germer, spies' attendance at picnics of Fisher Body employees, and spy reports on the reading habits of employees contributed to protection of its properties.

The strike which General Motors reaped from these practices had an inconspicuous start in the Fisher Body plant at Atlanta, Georgia. Four men who appeared in the plant with U.A.W. buttons on their workshirts were fired. A strike followed on November 18, 1936. The Atlanta unionists wanted the walkout extended to other plants, but the union and C.I.O. strategists felt such a move would be premature. A month later, the Kansas City Fisher Body plant discharged a unionist for an infraction of what was felt to be an unimportant, constantly violated rule. The response to the C.I.O. organizing campaign had meanwhile become so great, that Lewis and the auto union leaders on December 21st wired Knudsen, asking for a collective bargaining conference. They took as the text of their request, an address in which the corporation's executive head had said that "collective bargaining should take place before a shut-down, rather than after." General Motors replied that the respective plant managers should be approached with grievances that came within their jurisdictions. The U.A.W. locals thereupon handed in contract forms to the plant heads, and met with universal rebuffs. There appeared to be no alternative to spreading the walkout.

The efficiency of the specialized production units of the General Motors system proved its fatal weakness in the strike. Simple strategy indicated to the auto-union leaders that with the key plants tied up, production would inevitably be brought to a halt throughout the entire system. The principal organizing efforts had therefore been directed at the key plants, and these were now brought to a standstill. The Cleveland Fisher Body plant stamped turret tops for General Motors models. Organized under the leadership of Vice-president Mortimer, its workers had one of the strongest of the U.A.W. locals. On December 28th, all of the 7,000 Cleveland workers went on strike, more than a thousand remaining in the plant. The Cleveland local promptly announced that any settlement of its grievances would have to be part of a settlement for the entire General Motors system.

Flint was next in the line of the union's attack. In Fisher Body No. 1 plant were important dies, which, if removed to a less strong union center, might become the instruments for breaking the strike. On the evening of December 30th the night-shift men at Fisher No. 1 saw the dies being loaded on to trucks, bound for Grand Rapids and Pontiac. The events of that memorable day in Flint's history are detailed in the "Song of the Fisher Body No. One Strikers," a homespun parody to the music of "The Martins and the Coys," which soon became the epic song of the great strike. As the song told the story:

> Now this strike it started one bright Wednesday evening
>> When they loaded up a box car full of dies.
> When the union boys they stopped them,
>> And the railroad workers backed them,
> The officials in the office were surprised.

> CHORUS
> These 4,000 union boys
>> Oh, they sure made lots of noise.
> They decided then and there to shut down tight.
>> In the office they got snooty,
> So we started picket duty,
>> Now the Fisher Body shop is on a strike.

> Now they really started out to strike in earnest.
>> They took possession of the gates and buildings too.
> They placed a guard in either clock-house,
>> Just to keep the non-union men out,
> And they took the keys and locked the gates up too.

Closing of the Cleveland and Flint plants would have been enough to paralyze General Motors' sixty-five automotive plants, but the union in fifteen other units were too restive to await shut-downs by order of the Corporation. Sit-down strikers ensconsed themselves in the Fleetwood and Cadillac plants in Detroit, in Fisher Body No. 2, Flint, and in the Guide Lamp factory at Anderson, Indiana. The Cleveland local, strong enough to keep the plant closed without a sit-down, called its members out within a week after they had ceased working. In the last weeks of the strike the Chevrolet motor assembly plant at Flint also was occupied by the strikers. Strikes of the traditional type were called in Janesville, Wisconsin; Norwood, Atlanta, St. Louis, Kansas City, and Toledo, Ohio. A shortage of glass, brought about by a strategically timed strike of C.I.O. glass workers, closed several other plants. By January 11, 112,800 of the Corporation's 150,000 production workers were idle. Before the strike ended the total rose to 140,000.

A detailed statement of the union's grievances was forwarded to the Corporation on January 4th. It requested an immediate conference to discuss eight demands: signing of a national agreement; abolition of piece work and fixing of day rates of pay; a thirty-hour week, six-hour day, and time-and-a-half for overtime; minimum rates of pay; reinstatement of men discharged for union activities; a seniority system to govern employment and reemployment after slack periods; recognition of the U.A.W. as the sole bargaining agency of all G.M. employees; and regulation of the speed of the belt-line and other machinery by union plant committees and the management. This appeal, like the union's previous requests, was turned down, and the conflict became a belligerent endurance test. An effort by General Motors to create a united front of all automobile manufacturers broke down when the Ford Motor Company refused to coöperate. *Steel,* the trade journal of the iron-and-steel industry, reported on January 18th that the Automobile Chamber of Commerce had sponsored a meeting at which such a plan was broached. General Motors proposed that all companies cease operations. *Steel* reported the Ford management feared such a move would precipitate a national panic, responsibility for which would be placed at the doors of the auto industry.

During the second week in January, Governor Frank Murphy vigorously took over the task of peacemaker. Elected to office in the Roosevelt landslide of the previous November, he had received the endorsement of the auto union and the entire Michigan labor movement. The difficulties which Governor Murphy encountered were enlarged by the sit-down strikes. General Motors insisted that the sit-downs constituted illegal seizure of its property and refused to confer with the union until the sitters were withdrawn. The strike leaders and the C.I.O., on the other hand, declared they had no faith in the verbal promises of General Motors and would not order their men out of the plants until assurances of sincere collective bargaining efforts were given in writing and surrounded by conditions which would make resumption of operations impossible until collective bargaining conferences had been concluded. In this stand, the U.A.W. leaders had their backs stiffened by Lewis.

After days and nights of effort, Governor Murphy on January 15th announced that a truce had been arranged under which bargaining conferences might proceed. The union agreed to evacuate all the plants its members were holding; the corporation promised that negotiations would start at once on the union's eight-point memorandum of January 4th. This represented a substantial gain for the union, since the corporation had insisted that many of the eight points were not subjects for a general conference. The negotiations were to continue "until a satisfactory settlement of all issues shall be effected, if possible." In no event were the negotiations to be terminated in less than fifteen days. The corporation, meanwhile, was not to remove any dies, tools, machinery, material or equipment from any of the plants on strike, nor to endeavor to resume operations.

Hundreds of workers carrying blankets, radios, accordions paraded out of the Fleetwood and Cadillac plants on Saturday afternoon, January 17th. At the same time, the Guide Lamp sitters gave over the Anderson factory. The spirit of the strikers was high with the confidence that they had won important concessions. The Flint plants were to be surrendered the following day.

V

Flint held the key to peace as well as to the strength of the strike. The Cadillac, Fleetwood, and Guide Lamp plants had no great strategic importance, but the Flint Fisher Body No. 1 plant, which sprawled over half a mile, was an ace in the auto strikers' hands. Much of the bitterness of the battle was concentrated in Flint, where the C.I.O. and General Motors, respectively, despatched their specialists in striking and strike-breaking. The entire city of 165,000 men, women, and children was dependent on the local General Motors plants for its existence. More than 50,000 Flint workers toiled in Chevrolet and Buick plants, as well as in Fisher Body factories. Several times in the course of the six weeks' strike Flint was on the verge of serious violence. Early in the strike, the Flint Alliance came into existence. Chairmanned by George E. Boysen, a former General Motors' paymaster and owner of a spark-plug factory, the Alliance set itself up as the true voice of the Flint citizenry and its General Motors' employees. To translate this voice into propaganda and organization, Floyd E. Williamson, a New York promoter-publicity man, was imported. The Alliance attack varied from righteous appeals to civic pride, through Williamson's denunciation of outside agitators, to threats of violence against the strikers. Its financing has not been revealed to this date, but Boysen made no secret of its dependence on the business interests of the city. Before the strike had ended, the Alliance was publicly reprimanded by Governor Murphy as would-be instigators of violence.

The tense atmosphere of the city boiled over but once into bloodshed, in what has become known as "The Battle of the Running Bulls." "Fisher 2," two miles away and across the city from "Fisher 1," had been held by sit-down strikers since the day their fellow-unionists had "locked the gates" of their plant. During the afternoon of January 11th, while Governor Murphy was laboring for a basis on which the plants would be evacuated and negotiations set in motion, the heat in Fisher 2 was shut off. The need to protect plant equipment, including its water system, had hitherto led the corporation to maintain the heating supply without interruption. A few hours later, the Flint police surrounded the entrance and announced there would be no further shipments of food. A ladder placed to a window by strikers was immediately torn down. Dinner time on a cold day came with the police still at their stations. The strikers faced an effort to freeze and starve them out of the plant. The Fisher 2 sitters, captained by William (Red) Mundale, a union rank-and-filer, had been considered one of the weak links in the strike. The shutting off of heat and food for them, the union felt, would be followed by similar efforts at Fisher 1.

A union sound truck pulled up at Fisher 2 in the early evening.

Scores of strikers soon surrounded it. Victor Reuther, U.A.W. organizer, was at the microphone. The police were asked to permit delivery of food. The voice inside the car, carried to the strikers in and out of the plant, as well as to the police, first made pleas of labor solidarity to the officers. These failing, more belligerent appeals were uttered. Shortly before seven P.M., pickets rushed the door, swept the police aside, and moved coffee and bread into the plant. Two hours later, fifty policemen, almost half of Flint's entire force, attacked the pickets at the doors with clubs, driving some inside the building and attempting to scatter the others. A policeman shattered the glass pane in the door, poked a tear gas gun through the crevice and fired it. The gassed strikers inside fell back, and the battle was on. The police poured buckshot into the pickets and through the windows of the plant. Tear gas discharges alternated with the crack of the guns. The strikers fought back with sticks, metal pipes, nuts and bolts, soda-pop bottles, coffee-mugs, and a continuous rain of two-pound steel automobile door hinges. Throughout the three hours of fighting which followed, a group of stalwart strikers surrounded the automobile with the loud speaker and resisted efforts to dismantle it. First one strike leader, then another, took the microphone, directing the strategy of the battle, cheering on the strikers and shouting pleas and threats at the police. "We wanted peace. General Motors chose war. Give it to them," the voice would shout.

Sheriff Thomas Wolcott drove his sedan into the battle zone. Before many minutes, strikers turned it on its side, its headlights still glaring and lighting up a wide path strewn with broken glass, rocks, and door hinges. Before the battle had ended, three other police cars had been captured. The police reformed for a new attack at midnight, but at a shouted signal from the car the nozzle of a rubber hose appeared at the door of the plant, and the strikers turned a powerful stream of cold water on their attackers. The Flint police retreated under the barrage of water and door hinges. They ran fifty yards to a bridge that approached the plant gate; then they went fifty yards more to the far end of the bridge. The fighting was over.

The strikers' guard continued their vigil through the wintry night while the strident battle cries from the plant and the car gave way to labor songs and cheers of victory. Fourteen strikers were removed to the hospital with bullet wounds, but by dawn the strikers were unchallenged in their possession of the plant. "Solidarity Forever" and cheers for the C.I.O. from tired voices pierced the cold morning air as determined bands of men and women, huddled around two street fires, guarded against a possible new attack on their fellow strikers in the plant. "The Battle of the Running Bulls" proved to be the only effort forcibly to remove sit-down strikers from General Motors plants.

The battle brought 1,500 Michigan national guardsmen to Flint, but Governor Murphy refused to yield to demands of the Flint Alliance and local authorities that the troops be employed to dislodge the sit-down strikers. Instead, the Governor ordered the corporation to make no further efforts to halt the food supplies. While Boysen bitterly denounced him, Murphy summoned union and corporation heads to meet him in the state Capitol at Lansing. There he worked out the truce of January 15th which brought the sitters out of the Detroit and Anderson factories.

The Flint strikers were to evacuate their plants on Sunday, the 17th, and negotiations, under the terms of the Lansing truce, were to start the following day. Sunday morning, the auto union leaders learned of an exchange of telegrams between Boysen and Knudsen. The chairman of the Flint Alliance, assaying the rôle of unionist, wired the General Motors' executive asking for a conference in behalf of G.M. workers said to be members of the Alliance. The request was written to challenge the growing confidence of the auto union that it might win sole bargaining rights in the negotiations. Knudsen's reply sought to assure Boysen that no such rights would be granted. He agreed to meet with Boysen and asserted, "we stand ready always to discuss with your group or any group of our employees any questions without prejudice to anyone." The strike leaders now charged a "double-cross." The telegrams were not to have been made public until Sunday evening, after the Flint strikers had given up the plants. It was only by accident that a reporter learned of Boysen's wire on Sunday morning. He had then sought Robert Travis's comment and the entire auto union knew within a

[157]

few hours that the Flint Alliance had been promised a collective bargaining conference.

The national and Flint strike leaders, after acquainting Lewis of the development, declared that General Motors had presumed to rule out the union's demand for sole recognition before negotiations had even started. Sole recognition was, in fact, one of the eight points which were to have been debated at the parleys. The truce had been violated, the strike leaders announced. To the Flint incident they added charges that in Anderson local police had dispersed a picket line and demolished picket shanties, and that in Detroit some employees of the Cadillac plant had received instructions to return to work. Knudsen denied all three charges, but the Flint strikers reinforced their makeshift "fortifications" of the plants. The negotiations of the following day consisted of Knudsen's handing Brophy, Martin, Mortimer, and other U.A.W. officials a refusal to meet until the plants were evacuated. A few days later, G.M. promised not to confer with the Flint Alliance until U.A.W. negotiations had ended, but the union responded that it no longer had the slightest faith in the corporation's words. It insisted on an agreement before evacuation.

VI

With the breakdown of the Lansing truce, Governor Murphy turned to Washington for assistance. In the national capital General Motors was impatient for word from Secretary of Labor Frances Perkins that the sit-downs were illegal; and the C.I.O. was as vigorously seeking intercession of the federal government in behalf of recognition of the auto union. Miss Perkins persuaded Sloan and Knudsen to meet with her. She was making slight progress when the conference recessed. Meanwhile, Lewis had told a full complement of the Washington newspapermen that labor was expecting Presidential support for its crucial struggle.

"For six months during the Presidential campaign," said Lewis, "the economic royalists represented by General Motors and the Du Ponts contributed their money and used their energy to drive this Administration from power. The Administration asked labor for help to repel this attack and labor gave it. The same economic

[158]

royalists now have their fangs in labor. The workers of this country expect the Administration to help the strikers in every reasonable way."

Scanning a newspaper as he left Miss Perkins' office, Sloan read Lewis' pointed remarks, which included also a reiteration of his refusal to urge evacuation of the plants pending a settlement of basic union demands. The General Motors' president seized upon the statement and announced that it made further peace efforts futile. Pressed by interviewers, Sloan said he particularly resented Lewis' references to the President. That evening Sloan left the capital for New York.

At a White House interview, the next day, President Roosevelt indirectly but deliberately rebuked the C.I.O. leader for his plea that the Administration aid the strikers. Unperturbed, Lewis said that Miss Perkins' only success with Sloan was to have him meet with her in the Department of Labor Building, instead of secretly in the recesses of the plutocratic Metropolitan Club, where a first conference between the Secretary of Labor and the G.M. president had been held. The press, largely unfriendly to Lewis and the auto strikers, made much of the Presidential rebuke. A few days later the President spanked Sloan, evening things up but bringing a settlement of the strike no nearer. Miss Perkins had invited both Lewis and Sloan to meet with her. Lewis agreed, but Sloan declined, and President Roosevelt declared that the automobile magnate had made a "very unfortunate decision." A few days later Sloan returned to the city for a second meeting with the Secretary of Labor. When the conference ended, Miss Perkins was under the impression that a basis for ending the strike had been found. "Sloan had promised to have the corporation attend another peace conference in Lansing," said Miss Perkins. Later he called to say it was "all off."

"He ran out on me," said the troubled Secretary of Labor, providing avid headline-writers with ready-made text.

VII

The central stage of the strike had meanwhile shifted back to Flint, where General Motors for the second time turned to the courts for aid in recapturing its plants. The first court proceeding had reacted in the strikers' favor when it was revealed that Judge Edward D. Black, Genesee County's most venerable jurist, was the owner of G.M. stock worth $150,000 at the time he ordered the strikers to vacate the factories. The embarrassing publicity attendant on the revelation made Black's order a dead letter. The sitters laughed and jeered when Sheriff Wolcott read them the text.

On January 29th the corporation went before Circuit Judge Paul V. Gadola. The corporation told the court that the occupation of the two Fisher Body plants was maintained by force and violence as part of a conspiracy by Martin, Mortimer, and all other international officers of the union, Bud Simons and Red Mundale, leaders of the sitters in the Fisher Body plants, and Travis and Roy Reuther, U.A.W. organizers, to cripple the business of the corporation. This had been accomplished by the "continuous trespass" of the sit-down strikers, by the refusal of the strikers to permit G.M. executives access to the plants, and by the "clubs, sticks, and other weapons" of the strikers, it was alleged. Almost coincidental with the application for an injunction came a brutal physical attack on several auto union and C.I.O. organizers. Six organizers were driven by a mob from Bay City, Michigan, to Saginaw, both of them G.M. centers. Some were slugged and all were piled into a taxi which was forced to drive to Flint, thirty miles away, with a caravan of vigilantes behind them. As the unionists' car reached the outskirts of Flint, one of the pursuing automobiles forced the taxi to crash into a telegraph pole. Anthony Federoff, organizer for the C.I.O. and a Pennsylvania miner, had his scalp torn away; three others also had to be taken to the hospital with bad injuries. Ring-leaders of the mob were identified as G.M. foremen, but none were apprehended in the investigation which the Saginaw, Flint, and county authorities set in motion. The incident served to heighten the tenseness of an already jittery city.

Argument on the corporation's plea for an injunction took place before Judge Gadola on February 2nd. It dragged through the day as Pressman, Maurice Sugar, and Larry S. Davidow, U.A.W. lawyers, insisted that the corporation was violating the National Labor Relations Act, and thus came into the court with unclean hands. The guilt of trespass was denied, while the General Motors' lawyers insisted the sitters had violated every tenet of the law by seizing property which was not their own. Meanwhile, more potent affairs were transpiring outside the crowded courtroom.

The huge Chevrolet works in Flint had been operating a few days a week, stocking up a reserve of parts. Since no cars could be completed, the strikers had no objections to this work and urged their members to take advantage of the opportunity to earn a few dollars. Unionists employed at Chevrolet soon complained, however, that they had been unjustly fired. Strike-leader Travis requested a conference with the plant management. A meeting was promised, then postponed as more union men were sent home. Demands for a sit-down strike in Chevrolet began to be heard. The strike leaders weighed the possibilities of success of a sit-down, which in this case would mean capturing a plant. It would be a difficult task. The troops were still in the city and the strikers' ranks had scores of informers among them. Nevertheless, the strike strategists felt it would be a worthwhile effort. The strike was now more than a month old. Capture of another huge plant would enthuse all the strikers and set at rest reports that their spirit was weakening. It might have a salutary effect on negotiations for a settlement which finally appeared to be getting under way in Detroit. There was also the consideration that it would be a practical demonstration, in the midst of the court proceedings, of the strikers' contempt for judge-made law and injunctions.

With the increase of discharges at Chevrolet, U.A.W. members insisted that they be allowed to make a counter attack. Travis, Hapgood, and the other leaders agreed. The problem of how to plan and then take over a large plant worth millions of dollars without betraying the preparations to G.M. spies required consummate strategy. Travis, Hapgood, and Kermit Johnson, "Chevvy" union leader, were equal to it. Of the several buildings which made up the Flint Chevrolet works, Plant No. 4, the motor-assembly division, was the most important. Should the Fisher 1 strikers be ousted, possession of Chevvy 4 would still prevent a single shiny Chevrolet from rolling out of any G.M. factory in the world. The Chevrolet

[161]

workers insisted Plant 4 was the ideal place to sit down. The strike leaders knew this to be true, but since the project had been discussed by a large committee, they felt it necessary to keep the details a secret until the plan was ready for execution. Travis and Hapgood proposed that Chevrolet 9, a ball-bearing plant, was the one to be taken. The strikers set up a derisive howl. Ball-bearings could be gotten here, there, and everywhere, they said. It would do no good to take Chevvy 9, they argued hotly, sometimes with contempt for the ignorance of the outside organizers who presumed to tell G.M. workers that a ball-bearing plant was more important than a motor-assembly plant. The strike leaders stood their ground and their authority prevailed. Then came the problem of selecting a spy-proof committee which could be trusted with the truth, since their services would be needed at Chevvy 4. Each prospective committeeman was interviewed separately so that no striker knew what others had been considered for the task. Those appointed to the committee were ordered not to talk; those suspected and rejected were secretly and impressively told to proceed to Fisher 1, more than a mile away from Chevvy 4, on the afternoon of the projected plant capture.

Monday afternoon, several thousand strikers were in and near Pengelly Hall, the old three-story brick-and-wood structure which housed the union headquarters. By a prearranged plan word came to the strikers that some of their number were being attacked outside of Chevvy 9. Led by Hapgood, Roy Reuther, and an inevitable sound-truck, the strikers proceeded to Plant 9, arriving at 3:30 P.M. at the change of the shifts. Inside the ball-bearing plant, a group of unionists set up a shout for a sit-down strike. Warned by the false reports of informers, the plant management was fully prepared. The strikers in Chevvy 9, not one of the strongest union plants, staged a valiant battle for half an hour, many of them sustaining severe beatings from G.M. plant police, Flint detectives and other burly men who had been installed in the factory. Tear gas was thrown by company guards and police. Outside, several score members of the union's Emergency Brigade, made up exclusively of women and daughters of the strikers, smashed all windows within reach to permit air into the plant. Surrounded by hundreds of strikers, Hapgood was at the microphone of the sound-truck, keeping alive the impression that the striker's interest was concentrated at Chevvy 9.

Shortly after four o'clock, a union messenger brought Hapgood word that the occupation of Chevvy 4 had been accomplished peacefully and completely. The strike leader called upon the strikers to disperse, an order promptly obeyed. He then joined the sitters in Plant 4, located several hundred yards from Plant 9. The strategy had worked, completing one of the most audacious bits of strike strategy the country had ever seen. Some 400 Chevvy 4 strikers, joined by a few score from near-by Chevvy 6, had taken the motor-assembly plant with no more difficulty than a few harsh words to amazed foremen. Within a few minutes union guards had been placed at the doors and gates and patrol committees organized to guard against surprise attacks. The sitters blossomed into expert barricade-builders. Steel-plant trucks weighing several hundred pounds were piled on each other in front of entrances and windows until they reached from floor to ceiling. By morning of February 2nd, national guardsmen patrolled the plant, but Chevvy 4 strikers, perched on the roof, were serenading Fisher 2 strikers, heroes of the "Battle of the Running Bulls," with "Solidarity Forever." And from the roof and windows of Fisher 2, across and fifty yards down the street, husky voices shouted the union song back. Below, in the street, khaki-clad troops with bayoneted rifles walked to and fro, while machine-guns were focused on the captive plants.

For an entire day, soldiers' bayonets barred delivery of food to the men in Chevvy 4 plant and Fisher 2, which had been included in the militarized zone. Pressure was again exerted on Governor Murphy to use the troops to clear the plants. Among some national guard officers plans of attack were being suggested. Some proposed simply to shoot the strikers out; another hoped to project vomiting gas through the ventilating systems. The intelligence division furnished the press with a lurid tale of 500 "loyal" Chevrolet employees being held as hostages by the strikers. The plans and military propaganda came to nothing, however, as Murphy's abhorrence and fear of violence continued to dominate his efforts. Again General Motors looked to the courts. On the day following the capture of Chevvy 4,

Judge Gadola signed an order directing the men to leave the Fisher body plants under pain of imprisonment for contempt and of having a fine of $15,000,000—the estimated value of the plants —levied against them. Sheriff Wolcott proceeded to Plant 2 to read the order. A few strikers came to the door, dropped a steel barrier they had erected, and listened to the labored reading of the legal edict. At Fisher 1, the strikers permitted the sheriff to enter and stood about him in the cafeteria, gibing and assuming poses of mock seriousness while the recital was repeated. The order gave the strikers until three o'clock of the afternoon of February 3 to leave the factories.

The sit-down strikers called meetings in their plants on the evening before the ominous deadline. Seated on boxes, cans of paint, and kegs of nails, determined men in gray shirts, overalls, and work pants, all with loved ones at home, discussed a problem which they knew held life or death for some of them. The entire nation watched, fearing the bloodiest of industrial battles. It was obvious that only an army of sheriff's deputies and militiamen could enforce the court's ruling. In Fisher 2, surrounded by troops who barred all civilians from approaching, the sitters could not take counsel with their outside leaders. Nevertheless, the discussion in both plants was brief and arrived at unanimous conclusions. The decisions were conveyed to Governor Murphy in two telegrams.

"We the workers in the plant," said the message sent by the strikers in Fisher 1, "are completely unarmed, and to send in the military, armed thugs and armed deputies . . . will mean a bloody massacre of the workers.

"We have carried on a stay-in strike over a month in order to make General Motors Corporation obey the law and engage in collective bargaining. . . . Unarmed as we are, the introduction of the militia, sheriffs, or police with murderous weapons will mean a blood bath of unarmed workers. . . . We have decided to stay in the plant. We have no illusions about the sacrifices which this decision will entail. We fully expect that if a violent effort is made to oust us many of us will be killed, and we take this means of making it known to our wives, to our children, to the people of the state of Michigan and the country that if this result follows

[164]

from the attempt to eject us, you are the one who must be held responsible for our deaths."

The temperature was again near zero in Flint the next day, but the vision of thousands of strikers battling armed deputies and possibly the militia was colder still. There was a spirit of a zero hour before an army's charge into enemy territory. Hysteria, mixed with eager anticipation, was evident in some quarters. Into the early hours of the morning plant executives, Flint Alliance leaders, and Flint police heads drank potent liquor in the exclusive Town Club at the Durant Hotel. Boisterously, they sang the songs of the strikers, giving them raucous, mocking accents. In the plants the strikers sat silently at their radios and card games. Wooden clubs and blackjacks produced with belt-line technique and speed hung at their waists.

Early morning of the ominous day, the roads to Flint were filled with strikers from near-by cities, some many miles away. Thousands of workers, many women among them, came with squared jaws to take their places on a picket line around Fisher 1. By noon delegations of workers had arrived in battered and new cars and trucks from Detroit, Lansing, Toledo, and Pontiac. Akron sent rubber workers, shock troops of the C.I.O. Walter Reuther came at the head of 500 strong from the West Side of Detroit. The Dodge workers from Detroit also arrived in disciplined phalanxes. Kelsey-Hayes Wheel unionists waved aloft a banner, "Kelsey-Hayes workers never forget their friends." As three o'clock approached, a long train of almost 5,000 workers, two abreast, circled the lawn that fronted the approach to Fisher 1. An American flag led the procession, then came members of the women's Emergency Brigades, their red and green berets the only color spots in a grim assembly. Men and women carried clubs and stout sticks; several had crowbars, stove pokers, and lengths of pipe. A few had knocked the base off clothes-trees, and carried the poles, with metal hangers, on their shoulders. Like the Minute Men of '76 and as fully determined that their cause was righteous, they had seized whatever weapon lay at hand and rushed off to do battle. The constantly-arriving auto-loads of workers soon blocked the street, and strikers, aided by sound-trucks, took over direction of traffic. Not a policeman was in sight. At the windows of the plant were the sit-down strikers, their number augmented from the usual 400 to almost 2,000. Strips of cheesecloth hung round their necks, ready for use as some slight protection against tear gas. Windows were barricaded by steel plate, pierced with holes for the nozzles of hoses which lay on the floors nearby. A street valve that controlled the plant's water supply had been enclosed by a new wooden picket shanty. A special detail of strikers guarded the shanty. Inside were drums of gasoline, fuel for a protective wall of fire should an effort be made to capture the valve and cut off the plant's water system.

The zero hour at Fisher 2 and Chevvy 4 was far different. Here there were no crowds of cheering comrades, only a dreary, deserted broad street dotted with soldiers carrying muskets in a ceaseless patrol. The strikers at the windows of the plants displayed no outward reaction to the machine guns and 37-milimeter howitzers poised in the gutters. For hours as the afternoon fraught with tragedy wore on, the Chevvy and Fisher strikers chanted back and forth, "Solidarity Forever, For the Union Makes Us Strong."

Thus the deadline passed, Governor Murphy, in Detroit, where he had finally prevailed upon Knudsen to meet with Lewis, wired Sheriff Wolcott that he was to take no action. The sheriff, more than eager to comply, thereupon became a legal authority and asserted Judge Gadola's order was directed at the strikers alone and did not yet call upon him for enforcement. Boysen and local General Motors' attorneys raged at both the sheriff and the Governor. Meanwhile, the strikers' battle lines turned into celebrating. The sit-down strikers' band in Fisher 1 played hill-billy airs, and before many minutes the pickets, men and women, were square-dancing on the hard-frozen lawns. Flint's day of fear ended in hilarious, nervous joy for the strikers.

Two days later, Judge Gadola, refusing to postpone action any longer, ordered Sheriff Wolcott to arrest all officials and leaders of the auto union, and every striker in the Fisher Body plants. The sheriff, refusing to swear in new deputies, declared he did not have a sufficient force to make the arrests and asked Governor Murphy for the assistance of militiamen. Murphy noted the request, postponed a decision, and resumed his efforts to effect a settlement.

VIII

The end of the General Motors strike came on February 11th. A request from President Roosevelt that the corporation meet with spokesmen of the strikers brought about a conference on February 4th, Knudsen stating that the wish of the President left no alternative but compliance. The conference met in Detroit, with Governor Murphy in the rôle of peacemaker. For a week he shuttled back and forth between Lewis, Pressman, Martin and Mortimer, and Knudsen, John Thomas Smith, and G. Donaldson Brown, the corporation negotiators. Most of the time the two groups did not meet together; frequently they were on the verge of a complete break. At one point, Knudsen insisted that the talks would go no further until the plants were evacuated. "You have an injunction which disposes of that issue," Lewis replied. The chief issue was the insistence of Lewis that the auto union be given exclusive recognition. As the possibilities of forcible eviction of the Flint strikers dwindled, the resistance of G.M. weakened.

The settlement which Governor Murphy finally announced included a written pledge by the corporation that it would not, without the Governor's consent, for a period of six months recognize or deal with any other employee spokesman than the United Automobile Workers in the seventeen plants closed by strikes. In all other G.M. automotive plants, the union was to be recognized as the agent of its members. There was to be no discrimination against union members, and all strikers were to be rehired regardless of their union membership or strike activities. Union members were to be permitted to discuss the union with other workers during lunch and rest hours in the plant. Injunction and contempt proceedings against the Flint sit-down strikers were to be dropped. Negotiations were to start at once looking toward a signed contract on those of the eight original union demands which were not disposed of.

The agreement constituted a monumental advance for unionism in the automobile industry. The mere fact of General Motors signing a contract with a union would in itself have been an historic victory. The exclusive recognition accorded the U.A.W. in seventeen plants, however, was the outstanding union gain. The plants affected were those which held within their grasp the entire G.M. system. The prestige of the union was enhanced in all union plants, and as Lewis had foreseen, led to enrollment in the union of a great majority of all G.M.'s production workers. The pledge of no discrimination against union men might have been a mere pious declaration were it not for the lifting of restrictions on the right to talk about the union and the right to wear union buttons on plant property. The right to talk during one's lunch hour and to wear the insignia of one's organization seems an obvious enough privilege in a free country but the auto workers had never enjoyed it. These were more than academic gains. They effectively ended the spy system, for every man could now talk freely and proclaim openly his union affiliations without fear of reprisal. The agreement to reëmploy all strikers was a reversal of G.M.'s determination that all the sit-down strikers had been fired. Coincidental with the signing of the agreement, General Motors announced a general wage increase of five per cent. This was fixed in the auto workers' minds as a by-product of the strike.

There was good ground for the night-long celebrations which filled Flint and the auto workers' halls in Cleveland, Detroit, Toledo, and other G.M. centers. The auto workers had won a great victory for themselves, and for the Committee for Industrial Organization they had created the psychology of success and the enthusiasm which were needed to raise a great campaign to the dimensions of a crusade.

8.

"SIT DOWN! SIT DOWN!"

I

KRON created a fashion; Flint popularized it. The sit-down
strike became a full-blown labor weapon by the end of 1936.
From September, 1936, through May, 1937, sit-down strikes directly
involved 484,711 workers and closed plants employing 600,000
others. Constantly the grievance was the refusal of employers to
observe the National Labor Relations Act and engage in collective
bargaining. Stemming from Flint's spectacular perfection of the
technique, the height of the wave came in March, 1937, when
192,642 men and women sat down at their machines and waited in
determined idleness in workshops, in mines, on steamships, in retail stores and in hotels and restaurants. Giving an inescapable impression of cause and effect, the March sit-down peak was followed
by the Supreme Court's approval of the Wagner law. Thereafter
a decline set in.

There was no formal adoption of the sit-down as a labor weapon.
Neither the C.I.O. nor the A.F. of L. ever discussed it in its councils. The movement started where the technique was most effective—
in the mass-production plants where one break in the operation of
the belt-line could bring an entire plant to a standstill. It was a
spontaneous, frequently unorganized, occasionally undisciplined
method—the only means available, in the absence of collective bargaining and plant grievance committees,—to slow up a speeding line,
bring an unfriendly foreman to heel, or protect fellow unionists
from arbitrary discharge.

The many foreign examples had only slight influence on the
minds of American sitters. When 1,000,000 French workers seized

automobile, textile, and other factories in the summer of 1936, the *Auto Worker's Journal* here gave the affair four inches. Before the French workers decided to cash in without delay on the popular-front triumph, other European workers, usually in desperation, had used the method. Five thousand coal miners entered the pits at Terbovlye, Jugo-Slavia, in the summer of 1934 and declared they would starve themselves in self-imposed imprisonment until their wages were raised. They won their demands within a few hours. In October 1,200 miners in Pecs, Hungary, also decided that immediate starvation was preferable to wages of $2 a week. They remained below for five days. Starved and delirious, some of them were chained to posts to prevent violent suicide. When they emerged after five days and nights in their tomb, many came out on stretchers and more than 100 were rushed to hospitals. During February, 1937, the Pecs miners again struck below the surface of the earth. The Pecs example was adopted by Polish miners in Katowice, in October, 1934. Toward the end of the year more than 300 Greek tobacco workers defiantly installed themselves in a Saloniki factory. The summer of 1935 saw 3,000 Spanish copper miners descend into the pits near Huelva, and remain in them for ten days.

Around the globe, the fashion was copied. Welsh miners, in the fall of 1935, struck in the mines for more than a week while friends and relatives brought them bread and tea; they brought 20,000 other coal diggers out in sympathy strikes. At the Taff-Merthry colliery it required a fierce battle between strikers and police, 800 feet below ground, to end a stay-down strike. Elsewhere in Wales and in Scotland, Poland, and France other coal miners seized their pits in 1936. Polish rubber workers, at Cracow, paid with the lives of six of their number when they took over a factory. In India, where Gandhi's passive resistance had given some inspiration to the whole technique, 5,000 Pondicherry textile hands took over a plant and held it for a week until they were rewarded with victory.

American examples were rare before 1935. The Industrial Workers of the World inspired an effective 65-hour folded arms strike in 1906 in the Schenectady plant of the General Electric Company. The strike brought wage concessions, but did not bring repetitions. Women's garment workers in New York declared "stoppages" of

[170]

work in 1910. The current cycle of American sit-downs started, it appears, when 2,500 workers at the Hormel Packing Company, in Austin, Minnesota, sat for three days during 1933 and won wage raises, reduction of hours and slowing up of the machines. In the White Motor plant at Cleveland, there was a short sit-down, a "quickie," in the spring of 1934. The years that followed brought so many "quickies," lasting from a few minutes to an hour or two, that they became commonplace. They were centered in Detroit and around the grievance that the line was too fast. Sometimes a more serious form of protest, the "skippy," was resorted to. Workers in a section of a plant would quietly agree to skip every sixth fender or leave untightened every fifth bolt. Before many minutes the line would come to a halt in complete confusion, with enraged foremen at a loss to single out the participants in the conspiracy.

II

The open, effective sit-down of truck-tire builders at Goodyear's Akron plant in November, 1935, is of special significance because it was followed by a second sit-down the following January and a third in February, which led to the historic Goodyear strike. During the remainder of 1936, there was almost a sit-down a week in the Akron rubber plants. One plant experienced fifty-eight lasting from a few minutes to two or three days. Meanwhile, Detroit automobile plants were going through the same experience and the sit-down began to appear in still other industries. In September, seamen, revolting as much against a moribund A.F. of L. union as against their employers, sat down in the engine rooms, bunks, and decks of the *President Roosevelt* as she lay in New York harbor. The liner was held to its pier by a second sit-down in October, causing it to sail two days late without passengers or cargo. C.I.O. shipbuilders in Staten Island sat down for eight hours in October, completely ruining elaborate exercises which were to christen a new naval destroyer. More than 9,000 workers sat down in October and then, after the November plebiscite had endorsed the New Deal, the number rose to 17,340 and continued for six months thereafter to be major industrial phenomena. Chrysler, Bendix Brake, Briggs, Fisher Body plants were tied up by sitters in November. The Bendix plant saw a stay-in as well as a sit-down. More than 1,000 members of the auto union remained in the South Bend plant for ten days, while 1,500 others constantly patrolled the plant in protective picket duty. Midland steel workers staged a ten-day occupation in December, and the Libbey-Owens-Ford glass workers at Ottawa, Illinois, sat for fourteen days and nights. In December the victorious Kelsey-Hayes sit-down, and the first strike of its kind in the South were staged. In Birmingham, 100 of the 135 employees took over the workrooms of the American Casting Company. Libbey-Owens-Ford glass workers in Toledo sat down in shifts, each shift leaving when the next arrived. At the end of the month came the seizure of the Flint plants and the sit-down at Fisher Body in Cleveland.

The January sit-downs, involving 43,910 workers, most of them in the automobile industry, succeeded in closing plants employing 140,000 G.M. workers, and throwing into idleness 90,000 who worked for other corporations. Other industries—hosiery and textile, oil-refining, shoes, steel, newspaper publishing, and transportation— were also subjected to the pressure of sitters. The discharge of members of the Transport Workers Union brought a fifteen-hour sit-down in the highly mechanized power plant of the Brooklyn-Manhattan Transit Company. Only the reëmployment of discharged union men avoided a strike which would have crippled one of New York's major arteries of passenger traffic. The Beaumont, Texas, *Enterprise* and *Journal* were tied up by sitting printers. Chicago printers called chapel meetings during working-hours. They were only slightly disguised sit-downs and won substantial wage increases. The meetings were unusually prolonged in the Hearst composing-room. Akron again made labor history by contributing the first stay-in strike of store clerks. In Philadelphia, 1,800 employees of the Electric Storage Battery Company took over two huge plants, installed their own cooks in the cafeterias, and settled down to sit until they won a wage raise. Two grooms spent honeymoons in the plants, and when the strikers emerged victorious after forty-one days six of them greeted new-born babes they had not seen before. Chicago electricians staged a sit-down that threw the entire city into darkness for several hours.

The General Motors sit-downs continued into February, as did the Electric Storage Battery mass sit, and when they were ended, other workers emulated the tactic. The month brought a total of 41,000 new sit-down strikers, and the first successful forcible efforts to oust some of them. Before the Electric Storage strikers gave up their plants, they left off sitting long enough to charge three 65,000-watt batteries which were needed for flood emergency relief work in Cincinnati. When the strike ended, the management found the plant in such good condition that an estimated four-day delay in resumption of work was cut to one day. The Flint strikers also passed a hat for flood relief and turned over more than $100. The Goodrich company in Akron, bedeviled by a new sit-down, issued passes which permitted the strikers to return to the plant after a night's rest at home. A fifty-six-day sit-down by employees of the Hercules Motor Corporation at Canton, Ohio, ended after having established an endurance record. Employees in the kitchen and laundry of the Israel-Zion Hospital in Brooklyn sat down, bringing particularly bitter criticism of the technique. To the charge of unlawful seizure of property and of trespass was now added the accusation that the health and lives of sick persons were being endangered. Others who sat and waited in February were Chicago pencil-makers, Bronx janitors, sailors, tobacco workers, pie bakers, fishing-tackle workers, newspaper pressmen—on the *Detroit News* and those employed by the Crowell Publishing Company—shipbuilders and steel workers.

Several hundred strikers left the plant of the Douglas Aircraft Corporation at Santa Monica, California, on a promise that their grievances would be heard at once by the National Labor Relations Board. They walked out into the arms of deputy sheriffs, who arrested them for forcible entry. The violent ouster of sit-downers occurred at the Fansteel Metallurgical Company in North Chicago. A first effort at violent ejection, a two-hour battle in which 150 sheriff's deputies hurled tear-gas bombs into the factory, had failed to achieve its end. The deputies returned a few days later with more tear gas and a large supply of vomiting gas. They brought with them a structure which the headlines immediately called a "Trojan horse." The "horse" was an armored truck on which a huge tower had been mounted. As tall as six men, the tower was pierced for guns. An early-morning attack hurled hundreds of gas shells through the windows of the plant. The strikers pulled on gas masks, tied wet handkerchiefs around their mouths, and fought back with nuts, bolts and pieces of scrap iron. After a two-hour engagement, they began to stagger out, sick and retching. A young Chicago lawyer, who had become company counsel, had devised the tower. He was now hailed as the man who had ended sit-down strikes for all time.

The next month, March, saw 192,642 workers join in sit-down strikes in 247 plants. Woolworth girls, rug weavers, miners, restaurant and hotel employees, watchmakers, bindery hands, garbage collectors, Western Union and Postal messengers, newsstand clerks, dressmakers, milliners, farm hands, opticians, die casters, bedmakers, timbermen, and food-packers caught the habit and copied the more experienced sitters in automobile and rubber plants. A seventeen-day sit-down strike in nine captive Chrysler plants brought a new wave of stay-ins in other auto plants. As in the General Motors and other strikes, court injunctions directing the strikers to leave the plants brought only a tightening up of defenses. April brought 98,562 new sitters, including thousands in General Motors plants who felt that the company was violating the agreement which had ended the general strike. A sit-down in the Hershey Chocolate Company in the model town of Hershey, Pa., brought violent ouster of the strikers. A mob lead by employees of other Hershey enterprises brutally attacked local strike leaders and a C.I.O. representative. Violence by Detroit police accomplished the ejection of strikers at the Yale and Towne key factory. Strikers who sat down in the Brooklyn Jewish Hospital were found guilty of endangering human life, under a statute enacted in 1881. Sit-down activity in May engaged 27,844 workers in thirty-nine factories, steamships, refineries, textile mills, auto plants, and retail stores. The J. G. Brill Car and Foundry Company, at Philadelphia, was closed when 1,700 struck, hundreds of them electing to remain in the plant. A sit-down which closed the Philadelphia mill of the Apex Hosiery Company and provided the basis for a federal court determination on the legality of sit-downs also started in May. Each month thereafter brought new sit-downs, but not to the extent that marked the period from December, 1936, to the following May. The fall of 1937 saw a

number of sit-downs of operators who locked themselves in the pro-
jection booths of movie theaters and announced, through electrical
amplifying apparatus, that the picture show was at an end until
union demands had been met.

III

The story of a typical sit-down—so easy to organize and usually
so speedy in its results—explains the popularity of the method with
a large section of American labor. The example is drawn from Flint,
the perfector of sit-downs. Friday, the 13th of November, 1936, was
an ominous day for the General Motors Corporation. The auto
union had been ploddingly building its membership in Fisher 1.
On the evening of the 12th, hundreds of workers went to a store
across the street which had been rented by the union and signed
application cards. The next morning three welders came to work
to find their time-cards missing from the rack. That meant, as they
would be told upon inquiry, that they had been fired. A fourth
union man protested to the foreman. He too was fired. As he was
being paraded through the plant to the gate, he passed Bud Simons,
torch solderer for G.M. and torch bearer for the union in Fisher 1.

"Where are you going, Sam?" Simons inquired.

"You come along, too, Bud," the foreman said.

Simons complied, but as he walked the length of the belt-line his
glance communicated a message. Each worker wiped his hands on
his overalls, turned from the moving row of Chevrolet bodies and
joined in a sit-down strike. The news spread through the plant. By
the time Simons had reached the end of his "last mile," seven
hundred men were idle. A committee of workers hastened after
Bud Simon and the foreman. They met in the office. Simon noted
the arrival of the committee and turned to the plant manager.

"Mr. Parker," he said, "you are now talking to a union."

While the manager was recovering from his surprise, the sitters
were formally voting, *vive voce*, they would not resume work until
the discharged men had been returned to their jobs. And they insisted also that they be paid for the time they had been "sitting."
After slight deliberation, both demands of the men were met and
work was resumed—but not until the lesson of the power of the auto

union had been driven home. Sit-downs proved also an effective check on the speed of the line in mass production plants. During October, 1936, the foreman at General Motors' Delco-Remy plant in Anderson, Indiana, announced that the number of armatures to be finished per hour was to be increased from 32 to 35. The union leaders had discussed the problem of the speed-up before and decided to resist any further increases in the work load. The union leaders spoke up, calling on all to "sit tight" until the foreman's order was recalled. He was stubborn. Before the 400 sitters, all of them women, had resumed their work, they were required to produce only 29 units an hour.

Not all of the strikes were spontaneous. Many were carefully planned in advance and the job of determining the hour and the circumstances handed over to the discretion of a captain or several captains placed throughout the factory. The Exide-battery workers who struck at the Electric Storage Battery Company came to work, following a secret union meeting, loaded down with magazines, food, blankets, books, decks of cards, violins, accordions, banjos and saxophones. Preparations for one of the Woolworth five and ten strikes included the distribution of mimeographed instructions:

WHAT TO DO IN CASE OF SIT-DOWN

The strike starts at a signal given by some authorized member of the union. Upon receiving the signal, you will finish whatever you may be doing at the moment. Then you will stay at your post, fold your arms, and inform any customer who may want to be waited on that you are on strike. There will be no more waiting on customers.

After the store has been emptied of customers, some one who has received instructions from the union will explain them to you.

DURING A SIT-DOWN IT IS IMPORTANT TO REMEMBER THE FOLLOWING

1. MAINTAIN RIGID DISCIPLINE.
2. UNITY IN YOUR RANKS.
3. ELECT A STRIKE COMMITTEE, WITH A CHAIRMAN. THIS COMMITTEE IS TO BE IN COMPLETE CHARGE WHILE IN THE STORE. THIS COMMITTEE SHALL MEET DAILY.
4. ELECT A PICKET COMMITTEE. THIS COMMITTEE IS TO BE IN CHARGE OF ALL PEOPLE ENTERING OR LEAVING THE STORE. THEY WILL ASSIGN

WHICH STRIKERS SHALL BE STATIONED AT THE DOOR. THIS WILL WORK
IN ONE-HOUR SHIFTS.

5. NO PERSON IS ALLOWED TO ENTER THE STORE WITHOUT AN OFFICIAL
UNION CREDENTIAL, OR LEAVE WITHOUT PERMISSION OF THE STRIKE
COMMITTEE. COLLECT ALL CREDENTIALS IMMEDIATELY AND HOLD
THEM.

6. THERE IS TO BE ABSOLUTELY NO DAMAGE DONE TO ANY OF THE
STORE'S PROPERTY.

7. ANYONE WISHING TO USE ANY OF THE MERCHANDISE IN THE STORE
WILL PAY FOR IT AS THEY DID ORDINARILY. ELECT ONE PERSON TO BE
IN CHARGE OF COLLECTING THE MONEY.

8. IF ANY OF YOU ARE APPROACHED BY ANY PETTY BOSS OR MANAGER
DO NOT CONVERSE WITH THEM, BUT REFER THEM TO THE STRIKE
COMMITTEE.

9. IF ANY NEW PROBLEM COMES UP OF WHICH YOU ARE IN DOUBT, CALL
THE UNION IMMEDIATELY—GRAMERCY 5-8875.

The sit-downs, easy to start, were somewhat harder to keep going, and here expert planning was needed. The first problem was to stay in the plant. The auto strikers developed a corps of barricade-builders. One has related the first hours of the sit-down at Kelsey-Hayes: "That morning we barricaded the Kelsey gates. The main gates were blocked by a solid three-foot-high wall of steel, formed from a dozen carefully placed steel containers. We loaded each container with a couple of tons of hub-castings—about the weight of a brick—and behind the barricade we set a dolly-load of eighteen-inch T-irons. . . ." The plant insured as far as possible against easy capture, the sitters then tackled the problem of food, discipline, of complete self-government. Hundreds and sometimes thousands of men in a plant for days and weeks developed problems. Plant government followed a general pattern. At the top there was the general assembly which met at least once a day to discuss new problems, check on committees, counsel with union leaders and perfect and maintain the defenses. An executive committee ruled in between sessions and acted as a trial board for sitters who violated sit-down rules. In the Fisher 2 and Cadillac sit-downs, during the G.M. strike, disciplinary powers were vested in a kangaroo court over which elderly auto workers, noted for their judicial minds, presided. Punishments meted out ranged from fines of small change and cigarettes, to exclusion from the plant for more serious offenses.

[177]

Chief of the committees after the executive was the patrol or picket committee. In Fisher 1, this group was known as the police department and the "chief of police" received far more consideration than the sheriff or any of his minions. Contact committees maintained communication with strike headquarters, a particularly difficult task where police or militia barred persons from entering the plants. Picket or patrol committees checked on all doors, gates, and approaches to the plant; they ferreted out the violators of the universal rules against smoking or drinking of alcoholic liquor in the plants. This committee also had the job of keeping all false rumors out of the plant. This gave it the right to examine food, blankets, or notes which wives or other relations might deliver for the sitters. Visitors, excepting sympathetic fellow unionists in time of possible attack, were barred. This rule rigidly applied to women. Where women and men took part in a sit-down strike, the rules on chaperonage were extremely severe.

All plants had their sanitation committees, maintained for the dual purpose of making the sitters comfortable and earning the respect of the community which might believe stories of damage done to plant or machinery. The kitchen committee was one of the dynamos of the sit-down strike. It received milk-pails of coffee or milk, pails of stew, fruit, and cigarettes from the union kitchen, usually located in a store adjacent to the plant. The committee served the meals, where possible using company cafeterias. A rule which Flint and Detroit sitters set and which prevailed universally was that no company food or cigarettes which might be around were to be touched. Most famous sit-down cook was Max Gazen, who, with Mrs. Henry Kraus, his assistant, sometimes prepared as many as 5,000 meals a day for hungry sit-down strikers. In some plants, educational committees flourished, but more often the strikers favored the efforts of the entertainment committees which provided shows, dances, and music. Almost every large factory held by sitters produced a band, sometimes only an accordion and a mandolin, frequently an aggregation that included guitars, mouth organs, and saxophones, as well as the inevitable "squeeze box." The auto sitters' bands applied themselves most diligently to mountaineer airs, homespun hill-billy lyrics with parodies singing the praises of the union and of solidarity. Popular in Detroit was the song composed by Maurice Sugar, the auto union's general counsel. It epitomized the sit-down as the workers' infallible prescription for all his complaints:

> When they tie the can to a union man,
> Sit down! Sit down!
> When they give him the sack they'll take him back,
> Sit down! Sit down!
> When the speed-up comes, just twiddle your thumbs,
> Sit down! Sit down!
> When the boss won't talk don't take a walk,
> Sit down! Sit down!

Countless were the songs to the glory and power of the C.I.O., and many were the stanzas in praise of John L. Lewis. In bitter tones were the endless parodies on "Mademoiselle from Armentiers," with the boss "just another man," or "on the run," or "headed straight for hell." Hundreds of owners of sit-down plants were hung many times over to sour-apple trees. Where the strikes entered bitter stages, effigies of several hung from windows of their own plants.

IV

A war of words, of editorials, of court arguments, of Senate debates and of C.I.O.-A.F. of L. crossfire became a constant, though academic, accompaniment to the sit-downs.

The C.I.O. leaders, from Lewis down, did not essay to pass on the tactics of the men and women in the plants. Where possible, they strove to take full advantage of them. The sit-down was part of the C.I.O. upheaval. Nevertheless, it was not purely a C.I.O. tactic. More than a score of American Federation of Labor unions, including those of electricians, restaurant and hotel workers, printing-pressmen, retail clerks, theatrical employees, and building service workers joined in sit-downs. Those in the Brooklyn hospitals, which brought down most criticism of the technique, were sponsored by the Federation's Building Service Employees International Union. Nevertheless, the Federation assumed first a critical and later a bitterly denunciatory attitude toward the method. Frey saw the entire General Motors strike as a strike not against the corporation, but against the A.F. of L. The less learned men of the executive council, however, restrained themselves for a time. The council, in February, 1937, instructed Green to prepare a report on the "history and significance" of the sit-down. The report was to be considered at a meeting in May. Late in March, however, Green announced that the Federation had never approved or supported the sit-down. On the contrary, he found "its grave implications detrimental to labor's interests" and as such "must be disavowed by the thinking men and women of labor." He argued, in support of his position, that public opinion would not support sit-downs, and secondly, that "temporary advantages gained through sit-down strikes will inevitably lead to permanent injury." He feared that persistent use of the method would force the enactment of legislation for compulsory arbitration of strikes, the incorporation of unions and other repressive legislation.

"Both personally and officially, I disavow the sit-down strike as a part of the economic and organization policy of the A.F. of L.," the head of the Federation said.

The Cleveland Metal Trades Council, composed of A.F. of L. unions, signed a contract with the Electric Vacuum Cleaner Company pledging that none of its affiliated unions would ever engage in a sit-down. The Brotherhood of Carpenters refused to charter a union whose members were sitting on the job. Later, the Federation pressed a bill in the House of Representatives calling for an investigation of the sit-downs. Despite this determined stand, the position of the Federation was being honored in the breach. One of its strongest unions, the International Alliance of Stage and Theatrical Employees, whose president is a member of the executive council, staged several well-organized sit-downs in New York motion-picture houses months after the council had outlawed such strikes as alien to the policies and interests of the Federation.

Lewis, asked to comment on Green's pronouncement of March, replied briefly with a quotation from Hamlet:

"He again sells his own breed down the river. He 'bends the pregnant hinges of the knee that thrift may follow fawning.'"

Earlier, Lewis had wired the Flint stay-in strikers that the C.I.O. and its affiliated unions "pledge you complete and unanimous support in the conduct of the strike. . . . You men are undoubtedly carrying on through one of the most heroic battles that has ever been undertaken by strikers in an industrial dispute. The attention of the entire American public is focused upon you, watching the severe hardships which you are suffering. . . . Every worker and representative of labor in this country owes a debt of gratitude to each of you."

Both the United Automobile Workers and the United Rubber Workers have officially sanctioned use of the sit-down strike. The rubber-union convention in September, 1936, voted, however, that the sit-downs must first be approved by the local executive board. The auto workers' convention in 1937 also refused to concede that the use of sit-downs was either illegal or unjustified. Sit-downs, like all strikes of auto workers' locals, must, under the U.A.W. constitution, have the approval of the international union.

The C.I.O. attitude on sit-downs was discussed by Len De Caux, editor of the Committee's official Union News Service, in what apparently was an accurate representation of the Committee's leadership. De Caux denied that the C.I.O. is "the father of sit-down strikes, or, vice versa, that sit-downs begat the C.I.O."

"As a matter of fact," De Caux wrote, "the first experience of the C.I.O. with sit-downs was in discouraging them. This was in the Akron rubber industry, after the Goodyear strike. C.I.O. representatives cautioned and advised the new unionists against sit-downs, on the ground that they should use such channels for negotiating grievances as the agreement provided.

"The attitude of the C.I.O. to sit-downs has from the first been consistently that of all responsible union officials to any form of strike. When employers refuse to bargain collectively with the union of their employees, and threaten, spy upon, and repress them in many illegal ways, the workers are driven to protect their rights with such means as are at their disposal. Union leaders worthy of the name—and this does not include such as cringe and fawn before the frowns of the rich to wheedle their favors—then lay the blame for such industrial conflict as may result where it belongs, squarely on the shoulders of those who provoke it by refusing the workers their rights.

[181]

"But when collective bargaining is fully accepted, union recognition accorded and an agreement reached, C.I.O. unionists accept full responsibility for carrying out their side of it in a disciplined fashion, and oppose sit-downs or any other strike action while it is in force."

De Caux quoted Lewis: "The C.I.O. stands for punctilious observance of contracts, but we are not losing any sleep about strikes where employers refuse to recognize the well-defined principles of collective bargaining. A C.I.O. contract is adequate protection for any employer against sit-downs, lie-downs, or any other kind of strike."

v

Liberal lawyers offered a defense of the sit-down as a legal instrument. Leon Green, Dean of the Law School of the University of Illinois, asserted that the case for the legality of the sit-down was predicated on four broad fundamentals: that employees have an interest in the industrial relation and "they sit to negotiate some affair pertinent to their relation to industry"; that sit-downs and other industrial disputes involve economic questions outside the jurisdictions of courts and that courts will therefore leave them to other government agencies and to the parties in the dispute; that courts will not prejudice the issues of a dispute by assuming jurisdiction over issues incidental to the main dispute; and that "occupation in good faith and peacefully of a plant . . . awaiting the adjustment of differences growing out of the industrial relation is but an incident of the industrial relation and in no sense unlawful." C.I.O. lawyers placed the "worker's right to his job," a concept which had been recommended for sympathetic consideration by the U.S. Commission on Industrial Relations in 1915, as the chief argument in favor of the worker sitting at his machine. This alone, they held, offered assurance against the introduction of strike-breakers. They pointed out that a century ago the right to organize was regarded as a conspiracy, and that strikes and picketing were equally illegal. The sit-down, they suggested, is perhaps the latest of labor's weapons to be added to its legitimate and legal methods of offense and defense. In the court fight against the Flint injunctions, Pressman insisted that G.M. had violated the Wagner Act, had come into court with unclean hands, and had, therefore, no standing before the law.

The outcry against sit-down strikes made itself heard in Washington, where Secretary Perkins' declaration, during the G.M. strike, that the legality of the sit-down had not yet been determined was resented by the conservative Republican bloc, Southern Democrats, and foes of the New Deal. Most of the congressional liberals doubted the legality of labor's new weapon, but were inclined to place responsibility for its emergence on the shoulders of die-hard employers. Resolutions denouncing sit-downs appeared in the Senate and in the lower House in March. Senator Byrnes, Democrat of South Carolina, offered a rider to the then pending new Guffey Coal Act, which declared that miners who refused to work were not to remain upon the properties of their employers. In the House, Dies of Texas, a Democrat, won A.F. of L. support for a proposal to investigate the "instigators of the sit-downs." Representative Dickstein, Tammany Democrat, sought to have all "un-American activities," including sit-downs, investigated. Senator Hiram Johnson warned that continued sit-downs would lead to dictatorship; J. Ham Lewis, Illinois' bewhiskered sage, submitted that the rights of property were in danger; King of Utah, summoned quotations from Green and Frey to bolster his contention that the sit-downs were a C.I.O. technique for Bolshevizing the nation. Vandenberg, Michigan Republican, and Tydings, Maryland Democrat, took the opportunity to denounce the Wagner Act as well as the sit-down. In the House, Representative Connery, Massachusetts Democrat and spokesman for the A.F. of L., lent his support to Dies, as did Clare Hoffman, Michigan's most vigorous foe of the C.I.O.

The Senate liberals were vigorous, though qualified, in their defense of the sitters. Senator Thomas of Utah roamed back to classical Confucius and Lao-Tze, founder of the Taoist religion, and came down to date with references to Gandhi to prove the ethical validity of peaceful striking on the job. Senator Wagner declared the strikes had been provoked "by long-standing ruthless tactics of a few great corporations who have hamstrung the National Labor Relations Board by invoking injunctions in the courts, who have openly banded together to defy this law of Congress quite independently

[183]

of any court action, and who have systematically used spies and discharges and violence and terrorism to shatter the workers' liberties as defined by Congress. . . ."

"The organized and calculated and cold-blooded sit-down against Federal law has come, as always, not from the common people, but from a few great vested interests," Wagner charged. "The uprising of the common people has come, as always, only because of a breakdown in the ability of the law and our economic system to protect their rights."

Senator Norris, dean of the progressives, declared himself surprised that under the provocative circumstances "labor had not gone further." The House heard defenses of the sitters from John T. Bernard, soon to become a volunteer organizer among his mining constituents in Minnesota, from Maury Maverick of Texas, and John M. Coffee of Washington, among others. Byrnes' rider to the Guffey Act was voted down. A few days later the Senate, by a vote of 75 to 3, found a common ground. Its resolution denounced the sit-down as "illegal and contrary to public policy," but added a declaration that industrial espionage, the denial by employers of the right of collective bargaining and the fostering of company unions were also contrary to sound public policy. The House tabled the proposal which would have enabled Dickstein to go on a new fishing expedition, and refused also to consider the Dies resolution.

The federal courts, in July, upheld the Senate viewpoint of the illegality of the sit-down. Judge William H. Kirkpatrick, in Pennsylvania, had ruled, on an appeal by owners of the Apex Hosiery Company of Philadelphia, that the federal courts had no jurisdiction in the dispute between the company and its sitting striking employees. He granted, however, that the sitters were committing trespass in violation of the laws of Pennsylvania. Kirkpatrick was promptly reversed by the U.S. Circuit Court of Appeals, which ruled that the 250 strikers who had been in the plant for a month and a half had conspired to interfere with interstate commerce. This gave the federal courts proper jurisdiction, the judges ruled. The strikers had not availed themselves of the opportunities offered by the Wagner Act, the court held, adding the injunction that they were to leave the mill without further delay. Despite the judgment of the court that

[184]

a minority of the company's workers had seized the plant, the strike eventually ended in a closed-shop agreement for the strikers, who were members of the C.I.O.'s American Federation of Full Fashioned Hosiery Workers.

With the ruling of the Court of Appeals before her and with the sit-down outburst having almost completely subsided, Secretary Perkins found the time had come when a considered stand on the issue might be taken. Replying to a request for comment on the Apex Hosiery case, the Secretary of Labor declared her department had never taken the position that sit-downs were "lawful, desirable or appropriate." Agents of the department had urged labor to abandon the method, which, she added, was "full of hazards to the progressive, democratic development of trade unionism and to the orderly process of collective bargaining."

VI

Although the courts and government officials have disposed of the sit-down by declaring it unlawful and undesirable, it is not unlikely that sit-downs will persist. The facts of the 1936-37 sit-downs —where they occurred, who took part in them, and why—indicates the circumstances under which they may happen again.

The anti-union industries which, unlike steel, refused to alter their attitude, were hardest hit. In the manufacture of transportation equipment, almost exclusively automobiles, 247,095 workers sat down in plants or seized them; rubber had 42,167 sit-down strikers; textiles was third highest, with 22,270. Iron and steel had but 12,996. Least disturbed were the largely unionized mining industries, where 300 workers sat down; and the clothing industries, where none were reported from September, 1936 to June, 1937. The method was most popular with workers in newly organized industries which had no background of collective bargaining. A tabulation shows that of the 484,711 sitters, 277,769 belonged to new unions whose members and employees were too inexperienced, or unwilling, to resolve their difficulties in a more pacific manner. Of the remainder, 182,219 workers belonged largely to unions established since the advent of the NRA; 7,667 were unorganized when they sat down. Concerning 17,056 other sit-down strikers, no information was at hand.

Why did they sit? 52,305 struck in support of demands involving wages and working hours; 49,289 sat down for one of a variety of reasons, including sympathy strikes and jurisdictional disputes. The reasons which actuated the larger number of strikers in the last named category were, however, unascertained. The major part of the sitters—381,779—quit work in protest against the refusal of employers to grant union recognition. In some cases wages and hours were also involved, but always, in this largest group of sit-down strikers, union recognition or kindred causes like the closed shop (in the case of 9,241 strikers), alleged violations of agreements or discriminatory discharges were the basic causes of the difficulties.

9.

PEACE AND WAR IN STEEL

I

ON SUNDAY afternoon, July 5, 1936, a throng of Homestead steel workers searched for hours amid weather-worn headstones that rose from a cemetery on the side of a hill. They had come to lay wreaths on the graves of the Homestead martyrs and pledge a new effort to right the wrong epitomized by the "Battle of the Barges" in 1892. On a rust-colored river less than two hundred yards from the burial-ground, stretched the black expanse of the Homestead mill. Smoking stacks reached high in the air, blackening a summer afternoon's sky as though to remind the steel workers that the task they contemplated was fraught with great sacrifice. Discouraging indeed was the failure for hours to locate the graves. The shrine of American labor had been forgotten and unvisited for years. Pat Cush, an old steel worker, had searched since early morning in the cemetery records and among the stones for the names of the six slain union men who were buried there. Finally, toward late afternoon, four graves were located. Cush told the workers who gathered bareheaded at the graves small details of the slain men's lives.

"William Foy was a very religious man. He was always counseling the men against violence. He was the first to fall from the bullets of the Pinkerton men," said Cush. "And Silas Wain was a member of the strike committee. He had a wife and two young children. They went away after he was killed and nobody ever heard of them again."

Patrick T. Fagan, president of District Five of the United Mine Workers of America, concluded the ceremonies at each grave.

[187]

"William Foy," said Fagan, "we have come to renew the struggle for which you gave your life. We pledge all our efforts to bring a better life for the steel workers. We hope you have found peace and happiness. God rest your soul."

A Homestead meeting which had preceded the visit to Franklin Cemetery presented further ties with the past and signposts to the future. It marked the first union meeting Homestead had seen since 1919; before then there had been none since 1892. Not only the lack of interest on the part of Homestead's steel workers explained the absence of meetings. Stronger than that was the uninterrupted rule of the borough by the U.S. Steel Corporation and the local authorities it unfailingly placed in office. Even Secretary of Labor Perkins, in 1934, had been refused the use of a public park for a meeting of steel workers. Outwitting Burgess Cavanaugh, whom she termed the "nervous Burgess," Madame Perkins took her prospective audience to the Post Office building and there listened to their timidly-spoken grievances.

The meeting of July 5, 1936, was to mark a turning-point. While similar audiences met in South Chicago and elsewhere, the Homestead attendance of some 1,000 steel workers and as many miners from near-by towns heard leaders of the United Mine Workers sound the call for a new steel union campaign. Lieutenant-Governor Kennedy told the Homestead workers that the Pennsylvania steel towns were henceforth open territory for union organizers. Speaking in behalf of Governor George H. Earle, Jr., he said that if the steel campaign necessitated a strike, the strikers could count on government relief funds.

A miners' band from Morgantown, Pa., wearing picture buttons of President Roosevelt, played music; first a dirge for the Homestead martyrs, then strident marching airs. John Scharbo, a rebellious company union leader from U.S. Steel's mill at Rankin, read in Polish accents an indictment which held that the steel companies had, through violence, suppression of civil liberties and company unionism, deprived the steel workers of the promise of the Declaration of Independence. He proposed a new bill of rights. Even as the "Steel Workers' Declaration of Independence" was being approved by shouts and cheers, hundreds of mill hands hung back on a curb

[188]

a hundred feet from the speakers' stand and listened doubtfully. Among them stood the superintendent of the Homestead mill. The next day he asked a Pittsburgh newspaper to supply him with enlargements of a panorama photograph of those who had gathered around the speakers' stand.

II

The machinery of the C.I.O. steel drive was announced on June 13, 1936, ten days after Lewis had concluded the understanding with the Amalgamated Association of Iron, Steel, and Tin Workers. Philip Murray was named director of the Steel Workers Organizing Committee; his associates were Hochman of the International Ladies' Garment Workers; Tighe and Joseph K. Gaither of the Amalgamated Association; Krzycki of the Amalgamated Clothing Workers, Brophy and Fagan. Clinton S. Golden, machinist, but more recently director in Pittsburgh for the National Labor Relations Board, was made regional director for the eastern steel area. Van Bittner took over the Chicago sector, and William Mitch, also a mine union leader, was placed in charge in the South. Modern publicity methods were assured when Vin Sweeney was weaned away from the Scripps-Howard *Pittsburgh Press*. With an eye to civil liberties problems, Pressman moved his staff and his files to Pittsburgh. The S.W.O.C. installed itself on the thirty-sixth floor of the Grant Building, several floors above Ernest T. Weir's commodious business appointments in the most expensive of Pittsburgh's skyscrapers.

With funds supplied by the miners and the two large unions in the needle trades, a staff of 433 full-time and part-time organizers were placed in the field. They worked by a carefully planned strategy designed to gather the maximum of adherents without exposing any of them to discharge before the campaign had advanced to the point where protection could be offered. Thirty-five regional offices were opened in steel town stores and office buildings. A newspaper, *Steel Labor,* was issued.

Early in the drive, before "C.I.O." had become almost magic letters sweeping hundreds of thousands of steel workers into its ranks, the problem of leadership was a serious one. The abortive revolt of 1934 and 1935 was fresh in the memory of the workers.

[189]

Many had paid tidy sums, in some cases as high as fifty dollars, in initiation fees and dues to the old Amalgamated. Almost 100,000 had paid some dues. For reward, they had been expelled. S.W.O.C. organizers were confronted with Amalgamated dues books showing the large payments, and frequently a shrug of indifference answered the argument that the C.I.O. was working on a different plan. Ignoring the provisions in the Amalgamated's constitution, the S.W.O.C. fixed the initiation fee at one dollar, which was also to cover the first month's dues. Nevertheless, the dues issue still rankled. Murray felt it had to be effectively demonstrated that the prime objective of the drive was the unionization of the steel workers and their economic advancement. Dues and initiation fee requirements, as a condition of membership in the S.W.O.C., were temporarily suspended. Thus while the anti-C.I.O. press and the steel companies charged that the C.I.O. was another dues-collecting racket, no funds whatever were being collected from the workers. This policy continued in effect until April of 1937, when success had crowned the C.I.O.'s efforts. A dollar a month dues went into effect in April, and in June, a three dollar initiation fee was provided. This made the cost of joining the union fifteen dollars a year, a fraction of the annual wage increase which the union had in the meantime placed in the steel workers' pay envelopes.

The S.W.O.C. campaign was aided by tactical blunders on the part of the American Iron and Steel Institute and several of its affiliated companies. The first mistake came on June 24th, when the drive was barely organized and when Lewis, Murray, and their steel staff were still worried about the response of the steel workers. The Institute placed full-paged advertisements in 375 daily newspapers at a cost of almost half a million dollars, announcing their opposition to the Lewis efforts. They charged that coercion and intimidation were to be used by the C.I.O.; that the closed shop would be imposed, and that the workers would be forced to pay tribute for the right to work. The Institute declared that the industry believed in collective bargaining and was practicing it through the universally organized employee representation system. For "background information," the Institute furnished the press with a quotation from one Morris Childs, said to be secretary of the Communist Party, to the effect that the Communists were ready to play "an important rôle" in a forthcoming steel strike. Most of the press dutifully printed the Childs statement without indicating that it had been furnished by the Institute. Steel-town papers developed the theme that Lewis and his aides were both reds and racketeers. The effect of the Institute's publicity barrage was to give the C.I.O.'s campaign far more attention than its strength deserved at the time. The campaign was placed on front pages and on the minds and tongues of all steel workers; and the union organizers were satisfied. William A. Irvin, president of U.S. Steel, took up the attack a few days later, and to the delight of the C.I.O., Secretary Perkins expressed the opinion that there was no reason for the steel heads acting so jittery.

With the stage set for him by his opponents, Lewis took to the air on a national network on July 6th, and in a blend of righteous appeal and stern determination, declared that a momentous "battle for democracy impends in America." He accepted the Steel Institute's advertisements as "a declaration of war" and accused the corporation of defying the Wagner Act, of mulcting consumers, of coercing and spying upon its workers, and of foisting company unions upon them. He pledged the C.I.O. efforts would be legal and peaceful. Lewis challenged the Steel Institute's strongest boast, that they paid higher wages than any other industry. Hourly wages in March, 1936, said Lewis, were 65.6 cents in steel, 79.3 in bituminous coal, 83.2 in hard coal, and 79.8 in building construction. Common labor in steel, he said, received 47.9 cents an hour, and in the matter of weekly wages for that type of worker, the entire industry occupied twentieth place in a list of twenty-one industries. Lewis' figures were challenged by the Steel Institute, but after a battle of statistics it appeared that the C.I.O. leader had accuracy on his side.

III

The steel industry's continuous emphasis on the employee-representation plan as proof of its acceptance of collective bargaining also served the strategy of Murray and Lewis. The C.I.O. program in organizing steel included a new approach to the problem of company unionism. The plan was not, as in the past, to denounce the com-

[191]

pany-union heads and rake their organizations over the coals, but rather to encourage them to make their bargaining machinery effective. The C.I.O. hoped thus to establish cordial relationship with sincere elements among the employee representatives, and by forcing issues of wages and hours, demonstrate the inadequacy of their machinery.

The employee representation plan in steel was the brain child of Arthur H. Young, a U.S. Steel vice-president, who called it a modern application of the Golden Rule. A few mills had set up the plan in 1919, but it was not until the enactment of the National Recovery Act had brought a revival of union sentiment that the device came into more general use. By the end of 1934 at least 90 per cent of half a million steel workers were "covered" by the plan. When the Wagner Act was passed, the steel companies hastened to stage plebiscites of steel workers on a revised plan which eliminated some of the more obvious appearances of company unionism. Nevertheless, the plan continued to be of no value to labor on the major questions of wages and working-hours; it provided no machinery whereby workers of one plant could pool their efforts with those of another. Final adjudication of even minor grievances lay in the hands of the management.

Dissatisfaction with the steel company unions was evident in January, 1936, six months before the S.W.O.C. had launched its campaign. In Gary, Indiana, on January 12th, thirteen out of the twenty-five employee representatives at the local Carnegie-Illinois plant met at the Labor Temple and formed a lodge of the Amalgamated Association. Appreciating the implications of the step they were taking and having some among them with a smattering of ancient lore, they called themselves "Rubicon Lodge." Among them was John Mayerik, a heater in the wheel mill, who became vice-president of the Amalgamated lodge, and remained to become a member of the mill grievance committee under a contract signed by the S.W.O.C.; Joseph Goin, a bricklayer, who became the president; Edward Ennis, first helper in the open-hearth and one of the highest paid men in the industry; Pat Coleman, boilermaker; Henry Yurin, machinist; and Arthur Adams, a Negro worker in the coke plant. They openly announced their "rebellion" against the company union. Before a week was out, all had been put on the carpet by mill foremen, but none were discharged. By July 5th, when the Homestead meeting was held, they had grown from thirteen to sixty-seven members, and their influence in the plant was great.

In the Pittsburgh area, the first open impatience of employee representatives was voiced by William Garrity, an electrician in the Edgar Thomas mill at Braddock. The Thomas representatives' grievance centered about a check-off of 10 per cent of their wages, which the company was collecting as repayment for relief baskets handed out during the depth of the depression. Carnegie-Illinois had announced at the time that steel workers would not accept government relief; instead, the baskets were distributed. Garrity's fight succeeded in easing the check-off—one dollar was to be deducted from each twenty-five dollars earned—but the rumblings of the company union Frankenstein did not cease. On Saturday night, February 15th, some twenty-five company union representatives in Carnegie-Illinois mills of the Pittsburgh-Youngstown area met at a "purely social dinner." John Mullen, then a heater in the Clairton works, had sponsored the convivial evening, but it soon developed that he had serious business in mind. He proposed the formation of a "Pittsburgh Central Council of Employee Representatives" which would make district-wide demands, through the company union set-up, on wages and hours. The company representatives, an integral part of the employee representation plan, were to be excluded. At the dinner were John Kane, Elmer Maloy, Ernest Fries of the Carnegie-Illinois Duquesne works; Garrity, Bill Ragalyi, and Neil McLaughlin from Braddock; Arthur (Swede) Junstrum, Bill Combs and Bill Laird of Homestead—all of whom eventually were to become S.W.O.C. advocates; and Fred Bohne, heading a Youngstown delegation, who later fought efforts of the S.W.O.C. to make the Pittsburgh central council function.

The council was formally set up in March. The company refused at first to recognize it and persisted in its stand until the S.W.O.C. campaign was in full swing, when recognition was accorded in the hope that it would serve as a buffer against the C.I.O. group. By that time the more effective and influential representatives in the council had enrolled under the S.W.O.C. banner, and the company was left with only a shell of a buffer.

Van Bittner in Chicago brought his area into line early in July, with the announcement that the majority of the employee representatives in Carnegie-Illinois' South Chicago works had joined the S.W.O.C. A short time later, a company union at Inland Steel, at Chicago Heights, also switched its allegiance to independent unionism. The Chicago pioneers included George Patterson, a Sunday-school teacher, and on weekdays a roll-turner for Carnegie-Illinois, who was later discharged for making an unauthorized trip to S.W.O.C. headquarters in Pittsburgh; James Stewart, Stanley Bazinski and Bill Anderson, of Indiana Harbor. The Chicago Carnegie-Illinois steel revolt brought 3,000 workers into a lodge of the S.W.O.C.

Carrying its fight directly through employee representatives, the S.W.O.C. by the middle of July had enough contacts with employee representatives to have them formulate and demand a minimum wage of five dollars a day for common labor and wage increases for those who received more than that. Later, again through S.W.O.C. inspiration, the company unions added a forty-hour week to their programs. This gave the steel workers a money-and-hour objective, without making it directly a part of the S.W.O.C. program. The idea was to have the company unions "biting at the heels" of the management. Faced by the growing insurgency, the industry announced on July 24th that thereafter the industry would pay time and a half for overtime—the overtime rate to start after forty-eight hours of work in a given week. Murray immediately declared the move an imposition of a forty-eight-hour week, and within three weeks approximately sixty company unions had denounced the offer and refused to accept it. Garrity's group at the Edgar Thomas works adopted a resolution indignantly denying the company's statement that the "concession" had been requested by the employee representatives.

Lewis and Murray sensed that steel management, in a new effort to stem the tide toward unionism, would soon announce an increase in pay. Murray publicly predicted such a raise was coming, and linked it to the growth of S.W.O.C. sentiment. From that time on, company-union representatives knocked almost daily at the doors of Benjamin F. Fairless, president of Carnegie-Illinois, and left demands and petitions for higher wages, shorter hours, and a revision of company-union procedure.

Crystallization of the company-union demands—made always with S.W.O.C. prodding—came in the formation of a so-called Central Council of Employee Representatives. On October 19th, Maloy, the craneman from the Duquesne works, who was known to have S.W.O.C. "leanings"—actually he and a dozen others called almost daily at S.W.O.C. headquarters to discuss next steps—was elected chairman of the central council. The consternation of the Carnegie-Illinois officials was deep, for they had encouraged formation of the council in the belief that it would be dominated by anti-C.I.O. "conservatives." Maloy's election was due in part to S.W.O.C. maneuvering and in part to a division within the council. It was hailed throughout the Pittsburgh-Youngstown area as a clear S.W.O.C. victory. A subsequent labor board investigation revealed the distress with which Ross Loefler, director of industrial relations for Carnegie-Illinois, received the news. He had immediately called a meeting of the representatives he thought were closest to him and started to discuss Maloy's removal. Among his supporters, as Loefler thought them to be, were several men who carried cards in the S.W.O.C.

"My God, fellows, I am disappointed! That's terrible—a vote like that," Loefler exclaimed. "Maloy will have to go."

A few weeks after Maloy's triumph, the steel workers won another election. President Roosevelt defeated Landon, and in the steel towns it appeared that the nation had voiced approval of the C.I.O. campaign. Murray for the first time revealed the numerical results of the S.W.O.C.'s campaign—82,315 had signed membership cards. The following day an "average 10-per-cent" wage increase was announced by U.S. Steel, a rise which was duplicated throughout the industry. Again "Big Steel" contributed to the onward sweep of the S.WO.C. The wage raise was tied up with a cost-of-living plan. Within certain limits, wages were to be geared to the cost-of-living figures of the U.S. Department of Labor. A second innovation was that contracts, embracing the sliding-wage-scale plan, were to be

[195]

signed by the company unions. The implication was that the increase would be withheld from those workers whose representatives refused to sign. Through its by now close-knitted contacts with the company unionists, the S.W.O.C. induced scores of important plant representatives to refuse to sign. They objected to tying wages to the cost of living, insisting that the current wage was far too low to serve as a fair base for such a plan; and they felt that the company unions were not called upon to sign contracts, particularly unsatisfactory ones. The rebellious ones pointed out that the corporation had never before offered to treat the employee representatives so gallantly. Maloy and George Patterson, their fare paid by the S.W.O.C., hastened to Washington to see Secretary Perkins. Out of their interview came an opinion by the Secretary of Labor that the employee-representation-plan heads had no legal right to sign contracts.

The Perkins statement was the first of several blows which led to the death of the company unions. The few representatives who signed the agreements were subjected to repeated, planned attacks from their membership. There were charges that certain of them had "sold out" the men in the mills. To further embarrass the "conservative" representatives, the wage increase was granted to all workers regardless of whether or not a "contract" had been signed. Moving to reap full advantage of the anti-company union tide, the S.W.O.C. filed formal charges with the National Labor Relations Board charging Carnegie-Illinois with maintaining a company union. The board cited the company, and highly educational hearings, starting in Washington a week before Christmas, confirmed the S.W.O.C.'s charges.

The S.W.O.C. was now ready to come out in complete and open war on the company unions. Fully 250 "progressive" employee representatives from forty-two plants, most of them Carnegie-Illinois units, met in Pittsburgh, joined the S.W.O.C., and set up the "C.I.O. Representatives Council." Similar groups were organized elsewhere in the steel centers, and all were linked together in regional councils. Murray announced to the Pittsburgh conference that the S.W.O.C. membership had grown to 125,000. The unrest within the company unions now became a full-fledged rebellion.

"Conservative" representatives in January, 1937, started their last stand. Borrowing a leaf from beleaguered labor unions of other years, the remaining company unionists set up a "defense committee." They succeeded in ousting Maloy, the S.W.O.C. chairman of the Pittsburgh district "general council." Nevertheless, by February, the Carnegie-Illinois company-union system was in a chaotic state. Several plants were led by "progressives" who had S.W.O.C. cards or followed its lead; others still retained "conservative" spokesmen. To add to the confusion in the Pittsburgh "general council," which had been captured by "conservatives," a S.W.O.C. man was elected head of the subcommittee on hours and wages. Hoping to bolster the crumbling machinery of Young's Golden Rule, and perhaps restore it to functioning life, Fairless visited the representatives in most of the plants and assured them again that the management would stand behind the company-union plan.

IV

A S.W.O.C. organizer in Aliquippa, Pa., called Murray at the Grant Building during the late afternoon of March 1, 1937, and said he had been hearing wild rumors.

"One of the steel workers just came in and said he heard over the radio that U.S. Steel was meeting with the C.I.O.," said the organizer. "I told him he was crazy and kicked him out of the office."

"Well, don't kick him out. It's true," said Murray.

The Aliquippa organizer's amazement was of a piece with that with which the nation greeted the news. "U.S. Steel Bows to Lewis Union," the pictorial *Daily News* of New York screamed in letters three inches high. What had been predicted as one of the bitterest labor struggles in America turned out to be no less sensational for its peaceful turn. The full significance of General Motors signing with the C.I.O. had been obscured when it took place. Many called it a defeat for the union, and it was not until weeks afterward that it was acknowledged as a great C.I.O. victory. There could be no doubt about the meaning of U.S. Steel's capitulation to the C.I.O.'s industrial union of steel workers, although Lewis and Murray did not crow over it. They diplomatically spoke words of praise for the coöperative spirit of Myron C. Taylor, chairman of the U.S. Steel's board of directors and his co-directors; but the entire world knew that "Big Steel," a billion-dollar corporation, industrial colossus of the world, which since 1892 had set the pattern of American heavy industry's ceaseless opposition to unionism, had yielded and signed a contract with the militant C.I.O. The contract was signed—first by Carnegie-Illinois, employing 130,000 workers and largest of the U.S. Steel units. Other subsidiaries signed soon after.

There were four major concessions to the union in the U.S. Steel contracts. The S.W.O.C. obtained recognition through a formal contract signed for the company by Fairless, and for the S.W.O.C. by Murray, Golden, Bittner, Pressman and David J. MacDonald, treasurer of the S.W.O.C. A general wage increase, bringing the basic rate to a minimum of five dollars a day was granted, as was a forty-hour work week, with payment at the rate of time and a half for overtime. The fourth outstanding concession was an agreement that all grievances not immediately adjusted were to be submitted for compulsory arbitration. Technically, the corporation maintained its open-shop policy. It retained the right to deal with other organizations of its employees, and the S.W.O.C. was recognized only for its members. As in General Motors, however, the prestige of the C.I.O. was so enhanced by the agreement that the company unions soon disappeared. The remaining company unionists found themselves unwelcome stepchildren. With the Supreme Court's approval of the Wagner Act, U.S. Steel formally withdrew all connections, refusing any longer to provide them with meeting-places and terminating financial contributions toward support of the plan. While the company unions disappeared, S.W.O.C. membership in the mills grew daily. The contract prohibited solicitation of union membership on company property, but this was interpreted as applying only to the actual signing of cards or collection of dues. No effort was made to halt talk about the union, and union buttons appeared openly on the overalls of a great majority of Carnegie-Illinois employees, where years before so much as the suspicion of union membership would have meant discrimination or discharge.

The greatest news event in American industrial history was almost a complete secret until it became an accomplished fact. Four

[198]

or five members of U.S. Steel and J. P. Morgan and Company—
Taylor, Thomas W. Lamont, a Morgan partner, and Edward R.
Stettinius, among them—knew what was in the wind. In the C.I.O.
camp the delicate negotiations and their progress were known only
to Lewis and Murray, who participated in them. Starting early in
December of 1936, Lewis and Taylor held numerous conferences
in Washington and New York. The C.I.O. chairman and the U.S.
Steel head had known each other since the early days of the N.R.A.
when both were members of the advisory board. Other researchers
into the lesser angles of the epochal developments have returned
with the report that Taylor, inspired to industrial statesmanship,
went to his Italian villa for a spell and returned with a magic
formula which at once recognized the C.I.O. and maintained the
corporation's open-shop policy.

Fundamentally, U.S. Steel signed with the C.I.O. because the
Committee had enrolled a substantial majority of Carnegie-Illinois
employees as well as those of other corporation units. The company
union had been wrecked. U.S. Steel had the choice of a costly
strike—which, because of the political situation nationally and in
Pennsylvania, would most likely have ended in a C.I.O. victory;
or of signing with the union, granting wage demands which were
inevitable anyway, and enjoying an uninterrupted production season which promised, after comparatively lean years, to be highly
profitable. Politically, the cards seemed stacked against U.S. Steel,
largely through Lewis' strength in Washington and in Pennsylvania, where Kennedy was Lieutenant-Governor and where Governor Earle had been elected by a combination of labor and liberal
middle-class votes. Earle had pledged that if a strike came, the
steel workers would enjoy complete freedom of picketing and assemblage, and, while striking, might expect aid from governmental
relief funds.

Other political pressures which Lewis had engineered or encouraged helped to make up the corporation's mind. There was the
Walsh-Healey Act which provided that no steel corporation which
operated on a longer then forty-hour-week schedule could receive
government orders for naval armor plate; there was the proceedings
before the National Labor Relations Board which looked as though

they would end with findings that the corporation's subsidiaries had violated the Wagner act; there was the threat of the La Follette subcommittee on civil liberties to probe into the corporation's espionage activities. And there was pending a resolution by Representative Harry Ellenbogen of Pittsburgh, calling for an investigation of the profits and price-fixing methods of the steel industry.

The principal fear of the corporation, however, lay in its conviction that the S.W.O.C. had done such a good organizing job that if a strike was forced, serious economic losses would result. The prospects of a war in Europe, with a booming demand for steel, heightened this fear. Lamont and Stettinius are said to have realized that, all in all, it would be better to give Lewis and the C.I.O. recognition. Taylor was won over by making it appear that credit for a statesman-like approach would be his.

The steel workers gave the C.I.O. the credit, and in the week that followed the signing of the contract, 20,000 more workers joined the S.W.O.C., and thirty steel companies, large and small, agreed to collective-bargaining conferences. By April 1, fifty-nine companies were under contract, membership of the union had passed the 200,000 mark, and 429 new lodges of steel workers were functioning. Early in May, Murray announced that the S.W.O.C. had 325,000 members, 600 new lodges and contracts with 90 companies, including all the subsidiaries of U.S. Steel and such important independent companies as Wheeling Steel, Timken Roller Bearing, Caterpillar Tractor, and McKeesport Tin-Plate.

The fourth largest steel producer in the nation, Jones & Laughlin, traditionally more hard-boiled in its opposition to unionism than even U.S. Steel, signed with the S.W.O.C. on May 20th, but not until a thirty-six-hour strike and a labor-board poll had showed the great sentiment of its workers for unionism. J. & L. workers in Pittsburgh and Aliquippa, for years darkest satrapy of the steel industry, went to the polls and voted their preference for the S.W.O.C. 17,028 to 7,207. By the terms of an understanding, the company thereupon signed an agreement recognizing the union as the sole bargaining representative of its 27,000 employees. The remainder of the contract followed the lines of the U.S. Steel agreement. The Sharon and Pittsburgh steel companies also subsequently doubted the strength of the S.W.O.C. and insisted on employee polls by the Labor Board. The union won in Pittsburgh Steel 5,297 to 645; and in Sharon Steel 1,773 to 721. The tide into the S.W.O.C. appeared irresistible. It was only partially stemmed by the development of the strike in "Little Steel."

V

"Little Steel" generally included Ernest T. Weir's National Steel Corporation, Republic, Bethlehem, and Inland Steel, and the Youngstown Sheet & Tube Corporation. Within the ranks of "Little Steel's" executives, U.S. Steel's accord with the C.I.O. marked Myron C. Taylor and his associates as "turncoats" only slightly less dangerous than Lewis and Murray. The American Iron & Steel Institute was split, the independent companies placing Tom M. Girdler, president of Republic, in the chairmanship. Girdler and his supporters had decided that recognition of the C.I.O. and the S.W.O.C. was unthinkable. They said it would be a betrayal of their "loyal" employees. Girdler had previously stated that he wished to run his business, particularly the fixing of wages, without any compromises which might be entailed by collective bargaining.

The chairman of Republic Steel became obsessed with the notion that he stood at the bridge guarding the liberties of the nation and its businessmen against the onrush of a destructive horde. In his long industrial career, Girdler had never brooked the interference of labor. Before his association with Republic Steel in 1929 he had served with two outstanding examples of a corporate individualism so rugged that they became classical cases of extreme anti-unionism. Girdler was with the Rockefellers' Colorado Fuel and Iron Company in the two years when its policies bore fruit in the Ludlow massacre during which helpless strikers, their women and children, were shot, burned, and suffocated to death by mercenary strikebreakers. After 1914, Ivy Lee persuaded the Rockefellers to neutralize the infamy of Ludlow with the sweet scent of charity. Girdler later went to Jones & Laughlin. At Aliquippa, J. & L. built a closed company town where union organizers were decidedly unwelcome and where the thousands of "Hunky," Negro, and other American steel workers lived in segregated, assigned sections under the surveillance of company police and spies, supplemented by the services of a collection of public officials recruited from company ranks. Investigators for the World Interchurch Movement included Jones & Laughlin in a survey they made in 1919, while Girdler was chief factor in its labor policies. The report of the churchmen illustrated the thoroughness of the J. & L. dictatorship:

"Agitating in the mill," they found, "may include the mail a man receives at his home. At the Jones and Laughlin plant in Woodlawn, Pa., one department had twenty-four Finns. Finns are known as especially intelligent workmen and especially likely to join unions. In February, 1919, the plant management learned that these Finns were visiting a great deal with each other at night, meeting in the cellars of their own houses. Finally it was observed that the Finns seemed to be getting more mail than other 'foreigners,' including newspapers and pamphlets. The twenty-four were called up one morning and fired without explanation. In September, 1919, the plant managers were congratulating themselves: they observed in the list of union workers deported by plant guards the names of some of their Finns."

The more recent Girdler labor tactics had not tarnished his old reputation. Soon after Republic Steel joined in the general wage increase which brought the rate for common labor to sixty-two and one-half cents an hour, the Girdler company announced a revision. It reduced the hourly rate for laborers to fifty-nine cents and added a "bonus" incentive. The company represented that under the bonus arrangement, the men might earn as high as sixty-five cents an hour. However, with less than a full week's work, the bonus-paying tonnage could seldom be achieved. The company finesse was based on the knowledge that the work week as a rule did not extend over more than four days. The Republic laborers at Youngstown found themselves fortunate if they could average sixty-two and half cents an hour. Republic had announced the sixty-two and a half cent rate in the press and had posted it on company bulletin boards. The employees considered it a pledge. The bonus arrangement proved a decoy from another aspect. It could only be earned when the men worked on machines. If they worked three or four days on machines and were then transferred back to the laborers' scale of fifty-nine cents an hour, their weekly average was pulled down, and again the bonus went glimmering. The sponsor of this plan was the company which now took the lead in the battle against the C.I.O. because, it held, C.I.O. could not be trusted to keep its word.

Having failed to persuade the "Little Steel" companies to enter collective bargaining negotiations, the S.W.O.C., late in May and early in June, called 70,000 of their workers on strike. The mills of Republic, Youngstown Sheet & Tube, Inland, and the Johnstown plant of Bethlehem were affected. Weir's mill at Weirton, West Virginia, possibly the greatest obstacle in the S.W.O.C. path, was reserved for a later effort. The "Little Steel" strike proved to be the bloodiest of the entire labor struggle which stretched from 1933 to the winter of 1937. Both the C.I.O. and the nation were given to understand that there still remained powerful industrial interests not yet ready to recognize the principle of collective bargaining.

The strike was broken by a combination of official and vigilante violence, the use of the National Guard, and a concentrated barrage of propaganda which the S.W.O.C. could not equal or counteract. Civil government in Johnstown, Pa., in Youngstown, Warren, Niles, Massillon, Canton, and Cleveland, Ohio, and in Chicago was sympathetic, if not thoroughly subservient, to the steel corporations. In Johnstown, Youngstown and Chicago, key strike centers, the cooperation was open. The deaths of eighteen steel strikers occurred in what independent, government, and labor observers agreed were unprovoked attacks. Almost 200 active strikers and local leaders were arrested in Youngstown alone, most of them to be released eventually without having had formal charges made against them. Official violence was supplemented by vigilante violence in Monroe, Mich., and Massillon, Ohio. Despite this pressure, the ranks of the strikers held fast. The National Guard was then brought into play in Ohio, although state laws had been enacted to prevent strikebreaking by the military. Following a secret conference between the Ohio National Guard commanders and the heads of Republic Steel, the troops moved systematically from Youngstown to Warren, to Niles, to Canton, to Massillon and then to Cleveland to harass and disband picket lines and arrest local strike leaders.

Meanwhile the propaganda of the steel companies went forward.

Johnstown, Youngstown, Warren and Canton were one-newspaper towns, and in each case the paper was opposed to the strikers. Trivial incidents on picket lines were enlarged to give the impression of a strike-inspired reign of terror. Hysterical outbursts of local public officials were given prominence. "Back-to-work movements" were promoted and heralded as successes. Eight-column headlines and four-column picture spreads told of "normal" and "near normal" operation of mills while they were still largely deserted. Endorsement of these "back-to-work" movements was given by so-called "independent unions" whose aim uniformly coincided with the objectives of the corporations. The movements were supported by vigilante and would-be vigilante movements in Johnstown, Youngstown, Canton, Massillon and Monroe. These were labeled "citizens" committees and constantly bespoke their impartiality in the dispute, but all managed, nevertheless, to serve the interests of the corporations.

Mayor Daniel J. Shields of Johnstown, one-time inmate of a federal prison following conviction for attempting to bribe a federal officer, headed the "back-to-work" movement in his city. The National Labor Relations Board was subsequently informed that he received $31,456 of Bethlehem Steel money while the strike was on. The corporation gave the funds to a "citizens" committee, it was testified, for the purpose of helping maintain "law and order." The money, ultimately, was turned over to Shields, the chairman of the "citizens" committee said. The strike brought Mayor Shields busy days. He issued tin hats and permission to carry clubs to hundreds of supervisory employees of the corporation. He appeared on picket lines and ordered pickets to "move on," directing the arrest of those who, he felt, moved too slowly. He mounted the bench in police court and sat as a magistrate on strike cases.

"Are you a member of the C.I.O.?" was the first question. "What were you doing up so early this morning?"

A union lawyer protested the seemingly needless violence of Patrolman Doc Krise, the "quick-draw" man of the Johnstown police force.

"Doc Krise did his duty wonderfully," Mayor Shields exclaimed from the bench. "We need policemen like him. A world without policemen would be like a world without music . . . a very dreary world indeed."

[204]

At the Johnstown City Hall Shields speechified for news cameramen on the "sacredness" of the right to work. He went on the radio —from the same station which denied time to the S.W.O.C.—announcing that "the 'back-to-work' movement starts from now on." When the movement did not start, the mayor ordered the strike leaders to leave the city. They refused, and he had them dragged before him by police officers. No charge was made against them. They were told they remained in Johnstown at their own peril.

The Johnstown newspapers, the famous *Democrat,* and its morning edition, the *Tribune,* referred to "dirty Mexicans" and "knife-throwing Mexicans" stirring up violence on the picket lines. There were fewer than 300 Mexican steel workers among the some 12,000 who worked for Bethlehem at the Cambria plant. These were imported by the corporation as cheap and docile labor. The *Democrat* and the *Tribune* editorials had the effect of creating the feeling that most of the strikers were "dirty" foreigners, knife-throwing aliens, and "greasers." The newspapers cooperated with the so-called "Citizens Committee of Johnstown," officered by the heads of the local Chamber of Commerce and the banks. Johnstown had been peaceful for days, when these sentences appeared in an advertisement signed by the "Citizens Committee":

"These dastardly attempts to scare the families of workingmen. . . . This throwing of stones and missiles at men who want to work. . . . This wrecking of workers' automobiles. . . . This cowardly ganging of one lone, willing worker. . . . These vile names hissed from the lips of human beings aimed at men who want to work. . . . This throwing of dynamite. . . . This breaking of windows in workers' homes—all these things, all these atrocities, must stop . . . Be assured that the Citizens Committee means business."

Youngstown's strike activities were directed by the sheriff of Mahoning County, Ralph Elser, a one-time school superintendent. He improvised armored wagons, pierced with holes for rifles, which he flaunted daily along peaceful picket lines. His wholesale swearing in of deputies was comparable to Shields' enlisting of his own army of armed men. The Youngstown *Vindicator,* only newspaper in the city, served the same purpose as the Johnstown *Democrat,* but did the job more cleverly. Its news columns were carefully but diligently partisan, particularly when the "back-to-work" movement was launched. Editorially, the paper was more restrained than the Johnstown publication.

The most effective of "Little Steel's" strike-breaking activities was its use of the National Guard. The troops came into Youngstown and other Ohio cities to prevent Girdler and the Youngstown Sheet and Tube from attempting forceful, violent dispersal of picket lines around the mills. Soon after, Governor Davey announced that the troops would be used to open the mills. R. J. Wysor, second in command to Girdler in Republic Steel, C. M. White, executive vice-president, J. H. Voss, director of employee relations, two Republic lawyers, and Elliott Hess, Cleveland's director of public safety, conferred unannounced with the National Guard authorities in the Youngstown armory. No strike leaders were present, and it soon became evident that the troops' intentions were solely partisan. Their intelligence division took over direction of the back-to-work movement. Daily press releases announced the time of mill openings, and circulated the companies' estimates of the number of strikers who had returned to work. When Captain C. M. Conaway, in charge of press relations at Youngstown, was asked why the union estimates were not also made public, he declared the union figures to be falsehoods. Here are a few excerpts from National Guard press releases: "We met first with Youngstown Sheet and Tube Company representatives, and later in the day representatives of the Republic Steel Company were here. At 6 P.M. the following estimate of the total number of employees now working in the Youngstown area was made, based on all figures available from the steel company offices: 18,328." The next day: "Statement by Major Gilson D. Light, Commanding: 'The Struthers plant of the Youngstown Sheet and Tube Company will start operations tomorrow.'" And again: "Women and children appeared on the picket lines in Warren early today when a crowd of some two hundred people assembled *some distance* from Republic's main gate of Niles plant. The crowd was dispersed without incident by a small group of National Guardsmen." The press releases of the National Guard became the principal propaganda of the back-to-work movement and were dutifully featured in Ohio's newspapers.

Martial law was never declared in any of the three Ohio counties affected by the strike. There never were enough disorderly or threat-

[206]

ening incidents to justify martial law. This difficulty was circumvented by the simple device of having the sheriffs of the respective counties issue "proclamations." Picket lines were disbanded or so drastically limited as to make them worthless. Public assemblies were forbidden without permits from the sheriff. Picket-line leaders were arrested and detained long enough to demoralize their rank and file. Encampment of troops in Canton, where the strike had been peaceful for weeks, was not accomplished without popular resentment. Children, driven from their playground by nervous troopers with drawn bayonets, shouted derisively and were pushed back. Three of the youngsters, all under sixteen years of age, were cut by bayonets and bled so profusely they had to be treated in the medical corps room of the Canton armory. The following day a captain in the military press headquarters asked newspaper men to "coöperate" by suppressing the incident. In Canton also the military made wholesale arrests of pickets, detaining scores for hours in a basement of the Republic plant. By mid-July, labor sources estimated, the state of Ohio had expended approximately $250,000 on strike-breaking efforts.

The details of the killing of strikers in Chicago, Youngstown, Massillon, and Cleveland indicated the ruthlessness of some of the steel companies and their willing accomplices, the local "law enforcement" agencies. The Senate subcommittee on civil liberties found that a Memorial Day attack on the Chicago strikers near the Republic plant, which resulted in the death of ten workers and the maiming for life of several others, was without provocation; that the strikers were proceeding entirely within their legal rights in an effort to set up picket lines at the plant; that following the brutal police attack, no attempt was made to aid the wounded; that the group could have been disbanded without loss of life; and that the subsequent investigation by the Chicago city authorities was farcical and prejudiced. The National Lawyers Guild declared that the Republic officials and the Chicago police were "actively coöperating to break the strike." Two strikers who died in Youngstown gave their lives, official explanation had it, because wives of strikers started a row by calling insulting names at sheriff's deputies. The mayor and Chief of Police Stanley Switter of Massillon told the National Labor Relations Board that local Republic executives and

[207]

members of the "Law and Order League" pounded away and "put the heat on" him until guns were placed in the hands of "special police." Finally, Switter related, he was led to leave town and in his absence "special police," under other leaders, precipitated a riot in which two strikers were killed and several wounded, and as a result of which 160 strikers were arrested, some of them dragged from their homes. Switter testified that a Republic official had demanded, "Why don't you take action like they did in Chicago?" He told also of the efforts of Gen. William E. Marlin of the National Guard to have him enroll the "special police." The eighteenth worker to give his life was killed in Cleveland when a strikebreaker's car crushed a picket against an iron fence. Immediately after, the Cleveland strike headquarters was wrecked by a mob.

Neither the expressed view of President Roosevelt that *bona fide* collective bargaining should be consummated by a contract, nor the position of Governors Earle, Townsend of Indiana, or Davey, that "Little Steel" was wrong in not negotiating an agreement with the C.I.O., nor days of persuasion by a Presidential mediation board swayed Girdler from his design. He refused to accept President Roosevelt as a mediator. He declared Phillip Murray "a liar," and said that Senator Guffey "does not know what he is talking about." At a select press conference in Washington, he called Myron Taylor "a lousy so-and-so." Charles P. Taft and Lloyd K. Garrison, members of the mediation board, he referred to in language which the *New York Post* correspondent said was "too obscene to print," and the *New York Daily News* reporters termed "gutter epithets." Later, Girdler said he had merely repeated characterizations made by others and that he had not intended to be quoted publicly.

The strikes against Bethlehem and Youngstown Sheet & Tube were lost, and late in June the S.W.O.C. called upon its members to return to work. Inland Steel modified, somewhat, the bitter-end opposition of the others. It gave Governor Townsend, who had refused to send troops into the strike areas, a signed pledge that all strikers would be rehired and that the company would abide by a memoranda on labor policy which generally coincided with the Carnegie-Illinois compact. This included Inland's agreement to submit grievances, where necessary, to compulsory arbitration. The

C.I.O. refused to call off the strike against Republic Steel. Although thousands of employees were back at work in the mills, the number of Republic strikers toward the end of October was fixed by the S.W.O.C. at 3,200 in Canton, 1,800 in Massillon, 3,500 in Cleveland, 1,100 in Chicago, 450 in Niles and 2,800 in Warren. The nucleus of the strike in Niles and Warren was one of the oldest and proudest lodges in the Amalgamated Association. The anti-strike violence continued, as pickets, fed and clothed and given small relief sums by the S.W.O.C., continued their patrol. At three o'clock one foggy morning in Niles, the flood lights from the Republic plant were switched off. Suddenly a bundle of flaming gasoline-saturated rags was hurled into the pickets' tent, completely destroying it and an electric refrigerator, a radio, stove, coffee-urn, tables, dishes, and food which the strikers had been using to lighten their ceaseless watch.

10.

THE C.I.O. UNDER FIRE

I

THE period of "Little Steel's" attack brought the C.I.O. its most severe test. Girdler's lead was taken up with varying degrees of intensity in the press and over the radio. Walter Lippmann contributed his learned prejudices, but Dorothy Thompson, a new devotee of what the *New Republic* called the "Cassandra racket," became an even more vigorous prophet of national ruin through the C.I.O. Both saw in the growth of the industrial unions and the techniques they used, the death of democratic processes. Westbrook Pegler, an amusing sports writer now turned economic oracle, vied with Boake Carter, business-sponsored radio commentator, in the most extreme attacks on Lewis, the C.I.O., and all their works. With scarcely more than four or five exceptions, all newspapers turned their editorial writers and cartoonists loose on the new labor movement.

Girdler became the hero of the anti-C.I.O. business men, but Ernest T. Weir and Henry Ford occupied lesser niches only because their opposition had not yet been expressed in the direct combat of strikes. Like-minded organizations, some founded by petty racketeers who ride every popular wave that promises an income, others supported by substantial business elements were launched. The "Little Steel" strike brought into existence a National Citizens Committee which aimed to be an anti-C.I.O. clearing-house. Its efforts were stridently supported by a Constitutional Educational League which loosed a flood of invective to prove the C.I.O.'s subservience to Communism, and Lewis' rôle as one of violence and irresponsibility.

Some Southern towns and cities saw the Ku Klux Klan riding again, this time to stamp out the "menace" of the C.I.O.'s Textile Workers Organizing Committee. The National Association of Manufacturers offered advice to industrial interests on how labor might be "dealt" with without recognizing the C.I.O. or violating the Wagner Act. Persisting in his self-designated life-mission to save the nation from the "Reds," the aged Ralph Easley maintained touchingly cordial relationships with the American Federation of Labor in its efforts to stem the C.I.O. tide. In the industrial cities and towns of the nation, local vigilante groups made their appearance. Some found expression through back-to-work movements where strikes were in progress, and in revamped company unions where C.I.O. efforts were still in the formative stage.

These sources and organizations linked their attacks on the C.I.O. with a drive against the Wagner Act, which they held to be "one-sided." Their constant theme was that C.I.O. unionism threatened the liberties of the American workmen. The sit-down strikes furnished them with their most prominent grievance, but where traditional forms of strikes took place, their resentment was no less vigorous. The great danger to the liberties of labor, they held, was the closed shop and the check-off of union dues from pay envelopes. When comparatively few of the new C.I.O. organizations sought these concessions, the opposition was not lessened. The reaction against the C.I.O. boiled down to the usual opposition to labor and collective bargaining.

II

The Girdler reply to collective bargaining and the C.I.O. was demonstrated during the "Little Steel" strike. The Weir and Ford prescriptions were indicated with equally clear emphasis during periods of C.I.O. organization efforts. Both have since been described in sworn testimony before referees of the National Labor Relations Board.

Soon after the S.W.O.C. launched its campaign in the summer of 1936, Murray sent organizers to Weirton, West Virginia, and Steubenville, Ohio, where units of Weir's National Steel Corporation were located. Claude R. Kramer, a S.W.O.C. organizer, was seized by the mayor of Holidays Cove, West Virginia, questioned, and ordered out of town. Returning to his hotel at Steubenville, he was set upon by eight men and placed on a train out of the city. Paul Rysen, another organizer, was attacked as he sat in his car on a Steubenville street. The identity of his assailants was known, but no one was apprehended. In September, Richard Riser and Anthony Kowalsky, members of the S.W.O.C. staff, were also seized at Holidays Cove and ordered to leave. En route to Steubenville they were accosted by three carloads of thugs and severely beaten.

A few days later, Steve Barron, steel union organizer, was attacked on Main Street, Weirton, by several men who tried to drag him into an automobile. Warrants for the arrest of the assailants were sworn out, but the grand jury refused to indict. On September 11th, Barron, joined by two others, were distributing union handbills among employees of Weirton Steel. They were attacked by six armed thugs. The identity of these men was also submitted to the grand jury, which again refused to return indictments. Kenneth Koch, one of those assaulted on the 11th, was the victim of another attack on October 16th. Traveling in a car, he was halted in front of the Weirton police station, across the street from the company's emergency hospital. Again he was attacked so severely that he required hospitalization. Once more the assailants were named by the victim, and once more the beating went unpunished.

The S.W.O.C. turned to the Labor Board for redress against these attacks and other alleged violations of the Wagner law, and on July 31, 1937, the board issued a complaint charging Weirton Steel with numerous law-breaking acts. The discharge of 350 unionists was alleged, as well as the resort to interference, coercion, bribery, and espionage, formation of a company union, and violence through a secret police force known throughout Weirton as the "hatchet gang." The board also accused the company of domination of the "government, administration of justice, business affairs, and social relationships of Weirton to the serious prejudice of the liberties of the employees in the exercise of their rights of self-organization and collective bargaining." In addition to the discharges, the board's complaint alleged, twenty-four capable workers who were union men had been refused reinstatement after lay-offs and four others had been demoted.

Lengthy Labor Board hearings, held at Cumberland, West Virginia, after facilities in Weirton had been withheld, started in September. One witness revealed the existence of a blacklist arrangement between the Republic and Weirton companies. Foremen were quoted as discharging men because they belonged to the C.I.O. or because they would not join in anti-C.I.O. activities. Men who wore C.I.O. buttons in the plant were seized bodily and ejected. The Chamber of Commerce, it appeared, had helped sponsor a "Security League" whose avowed object was to "present a united front and keep the C.I.O. out of Weirton." The Security League received $5,000 in January, 1936, from the company, it was testified. The League worked on a basis whereby its leaders received fifty cents "expense money" for each member signed up. The "hatchet gang" was blamed for the violence against the S.W.O.C. organizers in 1936. An employee representation plan was set up. Witnesses told of having been threatened with discharge unless they joined.

Jack Larkin, chairman of the employee representation plan, which paralleled the League's efforts, testified that the Weirton Company had been paying him $11.74 a day for over a year and a half, during which he performed no labor at the mill. After the Wagner Act had been found constitutional and employer contributions to company unions prohibited, Larkin admitted, the Security League made monthly contributions to the representation plan. Each of the representatives received a salary of twenty-five dollars a month from the League, it developed.

Like Weir, Henry Ford also placed his opposition to labor unions on the ground of his devotion to freedom. To safeguard this freedom for his 140,000 employees, 80,000 of them at the Dearborn River Rouge plant, he organized one of the largest private police and detective forces in the country. Visitors in the Ford plant inevitably have been struck with the picture of the workers, during rest and lunch periods, carefully avoiding contact with each other. Those who did venture to "talk" or join a union, found they had been more courageous than cautious. A National Labor Relations Board hearing in July of 1937 heard testimony from thirty Ford employees who had been let out following their association with the United Automobile Workers.

Fred Nygard, skilled crane operator, forgot he had some union application cards concealed in his cap. When he took it off to wipe the perspiration from his head, the cards fluttered to the ground. A foreman saw one, and Nygard was out. Joe Sable wasn't a union member, but he played on the union ball team. One day he saw two service men watching the game. The next time he went to work, a "big husky who looked punch drunk" was in his department, standing around, doing nothing, getting in the way. When Sable accidentally brushed against him, the husky said: "Who are you shoving," and started swinging. Sable was fired for "fighting." Anthony Schipper never talked union until after the Wagner Act was declared constitutional. "I thought I had a right then," he said. One day he saw an article in a newspaper quoting Henry Ford as guessing he couldn't do much about his workers joining the union with the Wagner Act upheld. Schipper told his foreman to read the article. Next day he was fired.

Clifford Sheldon, foreman in line for promotion when he was fired, described how he had been ordered by his department superintendent to organize the "foremen, bosses, and trusted men" in his department and hold them in readiness for strike action. If workers caused "strike trouble," Sheldon and his gang were to "pick them up bodily and throw them out." Sheldon was fired when it was discovered he didn't have his heart in the job. Another witness, Mack Cinzori, related how he had been forced to become a member of a "vigilante gang" in his department, under instructions "to pick up a lead pipe and start swinging" if there was any "strike trouble." Cinzori said his gang was drilled by a superintendent to see how fast it could be mobilized for action.

On May 26, 1937, a group of auto union members set out to distribute handbills at the River Rouge gates, located near an overpass to the plant. They were met by men whom Harry H. Bennett, Ford personnel director, called "loyal Ford employees." It developed that they included Angelo Caruso, leader of the Detroit Down River gang; Sarkisian, a professional wrestler; Oscar Jones, also known as Jackie Young; Ted Greis, another devotee of professional wrestling; a pugilist; several service men who later acknowledged their status; and a collection of perhaps one hundred men whom Detroit reporters described as "typical hoodlums" and "dago hoodlums." The unionists included Walter Reuther, for eight years a Ford foreman, and now president of the auto workers' Detroit West Side local; Frankensteen, a U.A.W. vice-president; Richard Merriweather and Ralph Dunham, auto workers. The events which followed were later described in testimony of the union men before the Labor Board. Their recitals were corroborated by six newspaper men.

Reuther and Frankensteen had paused on the overpass to meet a request of news camera men.

"After the pictures were taken, we were approached by men from all sides," said Reuther. "One called out that we were on private property and to get the hell off of here. Frankensteen and I started to walk towards the north stairway to get off the bridge in obedience to the command. I had hardly taken three steps when I was slugged on the back of the head. I tried to shield my face by crossing my arms. They pounded me all over the head and body. . . . I was knocked to the ground and beaten. The leader said, 'That's enough, fellows.' I thought I was released. But they picked me up and threw me down bodily on the concrete floor of the platform. Then they kicked me again and again. They tried to tear my legs apart.

"Seven times they raised me off the concrete and threw me down on it. They pinned my arms and shot short jabs to my face. I was punched and dragged by my feet to the stairway. I grabbed the railing and they wrenched me loose. I was thrown down the first flight of iron steps. Then they kicked me down the other two flights of stairs until I found myself on the ground, where I was beaten and kicked. . . . At about this time girls and women who came from Detroit with circulars tried to get off the street cars, and so the men seemed to lose interest in me."

Frankensteen's experience was similar. Dunham was attacked several blocks from the overpass. Subsequently he was confined to the hospital for ten days, during which he constantly bled internally.

While telling the Labor Board of his experience, he was overcome and had to be led sobbing from the room. Merriweather's back was broken and he testified while in a plaster cast. A reputable Detroit physician declared that Merriweather's injuries will cause him "incapacitating pains for many years to come." Dunham, he said, may suffer permanent brain injury. Tony Marinovich, a union man who arrived with the women and the handbills, and was also beaten, will probably never be able to work again and may eventually develop epilepsy as a result of the slugging he received, the physician declared.

The unanimous findings of the Labor Board upheld the auto's union charges of intimidation and brutality. Ford's antagonism to unionism, the board declared, was "brought home to its employees through constant hostility of foremen, through the systematic discharge of union advocates, through the employment by the respondent of hired thugs to terrorize and beat union members and sympathizers. . . ." The board asserted that within the "vast River Rouge plant at Dearborn the freedom of self organization guaranteed by the (Wagner) act has been replaced by a rule of terror and repression."

III

Ford, an individualist, fought the C.I.O. alone, although not by unique methods. Weir took at least a friendly interest in what he hoped would be the initiation of a national movement of business to halt the advance of the C.I.O. This was the National Citizens Committee, an outgrowth of the Johnstown Citizens Committee which took upon itself the task of helping break the strike against the Johnstown plant of Bethlehem Steel.

The chairman of the founding group was Francis C. Martin, president of the Johnstown Chamber of Commerce and banker, whose concept of fair play in industrial strife did not preclude his soliciting $31,456 from Bethlehem Steel to finance the maintenance of "law and order" during the strike. It was this fund, the National Labor Relations Board was told, which was turned over to Mayor Shields. Other testimony given the board revealed that Shields, during the strike, had purchased $6,000 worth of gas, guns, shells and grenades from Federal Laboratories, Inc. Lawrence W. Campbell, secretary of the Chamber of Commerce, was the secretary of the Citizens Committee; and a gentleman of the cloth, the Rev. John H. Stanton, its chief mouthpiece. Sidney F. Evans, resident Bethlehem manager, addressed the committee in its early stages and laid upon it the responsibility of seeing to it that non-strikers made their way through picket lines. Mayor Shields also spoke to the committee and dropped the suggestion that he would not feel it his responsibility to act "if a number of citizens attempted to evict a union strike leader from the city." As treasurer, the committee had George C. Rutledge, treasurer of the Johnstown Bank and Trust Company. He collected $62,586 within a few days and spent most of it on publicity and advertising. To handle the publicity, the Johnstown committee had the services of George Ketchum of Pittsburgh, president of Ketchum, Inc., which publicizes for Ernest T. Weir's steel interests, among others. Before taking on the Johnstown assignment, Ketchum guardedly testified before a Labor Board hearing, he talked things over with Weir. The day after Ketchum arrived in Johnstown, and before the Citizens Committee had as yet any large amount of funds, he felt confident enough to place advertisements at a cost of almost $50,000. The advertising, full-page attacks on the steel strikers published in thirty-five daily papers, was handled by John Price Jones, a leading New York advertising man and public relations consultant. The committee also contributed to the cost of strike "investigations" made by the Johnstown *Democrat*.

When the Johnstown Bethlehem strike appeared broken by a combination of back-to-work propaganda and Mayor Shields' personally-directed pressure campaign, the Johnstown committee had $4,000 left, and this it contributed to setting up a National Citizens Committee. At the same time, Martin on Jones' advice dispatched telegrams to 200 chambers of commerce, civic organizations and leading business men asking them to join in a crusade which would protect "the right to work for all who want to work." A conference of those interested was held in Johnstown. Several score organizations and a few individuals who feared for the safety of the nation were present. Mayor Shields welcomed them. J. G. Lester, of Massillon, keynoted: "Thank God for Girdler!" The function of the national committtee, as voiced in a resolution passed at Johnstown, was "to restore and protect those constitutional rights that have been taken from American citizens by certain unworthy officials." The committee chose as leaders, the Reverend Rembert Smith, who was suspended from his Methodist pastorate in 1931 for "gross imprudence and high unministerial conduct," and was later reinstated and transferred to a small pastorate in Oklahoma; Donald Kirkley, one-time writer for a Ku-Klux Klan paper; and Ormsby McHarg, of New York, who years before had been a somewhat inconstant follower of Theodore Roosevelt.

The noble purposes of the committee, and the intentions of its leaders (who went on a payroll) did not avail to save it from death. Kirkley, piqued because he was ignored by McHarg, resigned with the declaration that the committee was Fascist. A lack of finances complicated other differences and soon after Jones was eased out of control. He had favored an "educational" approach to the problem of combating the C.I.O.; McHarg, who had been installed as executive secretary, leaned toward a vigorous, if moderately voiced, vigilanteism. The principal function of the committee having been accomplished when the "Little Steel" Strike was broken, the interest of Bethlehem Steel and Weir had lapsed. Fifty thousand letters soliciting interest and funds brought McHarg 600 answers and no funds to speak of.

The rallying-cry of the National Citizens Committee was "the right to work." At hearings before a Senate committee, Girdler made it plain that he did not intend the "right to work" to imply that a working-man or -woman was entitled to a job, but only that they had a "right to work" when an employer desired that they might. The "right to work" was a shibboleth used only when C.I.O. strikes were declared. It then furnished the moral tone for back-to-work drives. The movement replaced the old type of strike-breaking which had been made odious by a series of exposures starting in 1934 and culminating in the investigations of the La Follette committee. The imported "finks" were revealed as a collection of incompetent mercenaries, who, like their "nobles" (guards) had many among them with criminal records. The popular revulsion against finks, nobles, and spies, the top of the rung in the profession, made them liabilities. The value of finks and nobles also proved doubtful in mass strikes involving many thousands of workers.

Pearl L. Bergoff, for almost thirty years the biggest of the professional strike-breakers, was the first to suggest a departure in method. During the 1934 Akron difficulties he proposed the stratagem of building up back-to-work movements which would appear to be supported by "loyal" local workers and their respective local communities. To organize, direct, and control these "native" movements, he supplied old-line professional strike-breakers and labor spies. Bergoff sold the idea to Remington-Rand in 1935, and in the strike of that company's employees it reached the dimensions of a new method. The National Association of Manufacturers listed its component parts and attempted to popularize it as the "Mohawk Valley Formula." Nevertheless, it was not a brand-new method of breaking strikes.

As revealed in the Remington-Rand strike and again during the "Little Steel" war, the aims of the back-to-work device was to undermine labor morale, create fear and suspicion, and demoralize the strikers. It stemmed from business men, a company union, hired labor spies or professional promoters. While sowing discord and defeatist spirit among the strikers, it ought to create a public feeling that the strikers were a minority which was preventing a majority of the workers from returning to work.

The Interchurch World Movement revealed that back-to-work movements were encouraged by spies and provocateurs on the payroll of detective agencies during the steel strike of 1919. Most of them were trained propagandists and were hired for that reason. "Operative X-199" estimated that he alone had "induced about one hundred men or more to return to work." The use of the company union in the formula was shown during National Labor Relations Board hearings in July, 1934, in the strike of employees of the Chicago Motor Coach Company. "When the few employees decided to cast their lot with the representatives of organized labor," the board was informed, "the Fraternity [company union] took up the bludgeon and carried the battle into the stronghold of the opposing forces." In the 1935 strike of the Tubize Chattillon Corporation, at Hopewell, Va., R. S. Burrows, works-manager, initiated a back-to-work movement by a tactfully worded "personal message" to each striker. The Radio Corporation of America, with a strike on its hands in Camden, N. J., during 1936, employed two veteran strike-breaking practitioners, Max Sherwood and George (Toupee) Williams, "to organize community sentiment." A company union, this time the Loyal Legion of Loggers and Lumbermen, was the focal point of a back-to-work movement in the northwest during 1935.

The Remington-Rand Company used local business men and its foremen, as well as company unions and private strike-breaking agencies to round out its back-to-work campaign. Bergoff "missionaries" were used in Syracuse, foremen at Tonawanda, business men at Ilion. At Middletown, Connecticut, the company used foremen, "missionaries" and men supplied by strike-breaking agencies whose task was to go back and forth through picket lines. The Flint Alliance, which also leaned heavily on foremen for the circulation of "we want work petitions," took up the plan during the General Motors strike. Business men also initiated the plan, under the protective coloration of a "Loyalty League" in Saginaw, Michigan, and received messages of encouragement from Sloan and Knudsen. At Anderson, Indiana, businessmen organized "A Citizens League for Employment Security" to help wean auto workers away from the strike. The League was headed by Homer P. Lambert, "banker and civic leader."

IV

Many company unions, upon the Supreme Court's endorsement of the Wagner Act, were replaced by so-called "independent" unions. Examination of the formation, structure, and procedures of the "independents" shows their kinship with the organizations which the Wagner Act intended to outlaw. Of eighty-five such organizations studied for the National Labor Relations Board, thirteen were found to be merely adaptations of company unions, and twenty-three others were formed by ex-employee representatives. In a number in the latter category, company officials or supervisory employees assisted in the birth of the "independent" union, and in at least one case the company president was a speaker at the first meeting. Usually, employee representatives or company union heads decided that when they met again it would be as heads of "independent" unions. Only five of the organizations came into existence before the enactment of the National Labor Relations Act; twenty saw the light of day between passage of the law and the Supreme Court's approval of it; and forty-six emerged after the Act had been upheld.

The condition of bona-fide labor organizations at the time of the formation of the independent unions is another significant indication of the latters' motives. Fifty-eight were formed while labor unions were staging organizing campaigns, fourteen while strikes by other unions were in progress, and twelve came into being during "loyalty" or back-to-work movements. The Department of Labor has declared that one earmark of a company union is the limitation of its scope to a single company and its failure to make fraternal or other connections with other groups of workers. This test applied to the "independent" unions showed that 77 were organizations of employees in a single company, most frequently of a single plant, and that only three included workers of more than one company. Fully fifty-eight out of sixty-one organizations upon which such information was available were not only opposed to labor unions, but in opposition to the general aims and activities of organized labor.

The financing of the "independent" unions, where information was available, also showed their affinity with the company-union idea. Dues, where charged, were too low to maintain an effective labor union; sometimes funds were borrowed from local banks; and in one case seven employees borrowed one hundred dollars each from a bank of which the company president was vice-president. Meeting-places for some of the "independent" organizations were made available through the coöperation of local business men. Here and there citizens committees intent on keeping unionism from their localities provided meeting-halls.

Only seventeen of the eighty-five "independent" unions revealed written agreements, but none of the agreements examined contained categorical statements on wages, hours, and conditions of work. Most of the agreements limited themselves to outlining procedures by which individual grievances of employees were to be handled by their employers. On the other hand, some of the agreements appeared to be instruments for binding the workers closer to the revamped company union. Several employers actually signed "closed shop" provisions which barred all but members of the "independent" union from working in their plants. Incorporation of trade unions, a step urged by business interests and resisted by the labor movement, was sufficiently popular with the "independent" unions to have at least thirty-two of them file papers of incorporation.

Carefully worded suggestions how company unions may be transformed into "independent" unions without running afoul of the Wagner Act were periodically transmitted by the National Association of Manufacturers to its 80,000 employer members. A bulletin mailed by the association in August, 1937, suggested a complete set of procedures, including the wording of membership appeals, application blanks, and a constitution and by-laws which fixed dues at fifty cents a month. The bulletin originally included a "typical announcement of the management of one company to its workers to acquaint them with the organization of an independent union." Before it was mailed, however, this item was blacked out. The suggestions remained. The bulletin cited some of the isolated victories of "independent" unions over C.I.O. organizations. There was also a catechism answering some "practical questions" involved in employer relationships. An "independent" union was defined as "a group of employees of a single company who are independent of the company and of other unions." A later bulletin issued by the association contained "Twelve Rules of Collective Bargaining," intended as guides for treatment of "independent" unions after they had been launched. Both etiquette and strategy were emphasized. "Be friendly in negotiation," said one rule, "introduce everybody. Relieve any existing tension. Know at least a little about the personal history of every man in the meeting." Another "rule" urged that employers "be willing to listen" and added: "It is time enough to worry about how you will say 'no' after you have heard the facts." The employer was urged also to "give everybody an opportunity to state his grievance" since "this often discloses the real champion of the movement or grievance."

A number of "independent" unions came together at Hershey, Pa., late in July to organize the Independent Labor Federation of

America. Spokesmen supplied varying estimates of the strength represented by eighty delegates. One said the membership was 300,000; a few days later it was placed at 500,000. Both figures appeared to be exaggerations. The conference was held behind closed doors and its officers were not announced until ten days after it ended. Congressman Clare Hoffman was one of the invited speakers. Charles Hallman, head of the "independent" union at Hershey, was elected president of the federation; Reginald Boote, of the Remington-Rand organization at Ilion, N. Y., vice-president; and Mrs. Maude Painter, of the Kantor Employees Association at Lebanon, Pa., secretary. An executive committee of fifteen, most of them speaking for organizations in factories where C.I.O. strikes had taken place, was also chosen. The organization declared that it felt sit-down strikes were un-American and that it would resort to strikes, if ever, as a last resort. It insisted it would be independent of employer domination and planned to set up a constitution and by-laws in the near future. The first public appearance of President Hallman came as part of an effort in August to break a strike called by the C.I.O. against Pennsylvania silk mills. Hallman invited non-strikers to a meeting at the Hazelton City Hall, but when he arrived he was confronted by strikers and coal miners who engaged Hallman's supporters in a series of fist battles ending in Hallman's precipitate departure from the city under police escort.

The Constitutional Educational League propaganda against the C.I.O. was contained in two lurid booklets—*Join the C.I.O.—and Help Build a Soviet America* and *The Hell of Herrin Rages Again*. The League declared that a map of the United States redrawn in Russia had changed the name of Detroit to Lewistown; that certain C.I.O. organizers, who were well known as non-Communist, were Communists; that Communist leaders, who never were employed by the C.I.O., occupied high positions in its councils. The burden of the booklets is that every violent act in industrial struggles of recent years was committed by the C.I.O. or its agents. Thus, by sleight-of-hand reasoning, the C.I.O. was held responsible for the deaths of all strikers during the "Little Steel" strike. Joseph Kamp, head of the League and author of the pamphlets, was previously the executive editor of *The Awakener*, advocate of Fascism for the

United States. One of Kamp's agents who hopefully solicited the membership of Charles A. Beard, the historian, declared that the League placed under-cover agents in labor meetings. On occasion, Kamp lent himself to direct strike-breaking efforts as well as to the printed word. Kamp's books sold by the hundred thousand for ten cents and twenty-five cents the copy, and the League solicited outright contributions to aid in its assumed task to "Stop Lewis and Smash Communism." It operated from an office in New Haven, and another in Birmingham, Alabama, but did not, in the two years of its existence up to 1938, publish any report of the extent of its income or the beneficiaries thereof.

V

The fires of opposition to the C.I.O. were stoked by the American Federation of Labor no less vigorously than by employer groups. The Federation's attacks also ran the gamut from accusations of Communism to physical violence. While attacking the C.I.O. as irresponsible, the Federation's teamsters' union broke hundreds of contracts in its uncompromising warfare on the Committee. Vigilante violence was used against C.I.O. metal miners, and the Federation promptly accepted into membership the company union which perpetrated it. C.I.O. picket lines were bludgeoned by A.F. of L.-approved strike-breakers, aided by police, in Cleveland. Where C.I.O. unions went on strike and company unions were at hand, the Federation offered to charter the latter and in many cases did so. Occasionally the A.F. of L. signed "contracts" in behalf of nonexistent locals. The titanic struggle of the C.I.O. in autos met with the opposition of Green and the craft union heads, the U.S. Steel victory was belittled, and the defeat in "Little Steel" brought forth crowing. Nevertheless, the Federation gained members from the enthusiasm for unionism which was engendered by the C.I.O. To the Federation's convention in Denver, in October, 1937, the executive council reported substantial gains, part of it the result of absorption of company unions or deals by which employers consented to "unionization" of their employees, and partly the result of the impetus given unionism first by the C.I.O. and later by the Supreme Court ruling on the Wagner Act.

[224]

President Green's Labor Day address in 1937 summed up the principal Federation counts against the C.I.O. He insisted that the Federation stood as a barrier against Communism, while "the C.I.O. welcomes Communist support and used its methods." The Federation condemned sit-downs, which, Green said, were a "C.I.O. weapon which was likely to pave the way to a Fascist dictatorship." Politically, he continued, the Federation is non-partisan, whereas certain leaders of the C.I.O. were "moved by a consuming ambition to establish themselves as political dictators." He asserted that Federation unions always kept their contracts, but that the record of the C.I.O. in that respect was "deplorable." Finally, Green charged, the Federation has sought to unite the labor movement, while the C.I.O. has insisted upon division.

Green's criticism was temperate when compared with that of Frey. The Federation's scholar pointed incessantly to the "red menace" which he felt was inherent in the C.I.O., but he sought also to stir the spirit of reaction and frighten the souls at the Union League and Navy clubs by picturing C.I.O. efforts to organize navy-yard mechanics as fraught with danger to the national defense. He pronounced a verdict of "treason" on any and all navyyard workers who joined a C.I.O. union. Poring deeper over his researches, Colonel Frey declared that "an analyzation of the official roster of the industrial C.I.O. discloses the fact that many of the organizers and directors are operating under assumed names or have in the past employed aliases to protect them from arrest and conviction upon charges covering the entire category of crime."

Not to be outdone by Frey's billingsgate, Wharton wrote the locals of his machinists' union referring to the C.I.O. members as "gangs of sluggers, Communists, radicals, soap-box artists, professional bums, expelled members of labor unions, outright scabs, and the Jewish organizations with all their red affiliates." Wharton, in his righteous fury, also denounced one of the C.I.O. internationals for having failed to pay interest on $15,000 which it had borrowed from the machinists' union during a trying period. The International Ladies' Garment Workers Union, which had committed this offense against business unionism, had itself lent and given outright millions of dollars to Federation unions and labor causes in its time. Religious issues were also raised by the A.F. of L. *Newsletter,* which on August 17, 1937, published a story headed "Christians Urged to Smash C.I.O." The story dealt with a sermon by the learned Reverend Dr. John Inkster of Toronto, who informed his congregation that it was "the duty of every Christian citizen to do everything in his power to smash the C.I.O."

This duty the Federation accepted with alacrity. During the General Motors strike, the *American Federationist* published a full-page paid advertisement in which G.M. glorified itself as a "public-minded institution." Meanwhile, Frey and several leaders of the metal and building trades unions were in communication with the corporation. As a result, G.M.'s publicity department was enabled to give out a series of telegrams signed by these Federation heads which asked that the auto union's demand for exclusive recognition be denied. Although the craft unions had never been favored with agreements by General Motors, H. W. Anderson, head of the corporation's labor relations department, assured them that G.M. "has no intention of entering an agreement with any organization interfering with legitimate jurisdictions of unions affiliated with the Metal Trades Department of the American Federation of Labor." While Lewis and G.M. officials were locked in negotiations in Detroit and guns threatened the sit-down strikers in Flint, the craft union heads prevailed upon Green to wire Governor Murphy urging him "to keep in mind the exclusive rights of the international unions." Green not only wired the Governor, but called him on the telephone to emphasize his point. The call came while the peace negotiators were in session and caused Lewis to ask for a showdown. He declared that if General Motors wished to negotiate with the A.F. of L. he would retire from the room. The craft union pleas were forgotten and peace was reached, whereupon Green taxed Lewis and the C.I.O. negotiators, because, he said, they had failed to win exclusive recognition for the auto workers' union! To complete the picture of Green's acrobatics, it should be recalled that when the A.F. of L. oil workers' union signed an agreement with Harry F. Sinclair's Consolidated Oil Corporation in 1934—an agreement which accorded the union recognition for its members only—Green hailed the settlement as a "treaty of industrial peace" of which he "thoroughly approved" and which "removed the fundamental cause of most labor conflicts."

True to his word in 1936, Green sat on the side lines and watched the working of the "experiment" by which the C.I.O. made startling progress in steel. Stunned like most others when the news of the U.S. Steel agreement was flashed, Green could only say, "I always like to see them [the steel workers] win exclusive recognition." The bitter-enders among the Carnegie-Illinois company unionists turned to the A.F. of L. after the C.I.O. pact had been signed, and Frey hastened to Pittsburgh to offer them membership in the craft unions. The company unionists insisted, however, that craft unionism would be a backward step, and Frey's efforts came to nothing. While the "Little Steel" strike was still in effect in several of the steel centers, Green proclaimed the strike broken. He declared it had been lost because of the C.I.O.'s "utterly subversive policies of minority domination and violence."

VI

Green's detestation of violence was not an even one. On April 11, 1937, some members of the Tri-State Metal, Mine and Smelter Workers Union, a company union of workers in the Oklahoma-Kansas zinc and lead area, were on the march. Starting in Picher, Oklahoma, and plentifully supplied with liquor and pick-ax handles, they sought to prevent the holding of a scheduled meeting of the C.I.O.'s Mine, Mill, and Smelter Workers' Union. The meeting was hastily called off, whereupon the members of the "blue-card union," as the company organization was called, wrecked a C.I.O. meeting-place, flogged a constable, and set upon miners wearing C.I.O. buttons. The mob proceeded to Treece, Kansas, where they first shot out the windows of a C.I.O. headquarters and then demolished it. A sound-car then called for a march on Galena, Kansas, where a C.I.O. union hall was located. At the Galena hall, the mob was repulsed with a volley of gun and pistol fire, which wounded nine of the invaders. Before the battle was over, the Galena hall also was a mass of debris. Four days later, the A.F. of L. granted a charter to the "blue-card union." When Green was informed that the president of the union was a mine operator who had served a term in jail for bootlegging, and that its secretary was personnel manager of the Eagle Picher Mining and Smelting Company, he shrugged his shoulders in surprise. But the charter was not lifted.

Nor did the "irresponsibility" with which the Federation's president taxed the C.I.O. appear to worry him overmuch when it came to fighting the Committee. Thus the Progressive Miners of Illinois, many of whose leaders were under federal indictments as dynamiters, was granted a Federation charter in June of 1937. The Progressive Miners, starting as a rank-and-file revolt against Lewis in 1929, had by 1937 become the most peculiar of American labor unions. Its members worked at less than union scales and were forced to pay kickbacks to some of the companies. Its publication, *The Progressive Miner*, held an unmatched record for red-baiting and anti-Semitism. It gave warm applause to Huey Long, dubbed Townsend a savior, eulogized Father Coughlin, and wound up, in 1936, by supporting the Republican party in the Illinois elections and Lemke for president. The paper has declared President Roosevelt a "Jewish agent" and the C.I.O. "an unholy conspiracy of international Jewish bankers to enslave the American people." The Supreme Court, the paper held, was being made the target of "sinister forces which sought to subdue American institutions." Attacks on the Wagner Act and the Guffey Coal Act were given extensive space. The executive council of the A.F. of L. cheerfully chartered the union as a full-fledged affiliate, and at the Denver convention its spokesmen were given the craft unionists' warm salutes. Two months later, 36 leaders of the Progressive Miners Union were convicted in the federal court.

The Federation's policy of approaching employers before organizing their employees and of chartering company unions was outlined by Wharton in the letter to his locals.

"Since the Supreme Court decision upholding the Wagner Act, many employers now realize that it is the law of our country and they are prepared to deal with labor organizations," he wrote. "These employers have expressed a preference to deal with A.F. of L. organizations rather than Lewis, Hillman, Dubinsky, Howard, and their gang of sluggers, Communists. . . . We have conferred with several such employers and arranged for conferences later when we get the plants organized. The purpose of this is to direct all officers and all representatives to contact employers in your locality as a preliminary to organizing the shops and factories."

Coleman Claherty, then special organizer by appointment of President Green, told a Labor Board hearing in 1937 that he was able to negotiate contracts for his A.F. of L. locals with knitted goods manufacturers before he had signed up a single one of their employees. William Schoenberg, Federation organizer in Chicago, reached an "understanding" with the Cement Institute in that city by which he was able to "organize" thousands of workers.

The Claherty boast was effected in Cleveland, where he had signed a "closed shop" contract for an A.F. of L. union of knitted goods workers while employees who were members of the International Ladies' Garment Workers Union were outside on picket lines. A group of men and women, led by Claherty and protected by professional "guards," set upon the pickets and tried to fight their way into the plant. Strikers were badly beaten, as mounted police sought to aid the Claherty group. The Labor Board stepped in and ordered elections, whereupon a majority of workers in two of three shops with which Claherty had signed "closed shop" contracts voted for the C.I.O. union. In New York City, meanwhile, Tobin's teamsters' union chartered the Parmelee Brotherhood, a known company union of several years standing. The company hastened to sign an agreement with the new local of the A.F. of L. The taxi-drivers employed by the company had not been consulted, however, and when the Transport Workers Union of the C.I.O. sought and obtained an employee election, the poll went overwhelmingly for the C.I.O. affiliate.

The Federation's molders' union followed the pattern. "Due to C.I.O. propaganda among the workers," said the A.F. of L. *Newsletter* for July 3, 1937, the plant of the Oriskany Malleable Iron Works, Inc., in Oriskany, N. Y., had closed its doors. It reopened two weeks later after Michael Walsh, A.F. of L. organizer had effected an "arrangement" with the management by which its employees were to join the molders' union. Frey and the metal-trades unions joined in negotiating an agreement with the United Shipyards, Inc., at Staten Island, N. Y., while C.I.O. unionists were doggedly pressing a ten-weeks-old strike. It required the growth of

[229]

C.I.O. sentiment in steel to enable the Federation's Bridge, Structural and Ornamental Iron Workers Union to win a closed-shop contract with three steel erecting firms, including Bethlehem Steel, which had been notoriously open shop for decades.

Employees of the Southern Chemical Cotton Company, at Chattanooga, were organized by the Textile Workers Organizing Committee and went on strike on June 25, 1937. On July 19, C. M. Fox, A.F. of L. organizer—who had not appeared in the city until the strike was fourteen days old—negotiated a closed-shop, check-off contract with the company. The A.F. of L. group, the Labor Board later reported, then obtained the assistance of the police in penetrating the C.I.O. picket line. "Considerable violence resulted, but the strike was broken."

The C.I.O. office workers' union in New York encountered a similar experience during a strike against warehouses of the McKesson-Robbins Drug Company, drug wholesalers. The most conspicuous example of this Federation policy came in July, 1937, when Floyd L. Carlisle, chairman of the board of directors of the New York Consolidated Edison Company, announced that he had accorded recognition, covering the system's 40,000 employees, to locals of the International Brotherhood of Electrical Workers. The electricians union had four members at the time the utilities magnate announced he had concluded negotiations with Daniel W. Tracy, president of the I.B.E.W. All other members of the union had a few months before deserted the A.F. of L. to affiliate with the United Electrical and Radio Workers of the C.I.O. Former leaders of a Consolidated Edison company union became business agents of the newly recognized A.F. of L. organization. Unmolested by a company which had always fought unionism, the agents went through the offices of the company, soliciting memberships for a "union" which enjoyed recognition even before it had members. The Labor Board in November declared the I.B.E.W. contract a fraud and voided it.

Comparing the features of collective agreements signed by the A.F. of L. and the C.I.O., the National Industrial Conference Board appeared surprised to discover that whereas 31.5 of the Federation's contracts called for closed shops, only 9.6 per cent of the Committee's agreements contained such clauses. The board declared that "one is led to wonder how much this result is due to success and irresistible pressure from the A.F. of L. union and how much is caused by a relatively willing compliance on the part of the management—a willingness springing from the hope that a closed A.F. of L. shop will serve as a bulwark against C.I.O. invasion." Other results of the tabulation were equally suggestive. Of the Federation contracts which were studied, 50 per cent provided for wage increases; among the Committee's contracts, 73 per cent put additional cash into workers' pay envelopes. Eighteen per cent of the Federation's pacts and 71 per cent of those of the Committee provided there was to be no coercion of employees by management. The C.I.O. agreements also contained a substantially higher percentage of provisions against discrimination because of union affiliations. The prime interest of the C.I.O., it appeared, was in raising wages and protecting the workers against discharge; the aim of the A.F. of L. to prevent members of other unions from obtaining employment. The survey found two A.F. of L. contracts with check-off provisions. None of the C.I.O. agreements had such features. The C.I.O. contracts included in the study covered workers in the automobile, steel, textile, rubber, and men's clothing industries; those of the A.F. of L., workers in public utilities, paper manufacturing, food products, electrical manufacturing and metal working—a fair sampling of agreements signed by the newer unions.

Where C.I.O. unions were too strongly intrenched to tolerate the A.F. of L. process of chartering company unions or signing agreements while C.I.O. strikes were in progress, the sympathetic strike, usually enjoined· by the Federation as radicalism, and the boycott were used. When the C.I.O. succeeded in signing agreements covering employees of the Freihofer and Ward bakeries in Philadelphia, six locals of the teamsters' international, ignoring their contracts, declared a city-wide strike which almost completely paralyzed the city's business activities, including the publication of seven daily papers, two of them in near-by Camden. The bakery workers' preference may have been with the C.I.O., but without the material aid of the teamsters their union could not function. The teamsters' strike ended with an agreement to hold a poll of the bakery workers, and they voted 631 to 519 in the Freihofer plant and 111 to 35 in the

Ward bakery against C.I.O. unions. The teamsters' union also took the initiative in the West Coast boycott of goods handled by C.I.O. longshoremen and timber cut by C.I.O. loggers.

An A.F. of L. threat of a boycott succeeded also in Ambridge, Pa., at the factory of the National Electric Products Company. While the company was refusing to bargain with the C.I.O.'s United Electrical and Radio Workers Union, it precipitately signed an agreement with a "B" local of the electricians' union, which had no members at the time, for the simple reason that it did not as yet exist. The contract was signed on May 22, 1937; Local 1073B of the International Brotherhood of Electrical Workers did not hold its first meeting until May 23rd. Asked by a Labor Board examiner whether he had ascertained the I.B.E.W.'s membership claims in his plant at the time of the contract signing, I. A. Bennet, an executive, replied: "No. We thought it was important that we shouldn't." There was clear evidence that workers had been coerced into joining the Federation union, and the Labor Board, voiding the contract, ordered an employee election. The Federation agents announced that unless the workers voted for the "B" local, the company's products would not be touched by the membership of electricians' union. Foremen told the workers that the plant might be forced to curtail its operations. One story, which was untrue, was that several carloads of pipe had already been returned "on account of union-label difficulties." Meanwhile, C.I.O. and Federation adherents, most of the latter brought in from out of the borough, staged a pitched battle at the plant gates. When the ballots were counted, they stood 918 to 685 for the electricians' union.

Where the elements of coercion were absent, Labor Board polls usually resulted in substantial majorities for C.I.O. unions. From October, 1936, to September, 1937, C.I.O. unions participated in 374 elections, winning 291 of them and receiving 124,691 out of a total of 181,573 votes. The A.F. of L. offered the C.I.O. opposition in but 133 of the polls, and of these the Federation emerged victor in 25 and the Committee in 108; the Federation obtained 6,923 votes and the Committee 22,641. The A.F. of L. contested but three elections in the auto industry and received thirty-nine votes (less than "independent" unions) as against 19,427 for the C.I.O.; out

[232]

of a total of 12,179 votes cast in shoe elections, the C.I.O. received 10,138 votes. In the steel industry, the A.F. of L. ventured on the ballot in only eight small elections in which less than 1,000 workers voted. Out of a total of 25,284 votes in all steel elections, the S.W.O.C. received 18,252: In the textile industry, the A.F. of L. did not appear on any ballots; the C.I.O. received 10,473 out of 16,905 votes. Maritime industry polls gave the C.I.O. 3,250 votes as against 179 for the A.F. of L. The Labor Board polls were not, however, completely indicative of the greater popularity of the C.I.O. In steel, autos, and other mass-production industries the C.I.O. won members and agreements covering hundreds of thousands of workers without finding employee polls necessary.

VII

Like the C.I.O. opponents in the camp of the conservative employers, the Federation also subjected the National Labor Relations Board to attack. The order for the election at the National Electric Products Company, coming against a background of C.I.O. triumphs in other elections, brought the A.F. of L. criticism out into the open. Where the Federation unions were weak, as in the maritime and transportation industry in New York City, the A.F. of L. demanded that elections be postponed. It insisted that the board recognize crafts within a plant as a legal bargaining unit, and urged that craft elections be held instead of plant elections. When the board hesitated, the Federation demanded amendments to the Wagner Act which would place it on the side of craft unionism. The Denver convention staged a full-dress onslaught on the board, singling out several regional directors for criticism and, it was urged, dismissal. The criticism was not without its effect on the board. It consented to craft union elections on the theory that where craft unionists in a plant wished to be part of an industry or plant-wide bargaining unit, they might do so by voting for C.I.O. unions. To this the C.I.O. raised objections, insisting that it granted a minority in a given plant the right to override the wishes of a majority of the workers. Unlike the A.F. of L., however, the C.I.O. criticism did not demand amendment of the Wagner Act, insisting that the Act as it stood gave the board sufficient discretion.

[233]

Behind the Federation's attacks on the board, which were key-noted by Green, Frey, and Woll, was a nostalgic feeling for the old days of "voluntarism." Both of the Federation's intellectuals had for years been attempting to stir up dissatisfaction with the Wagner Act. The refusal of the Labor Board to consider back-stairs deals between Federation agents and employers as the equivalent of collective bargaining, so enraged most of the Federation leaders that, late in 1937, Woll and Frey achieved their objective. If the Federation could not have the Wagner Act operate in its special interest, as against those of the C.I.O., it preferred to return to the old-style "voluntarism." The ascendency of the Woll-Frey outlook was evidenced by the Federations' repeated criticism of the Labor Board, but even more forcibly, in November, 1937, when the executive council came out against a federal bill providing for minimum wages, maximum hours, and a commission to enforce the fixed standards. Green declared that a board created by the "fair labor standards bill" would prove as unsatisfactory as the Labor Board. He accused the Labor Board of having "disrupted tried and tested principles of collective bargaining" and of having "brought turmoil into industrial relations, usurped the prerogatives of courts essential to our democratic form of government, and jeopardized industrial freedom and initiative." The spectacle of Green joining with manufacturing interests in attacking what a few years earlier he had termed "the Magna Charta of Labor," and of weeping for the "prerogatives of the courts," at whose hands organized labor had suffered severe punishment for decades, was the nadir of the Federation leaders' many shabby performances during their clash with the C.I.O.

The Federation's Denver Convention, ending the most trying year in its history, saw the delegates in a bitterly defiant mood. The Labor Board was denounced; Secretary of Labor Perkins, accused of undue friendliness for the C.I.O., was compared with Hitler; Lewis was called a would-be Cæsar, and Sidney Hillman a Machiavelli. (These comparisons in a convention decision were the words of Frey, who a year before had decided that Howard was the C.I.O.'s Machiavelli.) The C.I.O. was attacked in the most extreme terms yet used; it was accused of harboring "not only an

[234]

alien philosophy, but a most cunning and ruthless design that would have our workers and our abilities . . . bow to the will of an alien government, especially in a time of war." The executive council was authorized by a vote of 25,618 to 1,271 to "expel" the C.I.O. unions which had left the A.F. of L. two years before. Randolph rose to the defense of the C.I.O., while the craft unionists stared in angry amazement at the foolhardiness of a man who, in addition to committing the crime of being a Negro, was also siding with the new labor movement. Below the surface, however, all was not peaceful. Woll, slighted by Green in the choice of an American member of the International Labor Office of the League of Nations, was all for making an open attack on his president, but he was restrained. There was no stopping Hutcheson, however, in his decision to eliminate John W. Williams as the president of the Building Trades Department. Williams had been indiscreet enough to oppose Hutcheson in a contest for the presidency of the carpenters' union.

The membership figures of the Federation gave the delegates some elation, though they had to be maneuvered somewhat to uphold a boast that the Federation had gained 800,000-odd members since August, 1936. The membership of the Federation for forty years had been based on the average annual per capita payments. By this standard, the Federation had 2,860,000 members in the year ending August, 1937, as against some 2,400,000 in 1936, excluding the C.I.O. unions. A new system of reporting members used in the executive council's report to the Denver convention gave the "membership for August, 1937," at 3,271,726. The actual gain, based on the acquisition of what promised to be lasting members, was actually somewhere between 400,000 and 800,000. The largest gains in annual paid-up members were reported by the machinists', bakers', barbers', common laborers', restaurant workers', butchers', painters' and teamsters' unions. One of the vagaries of the report was Hutcheson's payment of dues for 300,000 carpenters, as in 1936, although he had lost almost 100,000 members to the C.I.O.

THE TRIUMPH OF THE C.I.O.

I

B Y THE end of 1937 the affiliated international unions of the C.I.O. had grown from the founding ten to thirty-two; its membership from less than a million in December, 1935, to 1,296,500 in July, 1936; to 1,460,900 in December; to 1,804,000 in March, 1937; and by September of 1937 to 3,718,000. Less than two years after its inception, it was the dominant federation of organized American labor.

Behind these startling figures there worked an upheaval that dwarfed the "great upheaval" of 1886. The C.I.O. became a new gospel of 4,000,000 American breadwinners. More than two million took to picket lines and to striking in plants in 1936 and 1937, flaunting banners of C.I.O. solidarity. In 1936, strikers totaled 788,648; the first eight months of 1937 brought strikes by 1,652,772 workers, the greater part of them members of C.I.O. unions. Around mammoth modern mills and at bleak old factories, on ships and on piers, at offices and in public gathering-places, men and women roared, "C.I.O.! C.I.O.!" with the gathering velocity of a massed football cheer, with the difference that their goal was more and better bread for the family table and a greater sense of freedom in affairs economic, political, and social. Millions of C.I.O. buttons sprouted on overalls, shirtwaists, and workers' hats and caps. They became badges of a new independence, bringing new gains for labor and new problems for both labor and employers. Labor was on the march as it had never been before in the history of the Republic.

Steel, automobiles, and rubber did not by any means delimit the sphere of the new movement. The hurculean job of bringing industrial order and some equity to labor in textile, wool, worsted, and silk was attacked, and notable progress made in a campaign that brought into alignment all the Southern forces of progress and reaction. Unions in the maritime industry, organizations of seamen, of ships' officers, of stevedores, of shipbuilders, and of the men at the keys of ships' radios were founded and fostered into compelling stature. The million men and women employed in the manufacture of electrical equipment and in the radio industry were given some organization for the first time. A new street-car men's union was launched and within a few months it had many more members than the 70,000 of the A.F. of L.'s urban rail workers' union. The appeal erased the lines of social snobbery and unions of newspaper-writers, of architects and engineers, of stenographers, bookkeepers, and of store clerks came into being. Neglected unions of oil-field laborers and of metal miners made great strides in new members. Shoe and leather workers, cursed by apathy, fear, and division for decades, hitched their wagons to the C.I.O. and produced vitalized new unions. Government employees braved the wrath of politicians and set up two C.I.O. internationals. Unions of glass and aluminum workers and makers of dies for metal objects took on new strength under the Committee's banner. The loggers of the Northwest wrenched themselves from the protectorate of William Hutcheson and said that thereafter they were beholden only to the C.I.O. and industrial unionism. Furniture workers also turned to the C.I.O. for leadership. True to its promise of solidarity for even the humblest of the nation's workers, the C.I.O. stretched out its hand to the share-croppers of the South and a goodly number joined with other wage-working farmers, with fruit and vegetable pickers, and with cannery hands to create still another union. Among a miscellaneous group of workers, the C.I.O. organized and chartered 605 directly affiliated local industrial unions. Many were to be the nucleus for new internationals. They included meat packers and butchers; sawmill workers; paper-makers; laundrymen, laundresses and dry cleaners; brick, tile and clay workers; hotel porters and maid; waiters, waitresses, and bartenders; road-builders, quarrymen, suspender, garter, thread, twine and leather-goods workers; makers of incubators, cemetery laborers, barbers, beauticians, photographers, nurses, and bootblacks.

The large established unions which formed the C.I.O., and those which subsequently affiliated, took on new strength from the wave of popular unionism they created. The miners, printers, clothing workers, hatters and furriers' internationals became stronger than ever before in their decades of existence.

II

From the point of view of numbers involved and complexity of economic problems, organizing the textile industry was the biggest of the tasks assumed by the C.I.O. Textile has been one of the "sickest" of American industries. Its malady, competition between Northern and Southern mills, with wages in the South undermining Northern standards, has been of the pernicious and lingering type. An investigator for *Collier's* toured the South in October, 1937, and returned with a story that he labeled "peonage." He discovered companies and company stores which brought thousands of workers "all work and no pay." By the time these workers had paid check-offs to the store, for rent in company-owned houses, and for social insurance, they received exactly nothing with which to provide for clothing, home furnishings, or medical care. One worker had been receiving a net wage of nothing a week since "six years ago Christmas." Taking advantage of this poverty, some of the company stores had hangers-on who joined with the store managers to do a profitable bit of usury. The *Collier's* reporter found a shirt factory near Greenville, South Carolina, which was paying workers $1.95, 91 cents, and 59 cents for all the work that was offered them in a week. There was "the mother of five children—a widow" who had worked 182½ hours in eight weeks in a Douglasville, Ga., garment factory and had received $37.08. The mill workers' diet left the reporter extremely uncomfortable; he ate hominy grits, sauerkraut, corn pone, "bacon almost wholly innocent of lean meat," and canned fruits. In the silk industry of the North, meanwhile, wages hovered around ten dollars a week and only occasionally higher. Entire cities felt the pinch. The business men of Paterson, New Jersey,

[238]

felt the local silk industry was a parasite on their good will and charity.

The job of lifting the textile workers nearer a subsistence wage level, and eventually above, was one that required also some effort to rationalize the industry. Sidney Hillman, stabilizing influence in the men's garment clothing trade for years, was assigned to the task. The United Textile Workers gave the C.I.O. full power of attorney, and in March, 1937, the Textile Workers Organizing Committee was set up. The C.I.O. blueprint did not contemplate a piecemeal affair, but rather the unionizing of more than 900,000 workers connected with textile and cloth in all its branches—linen, woolen, rayon, cloth, silk, rugs and carpets, thread, textile trimmings, yarn, and cotton materials. The Amalgamated Clothing Workers and the International Ladies' Garment Workers unions, most closely concerned economically, supplied the financial sinews. The Amalgamated's 200,000 members taxed themselves five dollars each and by October had contributed $400,000; the International gave $200,000 from its treasury. The T.W.O.C. set up thirty region and subregional offices North and South. The most alert and modern of the A.F. of L.'s Southern leaders, A. Steve Nance, Atlanta printer, who had joined with the C.I.O., was given the most difficult deep Southern territory to handle; as an aid he chose Franz Daniel, young Socialist graduate of Union Theological Seminary. John Peel was placed in charge of the upper South, while in the North, Hillman leaned heavily on Emil Rieve, head of the hosiery workers' union, and Carl Holderman, of New Jersey, progressive among the leaders of the old United Textile Workers.

The T.W.O.C. placed almost 400 organizers, men and women, in the field. At first they found the workers suspicious that previous futile efforts of a timid unionism were to be repeated. The steel campaign's policy of "no dues" was adopted. Workers merely signed cards saying they wished to be represented in collective bargaining by the T.W.O.C. To silence the mill owners' cry of "racketeers," all dues-collectors and treasurers of the new locals were placed under bond.

Within a month after the many-sided campaign had been initiated, Hillman was signing contracts for the T.W.O.C. Eighteen manu-

[239]

facturers of hatbands, comprising 85 per cent of the industry, signed up in April, granting a closed shop, wage increases, vacations with pay, and a forty-hour week. During the same month, he won an agreement covering the employees of the important Viscose Corporation of America and giving them a 10-per-cent wage raise, a minimum weekly pay of fifteen dollars, as against the thirteen dollars, which had been the rule; a forty-hour week, recognition of the union for its members, and a promise that the corporation would not aid any company union. On April 14th the T.W.O.C. was able to announce it had 50,000 workers covered by contracts; two months later 200 employers had signed contracts, incorporating wage raises and other benefits, for 100,000 mill workers. In July, the Committee engaged in one of its few strikes. Mobilizing most of the silk-mill owners of Pennsylvania and New Jersey behind a campaign to establish a uniform minimum wage rate as a basis for stabilizing the industry, the T.W.O.C. called a general strike to bring the hold-outs into line. At the end of a two-weeks' strike, 45,000 out of an estimated 58,000 silk workers were the possessors of contracts with increased, though still modest, wages. During July the T.W.O.C. completed a successful peaceful conquest of Lawrence, Mass., where it won collective bargaining polls at two large mills of the American Woolen Company. Signing of contracts followed. Soon after, eight Labor Board elections in North Carolina and New Jersey resulted in majorities for the C.I.O. In early October the T.W.O.C. had contracts with 905 firms employing 270,000 workers. Fully 450,000 were enrolled as members.

The South held the key to the success of the C.I.O. in welding together the elements of a permanent union of textile workers. It has for years been an axiom that the awakening of Southern labor and its organization will be a landmark in the history of the states, bringing a shifting of political and economic influence. This was fully realized by the mill owners and their business fraternity when the T.W.O.C. appeared on the scene. The realization took concrete form. In South Carolina, in Georgia and elsewhere, Ku Klux Klan night-riders appeared again. This time their hates were directed at neither Jew, Catholic, nor Negro. The enemy was C.I.O. "C.I.O. is Communistic. Communism will not be tolerated. Ku-Klux

Klan rides Again," said signs posted on telegraph poles. Fiery crosses burned as warning to C.I.O. organizers. Now and then hooded night-riders called at homes of known union men. A South Carolina school-teacher separated the children of "loyal American parents" from the offspring of those who had become infected with unionism, and instructed the loyalists to spy on the families of the "disloyal" ones. Distribution of T.W.O.C. literature was followed by the holding of early-morning anti-C.I.O. prayer-meetings at mill gates. The C.I.O. responded to the challenge of the preachers by claiming the support of the best in religion for its aims. The *T.W.O.C. Parade*, southern organ of the textile drive, published a special issue of several hundred thousand copies dealing with "Labor and Religion." Statements of support from courageous Southern preachers, quotations from the Bible exalting the poor and chastising the exploiters, and reports of T.W.O.C. progress filled the columns. One story told how "Human Rights Were Placed Above Property Rights by Early Church Leaders." Another, addressed to the fundamentalists, was headlined, "Old Testament, Labor Movement Closely Connected."

III

Another C.I.O. union appeared destined to play a rôle in the future of the South. It was the Southern Tenant Farmers Union, the largest section of the United Cannery, Agricultural, Packing, and Allied Workers of America, organized in Denver in July, 1937. The problem of 1,400,000 Negro and white families living as share-croppers in constant debt, many on starvation rations, was viewed by the C.I.O. as a problem in national economy as well as a matter of concern to the workers immediately involved. Entire families which earned two dollars and three dollars a week—usually less, in cash—eliminated a huge section of the nation as possible consumers of goods produced by C.I.O. industrial workers.

Several fruitless efforts to band the tenant farmers together were made before July, 1934, when twenty-seven white and black men met in a rickety schoolhouse at Tyronza, Arkansas to form the Southern Tenant Farmers Union. The wrath of plantation-owners and their riding-bosses, joined by local law authorities, soon made itself felt. Leaders of the union were forced to work in secret, meeting in fields and in deserted shacks in the dark of night. Some fled to Memphis, Tennessee, there to direct the union's efforts. The survival of the union and its emergence into a vigorous force was almost entirely due to the persistent advocacy and material aid given the share-croppers' cause by the Socialist leader, Norman Thomas, and a group of young Southern Socialists led by Howard Kester.

Dues were set at ten cents a month, and initiation fees at thirty cents. Local leaders, including J. R. Butler, H. L. Mitchell, and E. B. McKinney, were developed and by 1935 the union was ready to call a strike of cotton-choppers. The demands were $1.50 for a ten-hour day. Although 6,000 voted to strike, somewhere between 2,000 and 4,000 responded. The remainder were in no position to withstand the reign of terror which plantation-owners had set in motion. Meetings were raided and speakers deported from Arkansas towns; strike leaders disappeared. Negro strikers and others were convicted of vagrancy, jailed and leased to plantation-owners for work at seventy-five cents a day. The strike, nevertheless, helped raise the income during the chopping season which was at hand. An observer sent South by John L. Lewis in the spring of 1936, reported share-croppers living in miserable shacks, in tents and abandoned churches. Five families evicted in Earle, Arkansas, were dumped on a road. Entire families were found sleeping by a roadside in the winter months of January and February. A scheduled union meeting was dispersed by gun-fire and its leaders threatened with lynching. Less than 5 per cent of the tenant farmers, William J. Sneed reported to Lewis, were permitted to vote on election day.

A year later, the Southern Tenant Farmers Union met in convention at Muskogee, Oklahoma, and reported the miracle of the organization of 328 locals and 30,727 members in seven states; most of them came from Arkansas and Oklahoma. Large banners set forth in biblical language the delegates' demand for justice. "What mean you that you crush My people and grind the faces of the poor?" and, "Let justice roll down as the waters and righteousness as a mighty stream," some read. And by their side hung the terse slogans, "Land for the Landless!" and "The laborer is worthy of his hire." White and black workers, Mexicans and Indians, sat together in the most unique labor convention the country had ever seen.

[242]

The A.F. of L.'s interest in the Southern tenant farmers had been almost exclusively an academic one, and the union coöperated willingly in the formation of an inclusive C.I.O. union of farm, cannery, fruit, and vegetable workers. Delegates came to the Denver convention representing citrus pickers, packers, and peelers whose total weekly earnings sometimes were as high as $10.40, and frequently as low as $2.75. Colorado and Michigan beet workers who labored ten to fourteen hours a day during a season of five or six months for a wage of $200 to $400 were also represented. Fifty-six unions, claiming a membership of 100,000, sent delegates, who voted, with one objection, to join the C.I.O. Under the devoted leadership of capable men like Mitchell and Kester of the Southern tenant farmers, and Leif Dahl of New Jersey, the new union promised a stirring effort to mobilize the strength of the many millions of farm, cannery, and vegetable field hands. Promises of coöperation from spokesmen of small-farm owners, including those organized in the National Farmers Union and the Farmers National Holiday Association, accepted with a pledge of mutual assistance by Lewis, served to build a link between the new labor movement and the farming population of the nation.

IV

During the 1933 enthusiasm for the NRA a group of workers in the Philco Radio plant at Philadelphia organized a Walking, Hunting and Fishing Club under the leadership of ebullient twenty-one-year-old James Carey. Before long the club had accomplished its purpose of boring from within a company union and transforming it into an independent organization. Carey and the other leaders went to the president of Philco, said they spoke for a majority of his employees and asked for a contract. They insisted the NRA made collective bargaining national policy. The management disputed the point, and Carey asked whether proof from NRA Administrator Johnson would be satisfactory. The management said it would. Two old automobiles full of union enthusiasts immediately rattled off to Washington. En route they purchased a newspaper and tore from it a picture of the NRA administrator. Once in Washington, they systematically started on the first floor of the Department of Commerce Building, opened all doors, peered in and checked all faces against the newspaper photograph. After several hours they found a square-jawed face that fitted the picture, walked up to his desk, and placed an outline of their case before him.

"That's legal," said Carey, "isn't it? Haven't we got the law on our side?"

Johnson agreed the union had a right to a contract.

"Well, then, sign your name to it. The management won't take our word for it."

The NRA administrator signed, and the union's leaders triumphantly turned their cars toward Philadelphia. Soon after their arrival, young Carey and his colleagues won a closed-shop agreement from Philco, a thirty-six-hour week, and, eventually, increases in hourly rates of pay that ranged from 69 to 150 per cent of the previous rates.

The Philco union became a federal local of the A.F. of L. Radio manufacturing was perhaps the last industry where craft unionism could work. A single worker, during a single day, fashions a cabinet, paints it, wires it, tests it, and performs perhaps a dozen other operations. Logically, craft unionism would compel such a worker to join half a dozen or more unions. Nevertheless as the Philco union idea spread to other radio plants, the A.F. of L. sought to divide up the radio workers. An application for a charter for a new international union was denied. Early in 1936, the new federal unions of radio workers, joined by several independents—twelve unions in all—formed the United Electrical and Radio Workers Union. It had by that time become evident that workers on electrical equipment, by the nature of their tasks, belonged in the same union as the radio workers. The United presented the Federation with several additional requests for a charter. All of them were refused, largely through the insistence of the craft unions of electricians and machinists. Finally the executive council turned over most of the radio workers to the electricians' international, which offered the new locals a class "B," non-beneficiary status wherein each local of radio workers, no matter how large, would have a single vote in national conventions, as against the old locals which enjoyed a vote for each of its members. The United's members refused to be turned over, and in retaliation were expelled from the Federation. Affiliation with the C.I.O. was effected in the fall of 1936, though Lewis and Brophy had months before become the guiding advisers of the union.

Under the leadership of Carey, at twenty-six an ingenious but open-faced diplomat, addicted to cigars that seem almost as long as he is tall, the United grew from 14,000 members in October, 1936, to 100,000 in June, 1937. Five months later, Brophy reported its membership at 130,000. Thriving local unions had been created in thirteen Westinghouse and eleven General Electric plants, which together control 60 per cent of the electrical manufacturing in the country. Four locals had been set up in the electrical manufacturing divisions of General Motors. Contracts were signed with Philco, and with RCA-Victor, after a hectic strike, a Labor Board poll and negotiations lasting more than a year. Negotiations were begun with Merganthaler Linotype, Westinghouse Airbrake, and Allis-Chalmers. Five hundred plants were brought under contracts providing for substantial wage increases, vacations, and nine holidays annually with pay. In March of 1937, the United initiated a campaign which destroyed the company union at General Electric's huge Schenectady plant, and brought wage increases of $1,000,000 a year to all G.E. employees. It won a national agreement with the General Electric Company.

Having demonstrated its capacity to serve the radio and electrical appliance workers, the United was entrusted by the C.I.O. with a campaign to organize the working forces of the nation's electric utilities. In October, 1937, the union had sixty-three functioning locals among the utilities companies. Ten of the fourteen major utility systems were paralleled by locals of the United. Eight agreements had been signed, establishing the highest wage rates and best working conditions of all utility workers. The contract with the Mountain States Power Company of Wyoming, covering most of the power facilities of that state and of three adjoining states, provided for a closed shop, seniority rights, review of discharges, a forty-hour week, and vacations and sick leave with pay. The close of 1937 saw the campaign of the United's utilities division pressed with particular vigor among the 40,000 employees of New York's Consolidated Edison; the 12,000 working for the Pacific Gas and Electric

Company; and among the workers of the northern group of the Commonwealth and Southern System. In the latter sector, the majority of the workers in each affiliate had been signed up and a closed shop was being made an immediate objective. A written agreement had been won with Consumers Power of Michigan, the largest property, and a verbal agreement with Ohio Edison. Eighteen organizers directly assigned and paid by the C.I.O. aided in the utilities campaign.

Revolts in the International Association of Machinists in New York and Minnesota brought the United 15,000 members in the late summer of 1937, and at its September convention the jurisdiction of the union was extended to include the manufacture of electrical equipment, machine tools, instruments, light machines, and the utilities field. Carey and Julius Emspak, secretary of the United, reported that two hundred locals had been organized and that the staff of full-time local, district, and national officers totaled 110. To counteract the efforts of Frey, Wharton, and Tracy, of the electricians, who sought to enjoin their respective memberships to refuse to handle products manufactured by United members, literature directly addressed to the craft unionists, over the heads of their leaders, was achieving great success. The Philco workers Walking, Hunting and Fishing Club had brought into existence one of the strongest unions in the nation.

v

It seemed to Heywood Broun in the summer of 1933 that the newspaper men ought to make an effort to share in the promised benefits of the NRA. He accordingly announced in his syndicated column that he would hold weekly informal meetings Wednesday nights in his New York penthouse apartment where the problem of organizing the news writers would be discussed. The sessions produced two general points of view which lingered on in the American Newspaper Guild, which was soon to take shape, until the fall of 1937. The issue was: should the reporters, rewritemen, and copyreaders organize a union, much like "common workers," or should it be a select fraternity of "professionals" which would seek to raise the standards of the business and by some not clearly defined system

[246]

of mutual aid help improve the newspaper man's working conditions. The early sessions were largely vacuous meetings, with some of the "right wing" suggesting the revival of a Press Club which had become defunct. The "left wing," among whom was Broun and later Jonathan Eddy, of the *New York Times*, was too cautious to propose a union outright, so the compromise was to set up a "Guild." Broun from the start was for a union. The issue cropped up again at a first general meeting in the City Club, where several liquefied rightists reared up against the phrase "collective action" which the leftists boldly proposed to write into a statement of principles. The necessity of getting together on a proposed NRA code for the newspaper industry helped clear the air. The publishers wished to class the newspaper editorial department workers as professionals, who would not, in self-respect, allow themselves to be distraught over plebeian topics of wages and hours. A meeting in the National Press Club, in Washington, during December of 1933 organized the Guild on a national scale. Before long the publishers had helped decide the issue of whether the news writers were to organize a union.

First Louis Burgess was fired by a Hearst paper in San Francisco. Then Don Stevans, another west coast Guildsman, felt the ax. Morris Watson, star man of the Associated Press staff in the east, was let out because, the management suggested, he "might be happier elsewhere." Faced by the loss of employment, Watson said the A.P. had failed to indicate where "elsewhere" might be. The Watson and Burgess cases, among others, went to the Labor Board. Francis Neylan, Hearst counsel, remarked during the hearing on the Burgess case that the Guild had created a "state of revolution." Burgess, prevented by other Guildsmen from settling the issue by punching Neylan on the nose, left the room with a defi.

"Hearst," he said, "has twenty-six papers and I have twenty-six cents. But some day the Newspaper Guild will be bigger than William Randolph Hearst."

Watson's petition for reinstatement, filed by the Guild, was upheld by the Labor Board, only to have Donald Richberg intervene and countermand the decision. It took several years before the Watson case became the cause celebre in the campaign to upset the Wagner Act. In the end the Supreme Court denied the A.P.'s contention that the Act was illegal and ordered Watson's reinstatement with full back pay. The Guild had won a great victory for itself and for all of organized labor. Meanwhile, the differences within the Guild had been settled by a referendum decision for affiliation with the A.F. of L. The issue came up again in a poll on joining with the C.I.O. Again, the membership voted, this time not only that it was to be a labor union, but that it would be part of the progressive, industrial labor movement. It decided to seek the membership of all newspaper-office employees, clerks and bookkeepers, as well as reporters, and looked forward to the day when it might fuse its strength with the powerful unions of linotypers, pressmen, and stereotypers.

The fight of the Guild for recognition was made doubly hard by the publishers' introduction of the issue of "freedom of the press," the same issue newspaper-owners had used in seeking to win exemptions from the scope of child-labor legislation. Membership of the news writers in a labor union affiliated with other unions, the publishers contended, would lead to coloring the news in labor's favor. The "closed shop," which was ascribed to the leaders of the Guild, the publishers said, would make it impossible for an editor freely to select a staff. These charges the Guild countered with reference to its constitution, which opened membership to workers of any, all, or no shades of political, economic, or social views. Further, the fact was cited that no Guild "closed shops" were sought; but that the "Guild shop," established on several papers, provided that an editor might hire whomever he chose, provided that within a reasonable period the new employee joined the Guild. Despite the outcry against the Guild as an alleged threat to the "freedom of the press," no publisher under contract with the Guild—in 1937 there were more than 7,000 newspaper writers under collective agreements—has ever accused so much as a single Guildsman of doctoring the news. And many Guildsmen have been assigned the task of reporting reams of unfair and untrue attacks on their organization.

In the face of skepticism within the ranks of newspaper men and the opposition of the publishers—later joined by the A.F. of L.—the American Newspaper Guild had in the winter of 1937 enrolled 15,000 members, approximately 14,000 of them editorial workers.

It had agreements with sixty-one newspapers, bringing wages of upwards of 7,000 men to the highest in the business, insuring them a five-day week, sick leaves with pay, and liberal dismissal bonuses based on the number of years in servitude. Of broader significance, possibly, was the fact that the Guild, by its association with the labor movement and its necessary absorption in social problems and legislation, was developing a type of newspaper man keenly aware of the modern trends of industry and labor. Franklin P. Adams, Guildsman conductor of the *Conning Tower*, was heard to complain at a Guild convention: "Everybody knows what the Supreme Court did today on the minimum wage law, but nobody can tell me how we made out in the Davis cup matches."

Of potential wide significance also was the development of another C.I.O. union of white-collar workers: The Federation of Architects, Engineers, Chemists, and Technicians. Organized in 1934 among engineers and other technical men employed on WPA New York projects, it later branched out to workers in private employment. Affiliation with the American Federation of Labor was terminated in 1937, when the Federation threw in its lot with the C.I.O. By October, the Federation had 6,000 members, only a handful of those eligible, but constituting the heaviest swing toward unionism the professions had ever witnessed. Wages, hours, working conditions, and security of employment dominated the minds of the leaders of the Federation, but they posed other problems for their members to tackle. When the Federation convened in Detroit on October 7th, it devoted a session to the question, "What can the technical professions do through organized effort to secure the benefits of modern science and technology in relation to productivity and utilization of resources, human needs, employment opportunities, and 'the abundant life'?" William Green promptly denounced the Federation as a Communist organization.

Stenographers and bookkeepers poring over ledgers and pumping adding machines also sported C.I.O. membership cards. The Committee in June, 1937, issued a charter of affiliation to the United Office and Professional Workers. The organization had been set up at a heterogeneous convention in Philadelphia on May 30th of the same year. Twenty federal locals of A.F. of L. office workers, joined by

[249]

independent groups employed by insurance companies, book and magazine publishers, and advertising agencies were represented. Eight associations of employees in private social work also sent delegates. The total represented was 8,600 workers, 965 of them social workers. By October of 1937, the union boasted forty-nine chartered locals, with 25,000 members, virtually all of them covered by contracts setting up minimum wages and maximum working hours. To safeguard its principle of industrial unionism, the C.I.O. reserved the right to delimit the jurisdiction so that automobile, steel, and other office workers might eventually join the industrial unions in their respective industries. Meanwhile, organizers and funds were extended to the new union, which proceeded to launch special organizing campaigns among the insurance companies and in the financial houses of downtown Manhattan.

The C.I.O. threw open its doors to government employees in June and July of 1937. The United Federal Workers of America was created from among dissatisfied A.F. of L. affiliates, joined by new recruits to unionism. Its charter barred strikes or picketing of government offices. The aims of the new union, operating in a field of 800,000 workers, was to be achieved by enlisting public support for reforms, and organized solicitation and pressure on legislative and administrative officials of the government. All federal workers, with exception of those in military service, those having the power to hire and fire, "and, for the time being, postal employees" were eligible for membership. A gratuitous announcement by President Roosevelt that federal workers might not strike was given much publicity by the unfriendly press, but three months after the organization was created it had forty-four locals and 5,000 members. A sister organization of government workers, the State, County and Municipal Employees of America, was launched by the C.I.O. in July. A number of A.F. of L. locals and national leaders of the Federation's competing group deserted at once to the new union. Within a few months the organization boasted of 30,000 members.

An A.F. of L. museum piece, the Retail Clerks International Protective Association, decided in April of 1937 to expel its largest local and with it Samuel Wolchak, a probable successful contender for its presidency. The act was the signal for a revolt, and most of the active locals bolted the Association to set up the United Retail Employees, affiliated with the C.I.O. Fifteen thousand members formed the nucleus of the new union, and by October of 1937 it had reached a total of 40,000. Its locals held agreements with Woolworth stores, with chain cigar stores, and with large department stores in New York and Pittsburgh. The department stores campaign of the United Retail Employees tested the newspaper publishers' vaunted belief in the freedom of the press, and in its early stages the union found the columns of the papers largely closed to stories of efforts to organize employees of the largest advertisers. In October, 1937, the union entered into an agreement with the C.I.O. by which a Department Store Workers Organizing Committee, headed by Hillman, was set up. It projected a strategy in which the tremendous purchasing power of the C.I.O. millions would be mobilized to speed the campaign to victory.

VI

The espionage system of Tsarist Russia worked no more efficiently than the spy system of New York's large rapid transit corporations. Sporadic attempts of the A.F. of L. to unionize the employees of the Interborough and Brooklyn-Manhattan companies had been crushed consistently since 1905. Hardy souls who tried to organize them did so at clandestine meeting-places, in guarded attics of homes. The fear exercised over its employees by the Fifth Avenue Coach Company was far more potent than the protection offered by the federal government. When the Labor Board ordered an employee poll of the company's workers in 1934, less than half a dozen voted and the remaining twelve hundred carefully avoided even the vicinity of polling-places picketed, for once, by minor company executives and inspectors. There appeared Michael Quill, Austin Hogan, and a company of Irish-bred rebels. Sometimes they exchanged union news when mass let out of a Sunday. They might entrust admittance to the inner circle to a fellow Irishman because, as Quill said of one, "I saved him from a millrace as a boy in Ireland. He wouldn't betray me." Together with advisers John Santo and M. H. Forge, the little group of I.R.T. employees grew larger. They attacked the company union and by careful research exposed an employee pen-

sion scheme which promised returns to executives far out of proportion to the meager benefits it conferred upon the subway guards,
ticket-choppers, porters, and skilled repairmen in the terminals.

They organized the Transport Workers Union of New York as
an independent organization. They insisted on the industrial form
of organization, and the A.F. of L.'s Amalgamated Association of
Street and Electric Railway Employees was doubly glad to wash its
hands of a problem it had failed to conquer in other years. Faced
by the C.I.O. revolt in 1936, Wharton was on the lookout for all
members he might get and he obtained a waiver from the Amalgamated by which he was allowed to charter the Transport Workers
as a machinists' lodge. As the lodge grew, however, and swept the
I.R.T. company union into the discard, the Amalgamated began to
reassert its Federation-given jurisdiction. Wharton was furious when
he heard of it, and with the wrath that a jurisdictional fight can
stir in the breast of an A.F. of L. leader, he advised the lodge to
ignore both the Amalgamated and the A.F. of L. Green, however, supported the contention of the Amalgamated and other craft unions.
He decreed that the promising new union should have its members
parceled out. Both Wharton and Green proved belated advisers.
The union had already decided to join in the van of the C.I.O.
At a meeting addressed by Brophy and Pressman, 5,000 transit workers celebrated the death of the company union—symbolized by a
coffin on the stage—and the acceptance of a C.I.O. charter.

The Transport Workers of America became the C.I.O. union of
all workers in and about transportation facilities, excluding only
ships and railroads. Soon after its admittance to the C.I.O. the
union, by an overwhelming vote, won the right to speak for all of
the 15,000 I.R.T. employees. Now, with the negotiating skill of
Lewis thrown in the balance, they won a closed shop agreement
with the line. From then on it was an irresistible parade: Third
Avenue Railway bus and trolley workers voted 86 per cent for the
union, and within a few weeks won a closed shop. The Fifth Avenue
Coach workers paid off an old debt by voting 82 per cent for the
union; they also won a closed shop. More trolley and bus workers
joined. Taxi-drivers, scored as unreliable and undesirable by Tobin
and the International Brotherhood of Teamsters, caught the fever

and they too trooped to the polls to give the C.I.O. new victories. Reaching out through the nation, the union chartered locals in Akron—again with the aid of the rubber workers—in Cleveland, Detroit, Pittsburgh, Los Angeles, Harlan, Dayton, Buffalo, Norfolk, and scores of other cities. Its only setback was in a poll among employees of the Philadelphia Rapid Transit Company, where the union forced the issue before sufficient organization work had been done.

Five hundred delegates who met at the first convention of the new C.I.O. international in September, 1937, heard reports that the handful who had met for years behind shaded curtains in Quill's home, or who had exchanged furtive words at mass, had grown to a fearless army of 87,000 members, with applications from many thousand more pending. More than 34,000 of 38,000 New York transit and omnibus employees, and 15,000 taxicab drivers had joined the union, and thereby won wage increases of more than $4,500,000 a year. A wage increase of $1,200,000 was obtained for workers on the city's subway system, whose politically appointed board of directors were attempting to deny the collective bargaining recognition which private interests had already conceded. Of the 87,000 members, 38,-500 were employed on other than New York systems and the union had every right to call itself a national organization. The Transport Workers of America was the infant prodigy of the C.I.O.

VII

The International Association of Oil Field, Gas Well and Refinery Workers Union, like other small industrial unions within the A.F. of L., was threatened in 1935 and 1936 with dismemberment by the craft union leaders. Its progress was impeded by company unions at the Standard Oil and other refineries. In the oil fields a spirit of frontier independence gave rise, on the one hand, to an aloofness from unionism among the workers, on the other to the fostering of anti-union vigilanteism by some operators. The union became a charter member of the C.I.O., and in March, 1937, the Committee decided to make the organizing of the half-million workers in the oil industry one of its major objects. A Petroleum Workers Organizing Committee was set up, with Lieutenant-Governor Kennedy as

[253]

the chairman, and with Harvey C. Freming, president of the union, as one of its members. The P.W.O.C. received the services of twenty-four organizers from the C.I.O., and within six months after the campaign had been launched, the membership of the union had grown from 45,000 close to 100,000 members, of whom 65,000 were covered by collective agreements.

Following the raids on its Montana membership by fourteen craft unions and the calling of several ill-advised strikes, the International Union of Mine, Mill and Smelter Workers fought a losing fight until January, 1937, when its membership was down to 17,000. Its youthful leaders, Reid Robinson and Thomas H. Brown, refused to lessen their efforts, however, and with the upsurge of C.I.O. unionism in autos and steel the metal miners' membership started to climb upward again. Campaigns were launched among the zinc and lead miners of Missouri, Oklahoma, and Kansas, where the silicosis scourge was said to have made nine years in the mines the average working life of a miner. The organization of a vigilante company union failed to halt the efforts in the Kansas-Oklahoma-Missouri tri-state mining area. A strike in the Utah mines brought a twenty-five-cents-a-day wage raise, and a healthy increase in membership. With the setback to the C.I.O. in "Little Steel," the Committee assigned the metal miners' union the task of organizing Republic Steel's source of iron ore in Minnesota's Mesaba range, where Finnish and Slovak workers had for decades endured a perfected system of espionage and anti-union warfare. Congressman John T. Bernard agreed to divide his time between Washington and the job of directing the organizing work on the range. The first victory was the winning of a contract for the workers in the mines of the International Harvester Company, followed by negotiations with the Oliver Mining and the American Steel and Wire Companies, subsidiaries of U.S. Steel. With the winning of a Labor Board poll among the International Harvester miners, the entire district was opened for unionism. The metal miners' drive fostered other efforts of the C.I.O. to draw a ring of strong unionism around the steel industry of the Northwest. Four thousand Minnesota timbermen were brought into the C.I.O., and with them hundreds of Great Lakes sailors who controlled a great artery of transportation from the ore mines to the mills of Chicago and the East. Meanwhile, other efforts of the union were going forward among Eastern metal workers. A labor poll election gave the union a clear majority among the 3,000 employees of the Bridgeport Brass Company. By October, 1937, the union had increased its membership to 45,000.

Of prime strategic importance to the C.I.O.'s efforts in the automobile industry was the Federation of Flat Glass Workers. The A.F. of L. had no organization whatever in the industry when the union knocked on its doors in August, 1934. By that time the job of organizing had been almost completed, and the Federation's executive council blinked at the fact that the union was thoroughly industrial in character. Contracts were won in 1935 with the Pittsburgh Plate and the Libbey-Owens-Ford glass companies. C.I.O. affiliation was voted by the union early in 1936. A C.I.O.-inspired council of glass and auto workers was set up in the fall of 1936, and in December 14,000 employees of the two companies went on strike. Several of the General Motors plants which had not been closed by the strike of the auto union were forced to close their doors because of a shortage of glass. Seeking to give Chrysler and other G.M. competitors an advantage that might have an effect in helping settle the auto strike, the glass walkout was ended toward the end of January on terms that gave the workers an eight-cents-an-hour increase, overtime pay, and, in view of the elimination of all company unions, virtually exclusive recognition.

The Aluminum Workers of America, formed of six federal locals formerly part of the A.F. of L., applied for and received a certificate of C.I.O. affiliation in April and June of 1937. Behind these locals was the familiar story of an upsurge of unionism in 1933, followed by attempted craft raids and the refusal of the A.F. of L. to grant a charter to an international union of aluminum workers. A "national council" which had been set up by the A.F. of L. had not met for two years when the six locals decided to cast their lot in with the C.I.O. The union in October, 1937, had 14,000 members on its books, and contracts with four large companies. Its chief problem lay in the renewal of a contract with the Aluminum Company of America. A contract which had been obtained by the A.F. of L. expired in November, 1937, and indications were that the Federation

[255]

could no longer command the support of any substantial number of the workers affected. A strike called by an A.F. of L. federal local at the company's plant in Alcoa, Tennessee, in August, 1937, produced a conflict between strikers and deputy sheriffs, in which two workers were killed. Green sent Francis J. Dillon to the scene to take charge, and immediately upon his arrival in Alcoa, Dillon announced that the strike was to be called off without an agreement. The president of the local was forced by Dillon to resign his post, whereupon 2,000 workers reorganized under the banner of the C.I.O.

Closely allied with the Aluminum Workers of America in its problems, were the 3,400 members of the National Die Casters' League, also a C.I.O. affiliate. By the end of 1937, amalgamation of the two unions was being urged as a further step in organizing the estimated 100,000 workers in the aluminum industry.

VIII

The shoe industry, employing 200,000 workers, was before the advent of the C.I.O.'s United Shoe Workers of America, a battleground of small, bitterly competing units without the stabilizing influence of an effective labor organization. A.F. of L. conservatism had made its boot and shoe workers' union unpopular with most of the workers. The United was formed in March, 1937, when the C.I.O. brought about a merger of the United Shoe and Leather Workers and the Shoe Workers' Protective Union, both independent organizations. By November, the membership of 16,000 had grown to 52,000. The first job of the United was to demonstrate its superior effectiveness over the A.F. of L., and for this task Lewis picked Powers Hapgood, whose days and nights since his association with the United Mine Workers in the winter of 1935 had been given in service to the auto, steel, radio, shipbuilding, shoe, and half a dozen other unions. A constitutional convention of the United, meeting in St. Louis during November, 1937, received reports that closed shop agreements had been won from 199 manufacturers. Wages were increased 15 per cent in Eastern factories, and 18 per cent in New York City.

Led by Hapgood, the shoe union fought one of the sharpest of

[256]

the C.I.O. strikes, directed against nineteen companies in the Lewiston-Auburn area of Maine. A report of investigators appointed by the American Civil Liberties Union charged that the Maine courts and the local authorities had denied the strikers their rights to strike, to organize, to picket, to get bail, to have adequate representation by counsel, to freedom of speech, to freedom from excessive punishment, and to fair and impartial justice. Supreme Court Justice Harry Manser decreed that the strike was illegal because the shoe union had not sought Labor Board polls of the workers. Hapgood, William J. Mackesy, and John F. Nolan and others of the strike leaders defied the court ruling and were jailed for six months. Hour-long volleys of tear gas were thrown into strikers' ranks. The union persisted, however, and with the C.I.O. it spent $150,000 in the battle. Labor board elections finally gave the union majorities in most of the plants and resulted in the signing of union contracts by fourteen of them.

The November convention of the United projected campaigns in Maine and New Hampshire, central New York State and in the Middle West, where important initial gains had already been made. Proffers of coöperation advanced by the United produced hopes that well-established independent unions in Brockton and Haverhill, Massachusetts, might soon become part of the C.I.O.'s shoe union.

IX

The first strength of the C.I.O. in the maritime industry came in the fall of 1936 with the affiliation of the Industrial Union of Marine and Shipbuilding Workers. The organization had been founded in 1933 at Camden, New Jersey, where former shipbuilders from Scotland's Clydeside tackled a task which the A.F. of L. had avoided since the bursting of the wartime boom in unionism. John Green, ship-plater and sheet-metal worker, and Benjamin Carwardine, shipwright, were the driving forces behind the new union. To their wide experience with unionism in Britain, they added the energy of Philip Van Gelder, who became the secretary-treasurer. Van Gelder's background was typical of several, like Hapgood, Walter, Roy, and Victor Reuther of the auto union; Franz Daniel, Howard Kester, Lief Dahl; and Mervyn Rathborne of the radio telegraphers,

[257]

who found in the C.I.O. a new expression of ideals of young America. A graduate of Brown University, where he later became an instructor in philosophy, Van Gelder deserted the academic world for a close association with the working people. He harvested in Oklahoma fields, planted telegraph poles in the Colorado Rockies, gandy-danced in Montana tunnels, shipped as a seaman, and installed subway equipment in Philadelphia. His apprenticeship completed, he turned to organizing unemployed, clothing workers', and taxi drivers' unions. When a shipyard strike broke out in Camden in 1934, he became associated with it and remained as executive of the union which emerged.

Efforts of the union to join the A.F. of L. were thwarted by the demands of eighteen craft unions. Before the conflict within the A.F. of L. had come to a climax, the miners and the two large needle-trades unions, defying the crafts, gave the union moral and material aid. The path of the new union was a stormy one. Its adversaries were the Bethlehem and Todd companies, and others dominated by Morgan, Mellon, and Huntingdon interests. The organization failed also to win the support which other unions gained from the enactment of the Wagner Act. By the end of 1937 the Labor Board had still to enforce a single one of its decisions against a shipbuilding corporation, and the issue of whether the board had jurisdiction over the industry was still enmeshed in the leisurely procedures of the U.S. Supreme Court. A series of bitter strikes was made inevitable. Those against the Federal Shipbuilding and Dry Dock Company, at Kearny, N. J., and at repair yards in San Pedro, California, among others, were successful. The Federal's 3,000 workers won a union agreement for the first time in the history of the yard; the San Pedro yards were forced to grant wage increases and preferential union hiring. The biggest strike, that against the Todd and other yards in New York harbor, ended in defeat, although 10,000 workers stayed out for ten weeks. Strike-breakers, a plethora of police generously granted the corporations by the city authorities, and backstairs deals between the corporations and the A.F. of L. broke the strike.

Refusing to dwell on post mortems, the union set in motion a campaign to organize navyyard mechanics. Gains were made in other directions as well, and by the end of 1937 the union had grown to twenty-six locals and 20,000 members as compared with twelve locals and 10,000 adherents in January.

X

The revolt of the seamen belongs among the spectacular achievements of the C.I.O. With the smashing of the International Seamen's Union in 1920 and the passing of Andrew Furuseth as an active figure, the 90,000 American sailors had no union to speak of. The sailors' life, romantic but never economically satisfying, dropped to new depths during the depression. Most of them with no homes and with no more security than the next voyage offered, the men of the merchant marine became the truest type of American proletariat. Yet they had in them the independence of their craft. Old Andy, once hailed before a San Francisco court for sentencing in a labor dispute, spoke out: "You can put me in jail, but you cannot give me narrower quarters than as a seaman I have always had. You cannot give me coarser food than I have always eaten. You cannot make me lonelier than I have always been." Most sailors had something of that defiant self-reliance in them, and it was all the more surprising that they should have submitted to the type of labor leadership which traded on Furuseth's name from 1920 to 1936. Several officials became the willing recipients of shipowners' favors. They operated what was left of the union somewhat in the manner of a cheap employment agency.

Grange, Brown, Olander, and other leaders of I.S.U. suddenly came to life again in 1934. They were bestirred by two trends: the men were listening to talk of forming a new independent union, and the government in Washington wanted the shipowners to deal with a "responsible" union and prevent a strike. The officers of the I.S.U. rushed to sign agreements with the steamship companies, although they had few members and although the men for whom they signed the agreement had not been consulted. Unrest continued and soon burst into a steadily burning flame. In 1935, Joseph Curran, a six-foot seaman built on the physical lines of Jack London's Martin Eden, induced his mates to sit down on an east-bound ship in San Pedro harbor. They had complained, without benefit, about

[259]

food and pay. Long-distance telephone conversations between Secretary of Labor Perkins and Curran succeeded in ending the sitdown, but efforts to prosecute Curran for "mutiny" followed. The Curran incident was used as a talking point to spur the east-coast seamen into action. The sailors on the Pacific, defying the I.S.U. officials, had already taken matters into their own hands, and by an alliance with the longshoremen, made collective bargaining a reality on their vessels. The strategy in the Atlantic ports, particularly in New York, was to bring about a surge of members into the old locals of the I.S.U., and then effect a complete change of officers and tactics. "The Emperor" Grange, overlord of the cooks and stewards, and Gus Brown, official of the local of the firemen and oilers—the men in the "black holes"—sought the aid of police, courts, shipowners and the A.F. of L. to stem the revolt. They rewrote constitutions to suit their needs. Nevertheless, the seamen won out. Rank and file committees or "trustees" were elected where I.S.U. officials persisted in clinging to their titles and the recognition which the steamship companies continued to afford them.

The Atlantic Coast seamen struck in the spring of 1936, under the leadership of Curran. Despite replacements supplied by Grange, Brown, and the I.S.U., and pressure exerted on the companies by Joseph P. Ryan, longshoreman-tsar of the New York waterfront, the strike brought substantial gains. Later in the year when the west-coast seamen went on strike, the east-coast rank-and-filers struck again, this time in sympathy as well as in furtherance of their own demands for recognition, higher pay, shorter hours, and better food and living quarters. Denounced by the A.F. of L., the new leaders of the Atlantic seamen led a trek out of the Federation and set up the National Maritime Union, with Curran as president. Overruling requests of the A.F. of L. for delay, the Labor Board ordered elections which went overwhelmingly in favor of the N.M.U., which from the first had affiliated with the C.I.O. Votes on lines tabulated by December 28, 1937, gave the N.M.U. 9,060 votes as against 1,599 for the A.F. of L. The crews of the International Mercantile Marine, Luckenbach, Clyde, and Black Diamond lines were among those whose votes had been counted. It appeared certain that most of the 50,000 east-coast seamen would vote C.I.O. On October 11th, Curran reported to the C.I.O. that a total of 47,325 seamen on the east coast had been enrolled as dues-paying members. The organization of inland boatmen had advanced to the stage where 4,000 Great Lakes seamen had joined the organization.

Despite the early friendship between the east-coast sailors and the Sailors Union of the Pacific, a move to unite both groups encountered difficulties. Harry Lundeberg, head of the Pacific union, a full personality in his own right, resented what he felt to be too great prerogatives assumed by Harry Bridges, the longshoremen's leader, who was, with Curran, the outstanding figure in C.I.O.'s maritime organizations. The National Maritime Union tended to support Bridges' claim to leadership as against those of Lundeberg, and the resolving of the dispute between the two became one of the few knotty internal problems which the C.I.O. encountered. The sympathies of Lundeberg and his members were, however, clearly with the C.I.O. rather than the A.F. of L. and eventually unity of the sea-going unionists seemed likely.

The National Maritime Union faced a greater problem from another quarter. The Bureau of Navigation of the Department of Commerce and a new Maritime Commission appointed by President Roosevelt were less than friendly to the new union and the sit-down and strike tactics which it employed against the shipowners. Tied up with the problem was the feeling of the owners, fed by heavy governmental subsidies, that the merchant marine, as a possible "third arm" of national defense, ought not to be obligated to meet the usual standards set up by labor unions. The new union was harassed by efforts of the Bureau of Navigation to assume jurisdiction in labor matters, and particularly by the action of Chairman James P. Kennedy of the Maritime Commission in ordering the arrest on a charge of "mutiny" of the crew of the S.S. *Algic*, which sat down while their vessel was at anchor in the harbor at Montevideo, Uruguay. Conviction and imprisonment of the *Algic's* crew did not increase the seamen's faith in the new commission. Meanwhile Senator Royal S. Copeland, of New York, a friend of the shipping interests, took up the cudgels against the union in the Senate.

A report of the Maritime Commission in November, 1937, raised the entire issue of maritime labor conditions and strikes. The shipowners were denounced for having perpetrated wages as low as twenty-five dollars a month, hours as high as twelve a day, living-quarters that were "wretched" and food that was "unpalatable." These were depression conditions, the commission said, but during the years in question the shipping industry was "receiving substantial subsidies from the government for preservation of an American standard of living." "The shipowners," said the report, "were now paying for their short-sightedness," which for eleven years included even a refusal "to answer requests of their workers for collective agreements." The depression wages had by 1937 been brought to $72.50 a month, largely as a result of the N.M.U. strikes, but other conditions of which the union complained had not been remedied. To bring an end to the guerilla strike warfare, the commission proposed enactment of legislation patterned on the Railway Labor Act, which makes strikes impossible until months of mediation efforts have been exhausted. The N.M.U. looked with some suspicion on this proposal, insisting that the shipowners had not yet demonstrated that they were willing to go so far as the railroads in acceptance of collective bargaining.

The west coast stevedores came under C.I.O. leadership in the late summer of 1937. Hesitating needlessly to split the ranks of the longshoremen, the C.I.O. proposed to Ryan that he take his entire organization into the Committee. The offer was conditioned on an agreement by Ryan to submit to a democratically-conducted election of officers. The New York pier labor boss balked, and Bridges led the 17,000 west coast dockers out of the International Longshoremen's Association and into a new C.I.O. organization, the International Longshoremen's and Warehousemen's Union. The west coast men had been at odds with Ryan as far back as 1934, when they repudiated his settling of a strike over their heads.

The grievances of the longshoremen, largely eliminated in the West but still prevalent in the East, centered around the "shape up." In the early morning, strapping longshoremen "shaped up" before pier bosses. They stood, meekly hopeful in a large half-circle, while the foreman sized up backs, biceps and—with an eye to labor agitators—faces. The favored ones were chosen, the others, after hours of waiting were dismissed to await the arrival of another ship and a new "shape up." The system made possible gross discrimination, slashing of wages, favoritism and graft by hiring bosses. To end the "shape-up," Bridges and his west-coast longshoremen in 1934 demanded union-controlled hiring-halls, where available work could be rotated among all the longshoremen. They won the hiring-hall, as well as shorter hours, better pay, and limitation of the weight of loads each man was to swing.

Native of Australia, Bridges, a tall, slim, wiry man, won the warm loyalty of the west-coast stevedores. An hour-long speaker with a "down under" cockney accent, the dockers nevertheless hung on his every word and acted with the discipline and precision of an army in response to his commands, which, by a democracy hitherto scarce in longshoremen's unions, was also their own. An effort of the A.F. of L. teamsters' union to break Bridges' hold on the San Francisco piers ended in failure in the fall of 1937. "Marching inland," the new C.I.O. union had won the support of workers in warehouses. The A.F. of L. teamsters' union claimed jurisdiction, and failing to win the support of the Labor Board, declared teamsters would not truck goods handled by C.I.O. longshoremen. San Francisco and other Western piers became choked with goods, but the boycott was never completely effective. Time and again longshoremen crashed through the teamsters' picket lines. After several weeks of effort, the Federation union called off its embargo.

The C.I.O. longshoremen's union was meanwhile concentrating on Ryan's domain in the East. Thirty-five organizers were placed in the field, and succeeded within a few months in winning 6,000 I.L.A. supporters to the C.I.O. standard. The plan was to take over I.L.A. locals as a whole rather than to set up opposition locals of anti-Ryan men. With the refusal of New York City authorities to grant Ryan the police coöperation he had enjoyed for years, he appeared in the winter of 1937 to be headed for the discard.

The aim of the seamen's and longshoremen's unions in the C.I.O. was eventually to set up a powerful national maritime federation, such as had operated for years on the west coast.

Two other new C.I.O. unions found a community of interest with the maritime union. One was the American Communications Association, founded in 1935 as an organization of marine radio operators. The union, aided by the seamen, had several thousand members when it joined the C.I.O. in April, 1937. Under C.I.O. encouragement and aid in the form of organizers and funds, the union grew within six months to 14,000 members and won a number of contracts, including an agreement with the Radio Corporation of America. The union was given the task of organizing C.I.O. strength among the employees of the Western Union and Postal Telegraph companies, and in December won a national agreement with the latter.

The west coast swing to the C.I.O. brought the formation of the International Woodworkers of America, comprised of 100,000 ex-members of the A.F. of L.'s Brotherhood of Carpenters. The new union had more than two hundred locals in the lumber camps extending from British Columbia to California, and inland to Minnesota. The bolt from the A.F. of L., led by Harold Pritchett, who became president of the new union, followed more than a year of vain efforts to secure a status in the Hutcheson organization which would be commensurate with its membership. The woodworkers' union, soon after its formation, faced an attempted boycott by A.F. of L. teamsters and carpenters. Lined up behind it, however, was the strength of the C.I.O. longshoremen. The outcome of the conflict was to decide the leadership of the labor movement of the entire west coast. The A.F. of L. placed its hope to defeat Bridges and the C.I.O. on the squat shoulders of David A. Beck, head of the Seattle teamsters.

XI

The 4,000 rubber workers who remained in the United Rubber Workers of America when Green grudgingly conferred an international charter on them in 1935 had increased their number to 25,000 a year later, and to 78,000 members in October, 1937. Behind this growth stood a steady accumulation of gains in job security, in the reduction of working-hours and the raising of wage levels. The Department of Labor in 1937 reported an increase in rubber workers' wages over 1934 of 33 1/3 per cent, with raises in the lower brackets as high as 150 per cent in some instances. The six-hour day was established in tire and tube plants where the union had a majority; seniority rights were won, and unjust discriminations and discharges ended. Ninety-five per cent of the union's membership enjoyed vaca· tions with pay. Six Labor Board elections, including polls at the Goodyear and Goodrich plants in Akron and Los Angeles, were won by overwhelming margins. Following an eight-week strike in March and April, 1937, the union won its first written agreement from a major company, Firestone Tire & Rubber. Exclusive bargaining rights were incorporated in the agreement. While strikes had been waged against Goodyear and Firestone, the third major company, U.S. Rubber, entered into a union contract by negotiation. Written agreements were enjoyed by 85 of the 136 U.R.W. local unions late in 1937, and 12 others were working under the protection of written memoranda.

Although the rubber workers' union contributed some of its ablest leaders to C.I.O. campaigns in other industries, it retained the intelligence and discipline of its early months. In the midst of its unprecedented period of growth it did not ignore problems which were appearing on the horizon. These included removal of some of the plants to unorganized districts of the country where realtors and public authorities promised cheap and docile labor. The Los Angeles Goodyear plant, which included a textile mill, moved to the Southeast after the union had scored an overwhelming victory in a Labor Board election. The Goodyear company, of which Girdler is a director, gave the union strong resistance in Gadsden, Alabama. It was in this town that Dalrymple and other union leaders were assaulted by strong-arm men and deported. Gadsden, which also harbored a plant of Republic Steel, in 1937 earned a reputation such as had previously characterized the closed steel towns of Pennsylvania. A further step in the decentralization process was the opening of a modern plant of the Firestone company in Memphis, whose officials had previously announced a war on the C.I.O. Akron, however, still remained the seat of the rubber industry, and the first capital of the C.I.O. It had in 1937 become the best organized city in the country.

[265]

XII

The growth of the United Automobile Workers Union was fully as sensational. The aftermath of the General Motors strike brought an answer to the charge that the union and the sit-down strikers were representative of a minority of G.M.'s production workers. With the fear of reprisals for union membership removed, a great majority of the corporation's automobile workers rushed to affiliate. The tide of auto unionism was swelled by workers in other corporations, and before long Chrysler, the third largest corporation in the industry, Hudson Motors, Packard, Briggs Body, and countless others signed union contracts. Chrysler came to terms with the union after a four weeks' strike in which its nine Detroit plants were held by 20,000 sit-down strikers. After a Labor Board poll in which its 14,000 workers voted four to one for the U.A.W., Packard gave the union exclusive recognition. By September, the U.A.W. had contracts with 400 makers of automobiles or auto parts, as compared with the sixteen agreements of June, 1936. Material gains for the workers included establishment of minimum rates of pay of seventy-five cents an hour for men, and sixty-five cents for women; time and a half for overtime, and double rates for Sundays and holidays; a forty-hour work week; seniority rules governing lay-offs and reëmployment; joint committees to discuss the rate of speed of the machines; and the recognition of shop committees to handle grievances which arose in the plants.

The growth in less than a year of a labor union which won agreements with every manufacturer of automobiles except Ford, produced the C.I.O.'s most serious internal problem as well as one of its outstanding accomplishments. The difficulties lay with the owners of the industry, as well as with the new union. The industry met the heady democracy of the rank and file and the inexperience of some of the U.A.W.'s leadership with an arbitrariness of its own that did not make for the smoothest adjustment of difficulties. Arrayed against 140,000 workers were 20,000 foremen and straw bosses certain in their knowledge that G.M. had not willingly signed with the unions, and equally definite in their feeling that if the pact didn't work, G.M.'s executives would not be sorry. Knudsen admitted that partial responsibility for 200 sit-down strikes which occurred in G.M. plants, despite the existence of an agreement calling for mediation and arbitration, lay with some of his hard-headed plant foremen and managers.

G.M. representatives in the plants did nothing to untangle problems complicated by an obviously inadequate machinery for adjusting grievances. The contract called for grievance committees of not more than nine members in each plant. Some of these had to handle complaints of thousands of workers. In the Buick plant at Flint there were 15,000 workers. Later the grievance committee clause was amended to provide one representative for each 400 workers, but complaints still hung fire for weeks and months. Basic cause of the Pontiac sit-down, late in November, 1937, was the failure of the workers to win arbitration hearings on discharges which had occurred in June. The union had asked for a shop-steward system, wherein each division of the plant would have a spokesman. This, the company had rejected in favor of the plan which soon gave rise to seemingly unending difficulties.

Hundreds of complaints of broken promises by superintendents, of stalling on adjustments, of speeded lines and of favoritism to non-unionists piled up. A company unionist was permitted to go through a plant soliciting members. Unionists threw him out and he came back with company guards. A sit-down followed. A shop foreman who had brought trouble to Flint was sent to Janesville, where more difficulties ensued. Speeding up of the machines, soon after the settlement, was alleged to be a universal practice and the clause in the agreement which gave the union the right to "discuss" speed-ups failed to offer a solution. Union men were frequently precipitate in their action, but behind the "wild cat" sit-downs and the direct manner the unionists sometimes had with blatant anti-unionists there appeared to be a concerted policy of provocation.

"On our line," said a Pontiac unionist in explanation of a sit-down there in November, "we were all of us union men except one. He belonged to the National Guard. We argued with him and he just cursed us and said: 'I was with the National Guard up at Flint last winter and poked the likes of you in the guts.' We asked the superintendent to get him transferred, as it wasn't helping the work to have this argument going on all the time. The superintendent tried to get him transferred, but the management wouldn't do a thing about it. The fellow got to laughing at us and we decided that if he wasn't transferred by 6:30 that day he'd get a tarring. The superintendent begged the management again, but the management said that if that man was tarred, everybody mixed up would be fired. Well, 6:30 came and the management said we were afraid to touch him, and up jumped a little fellow and pinioned him and was going to dip him all by himself, but we stopped it. He did get some tar on him as we had promised. The management fired our executive committeemen and told us to go home, but we sat down instead."

His hands tied by a faulty agreement, Martin, U.A.W. president, was nevertheless faced with the responsibility of keeping his locals from breaking it. To complicate the difficulties, internal dissension brewed in the union. From the ending of the General Motors negotiations there had grown up dissatisfaction with Martin's qualifications for leadership. An emotional man, his value as an administrator was small. He could rouse great enthusiasm by eloquent addresses, but what the union needed during its great mushroom growth was a stronger man in whom all could have confidence. Martin replied to his critics by accusing them of responsibility for the unauthorized sit-downs and by labeling them indiscriminately as Communists. Richard T. Frankensteen, Martin's first lieutenant, had aspirations of his own for the presidency, but felt that his first move was to prevent the growth of the anti-Martin following. Both Martin and Frankensteen had shown their lack of judgment in the calling of the Chrysler strike. The recognition for U.A.W. members and the death of the Chrysler company union system could have been obtained without a strike. It was not surprising that the Chrysler sit-down strikers balked at leaving the plants when the settlement was brought to them. They had been told that the union would insist on obtaining sole recognition in a contract, as well as in practice.

The forces against Martin and Frankensteen included most of the G.M. strike leaders, the heroes of the Flint battle and of the early sit-downs in Detroit. Communists, supposedly led by Wyndham Mortimer, were only a small part of them. There were not sufficient

[268]

Communists either among the leadership or the members seriously to seek the job of running the union. A more formidable opponent was Walter Reuther, young Socialist, president of the Detroit West Side Local of 32,000 members. Most of the elements of the opposition to Martin, such as the group around Secretary George Addes, had no particular political coloring. They felt that Martin was attacking militant locals when he should have directed his fire at G.M.; that he was inconsistent and vacillating on important issues; that he was badly mishandling a drive to organize Ford; and that he was too temperamental for the job of president of a union of almost 400,000 members. The revolt was fanned when Martin removed organizers Roy Reuther, Ralph Daly, and William Cody from Flint; reduced Robert Travis, director of the strike there, to a subordinate position; and fired, transferred, or demoted other opposition leaders. Frank Winn, whose conscientious handling of publicity had won the union many friends among the reporters, was dropped because he was a Socialist.

The two groups clashed at a national convention in Milwaukee in August, and only the appearance of John L. Lewis and a committee of C.I.O. leaders from other unions prevented a serious breach. Lewis prevailed on the Martin-Frankensteen group to give up their plans to remove Mortimer and one other from vice-presidencies. The Reuther-Mortimer section, called the "Unity Group," had not opposed Martin for reëlection. It gave assent to Lewis' proposal that conventions thereafter be held biannually. Thus both groups made concessions. Efforts by Martin to reduce the convention representation of the large locals was defeated; a move to eliminate the locals' rights to publish their own papers was referred back to a committee. Refusing to permit a roll-call after a close viva-voce vote, Martin captured the executive board of the union, 14 to 8. On the last day of the convention, when the roll-call had been refused, the 1,000 delegates milled about in a near-physical battle. Reuther took the floor and in the interests of harmony withdrew the roll-call demand. Previously, a peace arrangement had been worked out, with the aid of the C.I.O., and the "Unity Group" was in hopes that it would work.

After the convention, however, Martin discharged other leaders of the opposition, among them Stanley Novak, who had organized fully 10,000 Ternstedt plant employees in Detroit. Novak was immediately engaged as an organizer by his local union. Leaders of affected locals attempted to lodge a protest with Martin, but he confronted one of them with a drawn revolver.

Martin and Frankensteen meanwhile were receiving most of the blame for the failure of the union to make headway at Ford's River Rouge plant. During the summer, members of the West Side local, led by Walter Reuther, had shouldered most of the work at Ford's. Reuther and Frankensteen, who had not previously played an active part in the campaign, were severely beaten at the Ford gates. Several weeks later, when Reuther planned to return to the Ford plant, he was ordered by the executive board, under pain of expulsion, to stay away. Frankensteen and Martin had evidently decided that Reuther was not to have the opportunity to lead the Ford campaign and, possibly, gain the additional following which might result. Martin and Frankensteen advanced a strategy of their own. They felt that the elder Ford did not know the true conditions in his plant, and that if he could be reached his heart might be so touched that he would foreswear his opposition to the union. Martin knew a minister, who knew W. J. Cameron, Ford spokesman. The minister was to prevail on Cameron to educate Ford. The contacts had not been made by December, when the C.I.O. appointed an "advisory committee," which included Lewis and Murray, to function in the Ford campaign.

The internal differences in the U.A.W. were most serious from the point of view of the General Motors difficulties. With the development of a business recession in October, Lewis advised Martin to seek a stop-gap agreement until economic conditions in the automobile industry might make a strike, if one was found necessary, more likely to succeed. Martin, however, joined with the opposition group in rejecting a new contract which had previously been reached with the corporation. A high point of the proposed contract gave the corporation final disciplinary powers over employees felt to be responsible for causing unauthorized strikes. A conference of G.M. unions unanimously rejected the pledge. Demands for improvement on the grievance machinery, as well as for sole recognition, a thirty-five-hour week, and wage increases were substituted. The corporation was urged to give guarantees that its foremen would be disciplined for provoking sit-downs before the union made any pledge to discipline its members. The drop in production postponed a showdown. The business recession and the necessity for closing union ranks also lessened the internal conflict. Martin and most of the "unity group" adopted more conciliatory attitudes, while the Comunist party, much to the bewilderment of its auto union members, began to woo Frankensteen on the supposition that his power was in the ascendency.

Despite the sharp intra-union conflict, the union idea had so gripped the auto workers that there appeared no serious danger of disruption. During September, when the internal differences had already reached a troublesome stage and when the industry was at a low ebb in employment, the U.A.W. membership totaled 375,000, of whom 299,999 were paid up in their dues. The union's troubles appeared to be nothing more than growing-pains aggravated by its ill-wishers on the management side of industry.

XIII

The keystone of the C.I.O.'s strength in the newly organized industries at the close of 1937 was in the 1,047 lodges of the Steel Workers Organizing Committee. To the 140 steel companies under contract when the "Little Steel" strike was called, the committee subsequently added agreements with 294 others. The committee had 510,000 members, almost all of them covered by collective-bargaining agreements, and fully 50,000 of them in "Little Steel." Next to the United Mine Workers, the S.W.O.C. was the largest union in the country. Fifty of the agreements covered 260,000 out of 590,000 workers employed in August in the production of steel or iron as a raw material for further processing; the remainder of the contracts were with companies in metal manufacturing trades, including the fabrication of springs, boilers, stoves, bridges, ranges, tractors, refrigerators, valves, steel railroad cars, and malleable iron fittings. The jurisdiction cut out for itself by the C.I.O.'s industrial steel union included approximately a million workers in 1937. The major strength, inasmuch as it was a key to the entire industry, lay, however, in employees of

[271]

the major steel producing and fabricating companies. Among these, the S.W.O.C. had agreements with all but Republic, Bethlehem, Youngstown, Weirton, and the American Rolling Mill. Its standing and prestige in Inland Steel were secured by that corporation's memorandum given Governor Townsend.

The wage increases won in S.W.O.C. agreements brought an industry-wide raise. The basic rate stood at a minimum of five dollars a day, which meant at least a raise of $1.25 a day for some, and as high as $3.20 for others, over the rates in 1936. The wage for common labor had been brought up to 62½ cents an hour. In April, 1937, the average hourly wage for all steel workers stood at 85 cents and only three manufacturing industries (rubber tires, automobile, and petroleum refining) paid more. The average weekly wage in steel was $36.20—which was $10 above the next highest weekly average in any other industry. The wage bill of the steel industry was 34 per cent greater than in 1929, and at least half of the increase was the result of the campaign and agreements of the S.W.O.C. All steel workers enjoyed a forty-hour week. The 522,000 employed by the members of the American Iron and Steel Institute in August, 1936, had been increased a year later to 590,000, most of the gain necessitated by introduction of the shorter work week. In the field of job security, the S.W.O.C. had established rules whereby disputed discharges were to be adjusted within five days. Final decisions lay not with the management, as before the advent of the C.I.O., but with an impartial arbitrator chosen by both union and management. Vacations with pay had been liberalized, and a system of plant grievance committees—which had surprisingly few complaints to handle—had been set up. None of the S.W.O.C. contracts among the steel-producing companies called for either the check-off or the closed shop. In the miscellaneous trades, there were no more than a handful of closed-shop agreements.

The attitude of steel management toward unionism was undergoing a change, though there was no complete conversion to the idea of collective bargaining. A survey of employer opinion included in a report issued in October by the Industrial Relations Section of Princeton University found that most executives were not unconditionally opposed to collective bargaining with an outside labor organization. In fact, "some executives went so far as to admit that national collective bargaining might be beneficial in stabilizing labor conditions in the iron and steel industry if only it could be carried on with a conservative and responsible labor organization, and if there was some assurance that there would be no closed shop." In general, however, the executives felt that the closed shop would eventually be demanded. Princeton's investigators found only a few employers "pessimistically sounding the warning that the present drive for industrial organization is the first step in the establishment of a Soviet America." In the union camp, unlike the situation in the automobile industry, the leaders of the S.W.O.C. found that the executives of large and influential companies were compelling foremen to live up to the agreements. A few companies had requested permission to have some of their supervisory employees attend an S.W.O.C. training-school for local leaders so that their own plant representatives might better understand the problems and procedures of collective bargaining. Summarizing its own impressions, the Princeton report said that "considering the number of agreements signed and the newness of the union, up to midsummer, 1937, it appeared that the S.W.O.C. record, as far as living up to the contracts was concerned, was very satisfactory."

The problem of maintaining the steel union and building it into an effective and disciplined group, in so far as the economics of the industry permitted, was attacked by the S.W.O.C. as soon as it recovered its breath from the whirlwind campaign it had staged. Study classes and orderly, intelligent lodge meetings were held regularly. An organizers' school, at which vacations might be utilized, was projected. Where interest lagged in union affairs, as was the tendency when issues of wages, hours, and contracts did not press for immediate action, social and recreational activities centering around the union were planned and to an extent carried out. The C.I.O., wisely, did not contemplate at once turning the new organization loose to carry on with its own resources for leadership. The organizing of the steel workers was largely the work of the miners' union and its trained local and national leaders. This relationship, it was planned, would continue until the developing steel leadership was ripe for responsibility. To this plan, the steel workers raised no objection. On questions of wages and hours, they were regularly consulted. Facing expiration of its contracts on February 1, 1938, the S.W.O.C. convened a convention of all its lodges in December, in Pittsburgh, where a new program was drawn up and Philip Murray and the S.W.O.C. given the authority to continue the task of unionizing all of steel.

The full implication of the revolution the S.W.O.C. had wrought was brought home in the Pennsylvania local elections of November, 1937. Riding the crest of the new democracy which the steel union had brought in its wake, twelve steel and near-by coal boroughs and cities elected C.I.O. mayors and burgesses, all of them running on the Democratic ticket. Pittsburgh returned a C.I.O.-supported candidate for mayor. But in the smaller steel cities the victory belonged to the steel union exclusively. John J. Mullen, S.W.O.C. organizer and early rebel against the company union, was installed as Mayor of Clairton, for decades the unquestioned property, politically as well as industrially, of U.S. Steel. Maloy, another of the S.W.O.C. leaders, ousted Mayor James Crawford of Duquesne, who had reigned since 1919, when he had proclaimed that "Jesus Christ himself could not speak in Duquesne for the A.F. of L." William A. Fisher, a C.I.O. glass worker, was reëlected burgess of Brackenridge. The C.I.O. victory in Aliquippa devastated the opposition, composed of Republicans openly beholden to Jones and Laughlin. One city official who had sponsored a vigilante committee, a "justice of the peace" who had terrorized the steel workers for eight years, and a third officeholder, an editor who had called Lewis "that mad dog," were defeated for reëlection. Four years before, there had been only four Democratic voters in all of Aliquippa, and they were "stooges" designated to hold the franchise of Jones and Laughlin's only opposition party. John J. Cavanaugh, the "nervous burgess" of Homestead for sixteen uninterrupted years, was also sent into retirement to ruminate on the breakdown of a system which a year before had seemed as substantial as the Rock of Gibraltar.

The pledge made to the Homestead martyrs of '92 had been fully redeemed.

XIV

To effect the re-drawing of the picture of American labor and to guard, as far as economic conditions permitted, against any serious relapse, the C.I.O. had created a smooth-moving though ramified machinery of organization. Eighty-two Industrial Union Councils, five of them state-wide, others in cities and one in the New York maritime industry, had been set up. The Committee had also established forty-eight regional offices and ten sub-regional headquarters. Each had a director of activities, and under them served 198 field representatives. The latter worked exclusively among the 609 directly affiliated local industrial unions and in the miscellaneous industries not covered by a C.I.O. national or international union. The locals directly affiliated paid a per capita tax of fifty cents a member per month. This was a higher fee than the A.F. of L. exacted, but the returns on the investment in C.I.O. membership were far greater. The C.I.O. paid salaries and maintained offices for 256 full-time regional directors and field organizers. The A.F. of L., in 1936, had fifty paid organizers whose job was to "look after" the federal unions, and in 1937, had 229 paid organizers, a major part of their time devoted to combating the C.I.O. This smaller staff of A.F. of L. field agents ostensibly served the interests of 1,406 directly affiliated locals, while the 256 C.I.O. field men served the 609 locals. In addition to its field lieutenants in the miscellaneous industries, the C.I.O. paid 286 organizers assigned to international and national unions engaged in organizing campaigns. Eighteen worked under direction of the United Electrical, Radio and Machine Workers, twenty-four in the oil fields, twenty under the United Mine Workers among gas, coke, and chemical workers, thirty-five in the maritime trades. The national headquarters of the C.I.O. in Washington moved thrice in two years to ever larger accommodations and had a staff that increased from seven in March, 1937, to fifty by the end of the year. They worked in departments assigned to organizing, finances, charters, publicity and publications, legal problems, and research. These full-time forces by no means exhausted the executive and organizing man-power of the C.I.O. The steel union had 433 additional organizers, the textile union as many. The older C.I.O. unions, as well as those in automobiles, rubber, radio, shoe, and other trades, likewise had their own staff.

Salaries ranged between twenty-five dollars and fifty dollars a week for the organizers. None of the international officials in the new unions received more than $5,000 a year, while Lewis received $12,000, paid by the United Mine Workers. The services of the hectic years of 1936 and 1937 could not, however, be measured in dollars. The field organizers, younger men as a group, stood the test well, physically, but the wear and tear on the older leaders in positions of authority was keenly felt with the accumulation of weeks and months of fifteen- and twenty-hour working-days. The rank and file of the established unions gave funds as well as man-power, where they were needed. From June, 1936, to October 1, 1937, the C.I.O. disbursed a total of $1,745,968.96, $830,000 of it received from the miners. The U.M.W., the Amalgamated and International Ladies' Garment Workers' unions also gave directly to the textile and steel drives. The miners gave $1,404,000 in all to the C.I.O. and its sub-divisions. The rubber and auto unions largely supported themselves from their birth, but also received helpful sums from fellow C.I.O. unions. All internationals paid a per capita tax of 5 cents a month, as compared with the cent-a-month previously paid the A.F. of L.

XV

Summarizing the achievements of its campaigns among the organized workers, the C.I.O. reported to a conference of its unions at Atlantic City in October, that approximately one billion dollars in wage increases had been provided in C.I.O. contracts. The report did not estimate the increases indirectly won for workers whose industries had not yet been penetrated by the C.I.O. The steel contracts, Murray reported, had raised the workers' wages by a total of $250,000,000 a year. The auto union, meanwhile, had brought an increase in the annual income of its members of more than $100,-000,000; the contracts of the Textile Workers' Organizing Committee provided for increases amounting to $1,200,000 a week. The Transport Workers' Union, in its first five months, put roughly $6,000,000 a year additional into the pockets of its members; the United Electrical, Radio and Machine Workers' Union added

$12,000,000 to the earnings of its members. C.I.O. shoe workers enjoyed 15 per cent more in wages than before the inception of their union; maritime workers counted from five dollars to twenty-five dollars additional in their envelopes each month. Members of the American Newspaper Guild garnered increases that totaled $2,000,-000 a year.

Two million members covered by C.I.O. contracts had won shorter working-hours; nearly a million worked thirty-five or thirty-six hours a week. A six-hour day prevailed in the glass industry, and in large sections of rubber-products manufacturing. The establishment of a forty-hour week was virtually universal in all other C.I.O. contracts. Particularly noteworthy were the achievements in oil and textiles. In the former industry the Oil Workers' International Union had reduced the weekly hours of its field workers from a former eighty-four to thirty-six. More than 230,000 workers covered by textile-union contracts worked on a forty-hour basis, where forty-eight had been the rule. The shorter work-week gains were protected by overtime provisions. Time and a half for overtime was won by 1,500,000 of the C.I.O. workers under contract. Seniority rights were established for 1,000,000. An average of four holidays with pay, annually, had been created for 900,000 C.I.O. workers. Machinery for the regulation of the speed of machines had been set up for half a million. Protective clauses for safety and health applied to 900,000. Among the new C.I.O. contracts were clauses applying to 1,250,000 workers which militated against job insecurity, summary dismissals, discriminations, and other forms of managerial abuses. A number of contracts barred the use of spies and strike-breakers. An agreement between the transport union and the Parmelee Taxi Company, in New York, forbade the carrying of strike-breakers in its cabs. All of the textile contracts prohibited child labor. Vacations with pay, formerly enjoyed by white-collar workers and executives, were brought to a million industrial workers by the agreements. Fifty thousand textile workers, 70,000 in rubber, 65,000 in petroleum, 36,000 in the urban transportation industry won at least one week off a year, not through discharge or lay-offs, but with full pay. Contracts of the Transport Workers' Union called for two weeks' vacation with pay in 1938.

[277]

Assurance of the permanency of the C.I.O. was seen chiefly in the fact that all these gains were provided for in signed agreements. The new C.I.O. unions, in October, reported contracts with 30,000 companies employing 3,200,000 workers, most of them members of the C.I.O., but all, whether members or not, sharing the benefits alike. C.I.O. unions were recognized as sole bargaining agencies in contracts covering 2,100,000 workers; more than 1,500,000 others worked under closed-shop agreements.

The membership of the C.I.O., announced in September as 3,718,000, was, of course, not based on annual dues payments. The larger part of it had not formally joined the unions until after January. True to its design to act as an organizing force and scorning the necessity of balancing its budget in its early stages, the Committee did not start the collection of per capita dues until May and June. The dues-paying membership of the new labor movement could not, therefore, be computed over any significant period of time. The payment of dues by 299,000 of the 375,000 automobile unionists in September was, however, fairly typical of the other newly organized unions, and possibly a little poorer than their record, considering that the automobile industry was in a slack, lay-off period at the time. The older unions, the miners with their 620,000 members, the ladies' garment workers with their 252,000, and the men's clothing workers with their 200,000, paid full per capita of five cents a member per month.

Reports of C.I.O. affiliates in December, 1937, placed their total membership at 3,735,350. The A.F. of L. reported, on November 19th, that its affiliates had a membership of 3,441,340. Including the 518,397 members of bona fide independent unions, the total union membership in the United States stood at 7,695,087, the highest point in the history of the nation.

LEWIS AND THE PROGRAM OF THE C.I.O.

I

IT MIGHT have been expected that the speed and force with which the Committee for Industrial Organization burst upon American life would bring down upon it much misunderstanding. It need not have been so, for the twentieth-century vehicles for disseminating popular information should have made light possible. The Committee was not, however, an innocuous force. Though it intended no destruction of the capitalist order, it made demands on men and corporations which were loath to grant them. The press in the United States had long since, despite elaborate pretense, ceased to become a matter of public service. Daily newspapers must of their very nature be great financial undertakings; and like financial and industrial organizations which made no bones about it, the press and its owners were out to bring returns on investments, to make money. Inevitably, therefore, the business of publishing newspapers was physically and psychologically a part of big business. What appeared to menace General Motors or U.S. Steel or the Goodyear company was a menace also to the publishers of the nation. The C.I.O., cautiously welcomed in its earlier stages when it attacked the palpably outdated A.F. of L., soon became a common menace to the press and business.

John L. Lewis became the particular bogey. Here again the public prints mirrored the resentment of coupon-clippers and those on the ownership side of industry. He became the instigator of "minority strikes," a would-be dictator, an egoist with a ruthless will to power, a consorter with Communists, and a candidate for the White House. Most critics credited him with ability and acumen, yet fostered the idea that he was seeking his way to the Presidency by allying himself with the Communist party—which in the last national election polled 80,096 votes. Succeeding generations were able to get a perspective on the Knights of Labor, and today it is shorn of the horns and terror linked with it during its day. It ought to be possible, even at this early stage of its history, to get a reasoned view of the C.I.O. and its leader. Unlike the Knights of Labor, the C.I.O. does not appear to be a one-day sensation. It will be with us for some years to come. Its policies may undergo some changes, but a good starting-point for understanding and evaluating these changes, if they do take place, would be in knowing why and how it came to be, and what it proposes. The why and the how have been indicated.

II

While none but hysterical critics have attempted to label Lewis a Communist, there has been a more concerted effort to foster the impression that Communists exert some influence within the C.I.O. Excepting the few cases where Communist tactics have raised internal union problems, this line has been taken in the first place by die-hard employers and their apologists, like George F. Sokolsky; by Green and Frey, who were glad to have the A.F. of L. accept per capita fees from unionists they later denounced as Communists; and by members of the hot stove league of labor analyists and amateur strategists. This latter group finds it difficult to think of the labor movement except in terms of theoretical doctrines—Stalinist, Lovestoneist, Trotskyist, etc. Communists shape their labor union policies from a party line dictated by the needs of Soviet Russia in the field of international relations and from a belief in the infallibility of Stalin. Some anti-Communists formulate their trade union views on the basis of a belief in the innocence of Leon Trotsky. Attitudes born from such approaches are equally unhealthy.

Aside from the fact that shouting "Communist" tends to magnify the prestige of the Communists, which does not dismay them in the least, such procedure gives fuel to all enemies of the C.I.O. And it makes extremely difficult a square facing of the influence of the

Communists in unions where such influence exists. Although Communists are not an important factor in the labor movement of the United States, they do present problems in several unions. They place political considerations above the needs of the unions. Their current conversion to democracy is more professed than real. They have been unpredictable, zigzagging with the seasons, almost. In union, as well as in domestic political, and international outlook, they have become chameleon in character. Those unionists who listened to them in the last decade were told, in rapid succession, first, that dual unionism, then boring from within, then dual unionism and finally "popular frontism" was the correct attitude for class-conscious and progressive workers. In New York, within twenty-four months, they denounced certain racketeers within a group of A.F. of L. restaurant unions, then, denouncing District Attorney Thomas E. Dewey for prosecuting them, formed a united front with the racketeers. When Dewey succeeded in jailing the racketeers, the Communists re-emerged as their critics, took over their jobs and ended up with both feet on the Dewey bandwagon. The inception of the C.I.O. found the Communists sworn to a new policy of boring from within the A.F. of L. To this they gave a new twist, flattery of the conservatives instead of bitter criticism. They looked askance at Lewis and did not attempt to hitch their wagons to the C.I.O. star until the spring of 1937. They were then willing to pay any political price to be permitted to hang around in ever so unimportant capacities. In some unions they did notably good organizing jobs. In others, their accomplishments were mostly in the columns of *The Daily Worker*. Their willingness to forget their Communism and their practice of denying Communist affiliations brought good and evil to the labor movement. Over given periods they were indistinguishable from other progressive unionists, often cooperating in non-political fashion. On the other hand, no unionist who worked by the side of a Communist could be safe in the assumption that he was dealing with a free agent on union policies and not one who was subject to the manipulation of a party board of strategy.

The leaders of the C.I.O. felt that the way to combat Communism was not to indulge in red-baiting in the unions but to face each situation on its merits. On the whole, however, Lewis and the C.I.O. leaders were in agreement that the possibility of Communist domination of the labor movement was to be combated. However, there did not appear to be the slightest possibility of such domination. "Communist influence in the C.I.O." is a figment of imagination. Lewis' opposition to Communism is well known. The large C.I.O. unions—miners, steel workers, rubber and needle trades workers—have no trace of Communist influence in their ranks. In the auto union, the Communists are an active faction, but their party is so opportunistic and self-effacing, politically, that the final stage of the internal conflict of 1937 found it wooing the good will of the conservative Frankensteen. In the few unions where Communists held positions of influence they were checkmated by memberships which are by no stretch of the imagination Communist. Not one of these officers could hold his job if he were to ask for a vote of confidence in Communism. There is no such thing as a "red" or a "Communist union," any more than Hutcheson's Republicanism makes the Brotherhood of Carpenters a "Republican union," or Joseph P. Ryan's affinity with Tammany makes his longshoreman's organization a "Democratic union." American Communism, in or out of the labor movement, is most frequently a red herring used by political or economic demagogues; it is a Halloween goblin fit to raise the blood pressure of the men in the chairs at the Union League Club; it is a phenomenon to engross some of the intellectuals and literati; in a few minor instances it is a force to be reckoned with. As a major aspect of American political or labor life, it does not exist.

III

Lewis is neither the bull in the china shop his critics and enemies picture him to be, nor the meek labor leader they would like to see. Not that the anti-C.I.O. forces gave William Green any warmer reception than they would accord to Lewis. Essentially they are opposed to labor unions, and their yearning and preference for the supposed greater "reasonableness and responsibility" of the A.F. of L. was not apparent when that organization was alone in the field. The drive for leadership and power dominates American business and politics as well as the labor movement. The power Lewis allegedly wields over his followers is puny compared, say, with the authority of a big business man in his own establishment; or the power one of these does not hesitate to use when he is in a position to deal with competitors. For a Ford, a Weir or a Girdler to denounce Lewis as a despot is so ridiculous it needs only to be stated to reveal it.

The desire for influence in American life need not be dismissed as vicious. The test should be, power and influence for what? By his answer to this question, Lewis has marked himself apart from those who measure their power by wealth and the influence it brings with it. Lewis' area of influence, before 1933, was in the miners' union. During this period he might often have gone over to the side of management. His toughest mine-union critic and opponent, Frank Farrington, had done so. Lewis' ability might have enabled him to cross over to the other side, not by "selling out," but merely by exchanging his knowledge of mining and coal economics for a handsome salary. If it were political recognition he sought, he might have accepted the flattery of a post as Secretary of Labor from Harding, Coolidge, or Hoover. He stayed with the miners, and when some of them showed signs of wishing to part company with him, he stuck harder and refused to be pried loose. Labor leadership was his career. Ever through the later years of broader influence, when he "made a noise like the whole labor movement," and virtually became just that, this rôle dominated his thoughts and activities. He was the New Deal's labor advocate from 1933 to 1935; he was its welcome financial aide and public supporter in the campaign of 1936, but always because the interests of the workers appeared to him to coincide with the interests of the New Deal. In the campaign of 'thirty-six, Lewis again distinguished himself from the type of labor leadership the nation had known in other years. While Tobin and Hutcheson, as chairmen of the Democratic and Republican "labor committees," received substantial funds to dispense in behalf of their political loyalties, Lewis gave money. With the former, the object was to place men on a payroll and perhaps, with victory, win a place in the Cabinet. Lewis preferred to persuade the miners to donate money and reap the benefits in prestige and influ-

[283]

ence for all organized labor. Nor was the miners' contribution to the Roosevelt campaign fund the outrageous precedent which anti-labor editors professed to see. An organization of 525,000 members gave $469,668, less than a dollar apiece—certainly a modest contribution when compared with Alfred P. Sloan's gift of $5,000 and five Du Ponts' donation of $22,000 to the Republican party in Maine alone. Were it not that any stick was sought with which to beat the C.I.O., the miners' contribution, enthusiastically authorized by a national convention, might have been hailed as evidence of a devoted citizenship.

Lewis' objective was influence for labor, and when political opportunism in the summer of 1937 appeared to dictate to the President the need to dissociate himself from his militant labor allies, the C.I.O. chairman did not hesitate to voice his disappointment. After all, the "economic royalists" *had* turned their fire on the steel and auto strikers; they *were* pursuing a course which Roosevelt had denounced in 1936. The "plague on both your houses" which the President pronounced on C.I.O. and "Little Steel" in June was no more just than it was a way out of the difficulties. In a White House "spokesman's" modification of this sweeping condemnation, there appeared to be a softening of the rebuke. The "spokesman" explained that by "both houses" the President referred on the one hand to those who would not negotiate with organized labor, and on the other to those who practiced violence. The amended rebuke still condemned the tactics of "Little Steel," but limited its application to certain elements in the C.I.O. It was nevertheless as unfair as the original outburst. The fact is that those who would not negotiate and those responsible for the large scale violence were one and the same house, "Little Steel," its Girdler-led executives and the coöperative local authorities. The ringing of steel mills by pickets, their interference with mail provocatively filled with supplies for strike-breakers, and the aborted march of Akron rubber workers on Youngstown, paled into insignificance compared with this large-scale violence and the sacrifice of life and civil liberties.

Some among the C.I.O. leaders felt that caution would be the better part of truth in handling the President's letting down of the

"Little Steel" strikers. They felt that the C.I.O.'s strongest stock in trade was to continue the appearance of an association with the President. Lewis appreciated the value of that association in the minds of labor, but he understood, as he had when he demanded administration support during the General Motors strike, that real coöperation from the White House, if it was to be had at all, was not to be obtained by fawning. He went on the radio and denounced "those who supped at labor's table" and then assumed an air of fine impartiality when labor was under attack. The C.I.O. tie with the White House seemed to be broken. But an invitation to visit the White House, extended to Lewis before he made his address, was repeated after he had delivered it, and after the nation understood that Lewis had the President in mind during his radio address. The sequence of the White House invitation and the scheduled address presented Lewis with a problem. He had prepared the talk, including his thrust at the President, when the first invitation arrived. The White House appointment, because of other matters, had to be postponed for a few weeks. In the meantime, Lewis had the problem of whether to stick to his original intentions or, in view of the call from the President, eliminate the barbed paragraph. He decided against revising the address; the invitation was nevertheless repeated.

Lewis has no adviser favored over others; he has no personal publicity man, despite the urging of Heywood Broun and others who feared the result of the drum fire of criticism which sounded during the "Little Steel" strike. Yet, he is no one-man machine, self-satisfied or, even in his own mind, self-sufficient. In Murray, Kennedy, Van Bittner, Brophy, and a half-dozen others, the miners' union has given Lewis and the American labor movement the ablest group of union leaders. Murray, beyond a doubt, is the Number 2 man in the C.I.O., the successor to Lewis should fortune or events dictate the need for a new leader. His acute appreciation of the American psychology, his understanding of modern techniques in public affairs, and his selfless devotion to labor's cause, are a tower of strength on which Lewis has frequently leaned. The leader of the C.I.O. has surrounded himself with others who share his prob-

[285]

lems and contribute to his strength: W. Jett Lauck, the perspicacious economist; Henry Warrum, chief counsel to the U.M.W., and Lee Pressman, Harvard-trained lawyer not too steeped in the law of precedent to render himself useless to a movement which dares new methods and new concepts of law and social justice. Lewis counsels with all of these, and with others—Hillman and Dubinsky; Len de Caux and young James Carey; ebullient Joseph Curran and cautious Adolph Germer. Hours after the sun has set and marked the end of a working-day for the rest of Washington, the lights burn in Lewis' oak-paneled office at the United Mine Workers office. During the crises of the General Motors strike, of the U.S. Steel negotiations, of the battle in "Little Steel," he kept telephone wires open nightly, determined that no important detail should escape his attention.

Lewis was the nation's best news copy during 1936 and 1937, and his callers in Washington included journalists and students the world over. When the strain of a strike or a crucial conference did not prevail, he was usually available to his known detractors as well as to friendly writers. The effect of interviews on men in the former group was amusing. After Westbrook Pegler had devoted many columns to lambasting the chairman of the C.I.O., he decided to make a trip to Washington to find out what he really was up to. The effect seemed to be something of a conversion, though not a lasting one. Pegler felt impressed with Lewis' arguments at the time of his interview; later, he recalled that he should not have been "taken in." Preconceived judgments ran up against reality; a struggle ensued, and the prejudices prevailed. Toward the end of his months of radio diatribes against Lewis, Boake Carter adopted a suggestion, which had not occurred to him before, to call on the C.I.O. leader. The meeting was the work of the ingenious young Carey, who had hinted at the harm Carter might be doing the business of his radio sponsor, the Philco company. Carter left the United Mine Workers office to indite a column of praise for the man he had denounced as a menace.

The major part of his education, Lewis gained in meeting the daily problems of the labor movement. A New York editor, once a

[286]

reporter at the State House in Springfield, Illinois, recalls the answer to a question he had asked about young Lewis. It was back in 1910 or so, when the leader of the C.I.O. was the Illinois mine workers' legislative agent. Among the dignitaries at the capital, Lewis did not appear to be impressive. Yet he was always at the heels of legislators.

"Who is that man?" the reporter inquired.

"Oh, that's just John Lewis," was the reply. "He's always bothering his head about statistics and the miners' union."

Organizing for the A.F. of L. in steel, in rubber, in the glass, copper, and lumber industries made Lewis a diversified labor citizen. He met the American workers, though, in the mines for years himself, he had already laid a fundamental basis for his understanding of them. In the political atmosphere of labor lobbying, he sized up the genus politician, and came to know what ambitions and pressures made them work, and where their limits lay. He came to understand that few were or cared to be their own masters, and then was born the feeling, rather than in any later academic contemplations, that labor pressures, too, might with result be exerted on the seeker and holder of public office. Lewis' education in economics came with his accession to the job of president of the United Mine Workers, in the year-in-and-year-out almost hopeless task of making a "sick" industry, milked by the anthracite combine or by fly-by-night adventurers in soft coal, pay some measure of security to the coal-diggers. The miners were his first associates, and in his mature life he turned to them. In the uncompromising battle for labor's influence, and in defeat, he had in him the dogged independence of the miner whose every trip to the mines to earn his daily bread, may be an encounter with death. In the radio address which opened the steel campaign—"the battle for democracy which now impends in America"—Lewis called his miners "the household troops" of labor's forces. In this tribute to his coal-diggers, he also gave himself the fortitude for the momentous struggle which ensued.

In recent years, Lewis' reading has been exclusively concerned with the problems of the labor movement and in keeping track of "public opinion" as it is mirrored in the representative newspapers and magazines. Relaxation to him seldom meant the theater or the movies, but rather catching up on that type of reading. But in the years before his preoccupation with the New Deal and the C.I.O., Lewis' reading ran to history and the rich phrases of the classics. During the 1919 coal strike he read Homer's Iliad; during the dog-days of 1931, he distracted himself from the state of the nation by re-reading *The Decline and Fall of the Roman Empire*. His many quotations disclose his acquaintanceship with Shakespeare. His language, when the gaze of an audience is upon him—though he frequently holds large groups fixed and attentive by studied, impressive silence—is thus a mixture of graphic miners' talk and classical quotations. Bidding a frightened young unionist good luck as he made off to appear before the A.F. of L.'s august executive council, Lewis reminded him, "I'll be holding the light for you." In his youth at the mines he had many times held the light while his buddy hacked away at rock-encrusted seams of coal. A luckless opponent once heard himself characterized by Lewis as "a little slower in the head and fatter in the legs than he was." Now and then a bit pompous, he has of recent years overcome this tendency. Years ago, he told a miners' convention, "I come, I will always come, I will come on horseback even, if the miners of Illinois need me." To another gathering of miners he announced that he came with his "pit boots on" to put an end to their adversaries' disruptive tactics. Delightful sarcasm, if one is not the target, characterizes other moods. When he heard that his ancient enemy, Farrington, had been thrown out of a meeting of miners who had themselves been expelled by the U.M.W., he exclaimed: "My idea of going to hell in a trade union way is to be thrown out of a scab convention." When the A.F. of L. at Denver accused the C.I.O. of undeserved self-praise, Lewis observed, "He who tooteth not his own horn, the same shall not be tooted." Best of all, however, Lewis loves to fit classical quotations to modern events. Green, when he denounced the auto strikers, had bent "the pregnant hinges of the knees that thrift might follow fawning." When during the heat of the auto strike, Lewis set out from Washington for Detroit, he urged that "there be no moaning at the bar when I put out to sea."

The instinct for dramatization which Lewis exercises is not born of his own desires to project himself into a picture. More than a dramatic instinct, itself no mean asset for a public figure, his is an instinct for timing. A move to place Green on trial before the miners' union was not the result of a desire to lord it over Green— whom he does resent with what seems to be needless personal fervor —but rather an effort to crystallize the wide, latent resentment against the Federation president. If it had been self-dramatization he sought, Lewis would have followed through and seen to it that the trial was held. His sense of timing dictated the break with the A.F. of L. when it did come, and it has dominated his feelings on the subject of peace with the Federation. He understands the psychology of making himself inaccessible, thus making himself more effective, for public assemblages and gatherings. He realized that four or five wisely placed national radio addresses in a year are more effective than a weekly pouring forth of sentiments on a public not yet wholly concerned with his cause. During the "Little Steel" strike, his advisers pleaded with him to go on the radio and reply to the torrent of abuse. He realized, however, that a talk by him in the unreasoning atmosphere of that period would merely give his enemies further fuel, no matter how convincing his case might be.

The belief persists that Lewis' prime interest is to propel himself into the White House in 1940. To be President is an ambition which, supposedly, every American may legitimately hold. Yet in Lewis' case, those who say he wishes to be President also see something diabolical in the idea. The possibility of Lewis entering the lists in 1940 is a slim one indeed. Lewis would not be a candidate because it is not in the cards for him to be a labor President. Even before President Roosevelt turned away from the "Litle Steel" strikers, Lewis knew that public office—the Presidency in particular—cannot at this stage of American affairs be the unconditioned property of labor. Lewis is the chief spokesman of labor; in the White House he could no longer be that. While a labor President, backed by a majority in Congress could make great contributions toward winning security for labor's millions, a President dependent on the support of other strata of the population would have to heed various pressures. To be the leader of an aggressive, growing labor movement makes Lewis far more serviceable to the working-people than to be a captive in the White House.

[289]

Lewis does not, however, belittle the value of political strength for the C.I.O. and the labor movement. His contributions to the Roosevelt campaign, his fostering of Labor's Non-Partisan League and his steady accumulation of political influence in states like Pennsylvania, West Virginia, Ohio, Colorado, and Iowa, show his awareness of labor's need for political power. Though he does not picture himself as a candidate for the Presidency, he is acutely interested in the 1940 contest. Anxious for more and immediate gains for labor, he would like to see a President elected by a partnership of labor, the middle class, liberals, and the farmers. He is thus interested in the possible formation of a bloc which can control the Democratic party; or failing that, a new liberal or progressive party rather than a labor party. His own candidacy for the Presidency, if it comes about in 1940, would be with Lewis a second choice. He would rather back a progressive on whom labor can count, than take the field against conservatives nominated by the two old parties. The latter course would be pioneering without the prospects of immediate result. Lewis does not object to pioneering, but he does not see labor's pressing problems permitting a long span of spade work and defeats as a preliminary to labor rule in the distant future. Unlike the A.F. of L. leaders, who look upon the possibility of independent political action by labor as akin to Communism, Lewis does not bar the possible formation of a new party in which labor will dominate or be an important partner.

IV

The social and economic views of John L. Lewis, which may be certain to dominate the program of the C.I.O. for years to come, cannot by any stretch of the imagination place him in the company of radicals. These views have undergone a change since 1925, when he published his only book, *The Miners' Fight for American Standards,* but they still mark him as a believer in capitalism, of private profit and the wage system. When the "free play of economic law" which he defended in his book produced disaster in the coal industry and brought on the collapse of 1929, Lewis abandoned this *laissez faire* view in favor of some restraints. Still, he proposed no radical modification of capitalism, but rather an arrangement where capi-

[290]

talism might have more stability. The proposed Davis-Kelly Act, the Guffey Coal acts, and the NRA, which Lewis and his advisors helped draft, were based on a community of interest between capital and labor, and negated completely the class-struggle theory. But to modify the "free play of economic forces," Lewis proposed that labor, as a "co-partner" in industry, and the government as umpire and representative of the best interests of all, be given a voice. Psychologically, as well as economically, he rebelled against acceptance of the belief that labor's interests might lie apart from the owners of industry.

"I'm not interested in classes," he told an interviewer in 1935. "One man's as good as another in this country, and far be it from me to foster inferiority complexes among the workers by trying to make them think they belong to some special rigid class. That has happened in Europe, but it hasn't happened here yet. Of course, it's true that there is no longer equality of opportunity in this country, and it is conceivable that if this state of affairs is allowed to continue there will not only be 'class consciousness,' but revolution as well. But it can be avoided. The employers aren't doing much to avoid it. But the United Mine Workers are doing everything in their power to make the system work and thereby avoid it. We'll see. . . ."

While waiting to "see," Lewis, in another interview, defined the general aim of the new labor movement:

"For the immediate future we want a larger share in the increased income of industry and a more equal distribution of that income. This is a marvelous age in which we live. Science is perfecting machines and formulae which at once make for economy of production and a decrease in the number of jobs. The result is a development of a tremendous producing machine for which there will be no outlet unless there is a corresponding increase in consumer capacity. We must give more widespread employment, increased wages, create more leisure, if we are to compensate for the producing power of the improved machinery."

If Lewis ever believed that organization of labor alone would win the creation of more employment and a lasting increase of labor's share of the wealth of industry, the closing months of 1937 dissuaded him from such a view. Even while the C.I.O. was putting hundreds of additional dollars annually in the pay envelopes of millions of workers, part of that increase was being nullified by the rising prices for the necessities of life. Toward the end of the year, unemployment started to mount again. Neither complete security of work nor adequacy of income had been obtained, although labor's position was immeasurably stronger than it had been before the C.I.O. appeared. The constant menace to the gains of the C.I.O. absorbed Lewis' attention, but still he did not put forth any program for basic organization of the economic processes. He still held the faith that capitalism could yet be made workable. But there was also a visible growth of impatience.

"The modernization of industrial plants, the adoption of new formulae, the utilization of new energy displacing human needs," he said in October, 1937, "is proceeding to a degree that the nation will not realize the full impact of that change until sometime next year, and as a result we already have a slowing down of industry. . . . In most industries that have increased their dividends, those who have reduced their bonded indebtedness, and those who have paid off their preferred dividends on their preferred stocks have taken their money from the accelerated operation of their industries and divided it among the stockholders and creditors.

"Now there is not a dollar available for those men in those plants and those mills who have been turned out by their employers and who must live or die as they will without any help from corporate industry or from the government, because be it known that the government relief situation is now at a point where it is impossible for a man who has been thrown on the idleness rolls to get public assistance or public relief.

"One of the great principles for which labor in America must stand in the future is the right of every man and woman to have a job, to earn their living if they are willing to work. A citizen of the United States has a right to live. He has a right to work. We have heard much about the right to work. Well, let our people work. They have a right to a job. If the corporations which control American industry fail to provide them with that job, then there must be some power somewhere in this land of ours that will go over and above and beyond those corporations, with all their influence and power, and provide a job and insure the right to live for that American."

In other sections of his address to the Atlantic City conference of the C.I.O. in October, Lewis denounced the demand for lowering of taxation on the rich; he advocated a greater appropriation of wealth to aid the jobless and to furnish them with work. He revealed his cognizance of the integrated aspects of the problem when he eloquently pleaded the case of the sharecroppers, both for their own right to live and work, and for their rehabilitation as a great consuming bloc for the industries of the nation. But he did not indicate the "power somewhere in this land of ours that will . . . provide a job and secure the right to live for that American." Nor did he indicate what the program of that power would be. The gap in Lewis' program need not, however, be interpreted as either his failure to answer his question or his hesitancy to espouse it. Pragmatist that he is, Lewis' program for the future will depend to a great extent on how far he is forced to go to win security for labor. His economic development since the appearance of his book and his challenge of the deep-rooted policies of the A.F. of L., showed his to be no static mind. They revealed also, however, his characteristic absorption with immediate next steps and his hesitancies, as he phrased it, "to indulge in philosophical cogitations or academic meanderings about the philosophy (of the C.I.O.) or the academic benefits that might come to posterity through the work that you (of the C.I.O.) are doing in this pressing day and year."

Labor, in the period of its second great upheaval, did not demand an economic program nor a blueprint for social reorganization. American labor was neither class-conscious nor radical. Except to a limited extent, American labor did not even exist as an organized force. It had yet to learn first steps in unionism. Lewis became their teacher, their strategist and their commander in battle. His program answered their elemental desire to organize unified labor organizations and seek collectively the security which they could never attain singly. Economic and social conditions were ripe for the great upheaval of 1936 and 1937, the forces of labor were ready to inaugurate their spectacular march, but they might never have proceeded in orderly ranks, if at all, were it not for the devoted, skillful and determined leadership of Lewis.

To Lewis' program of industrial unionism, dictated by the simple requirements of the situation, he brought a crusading fervor. The warm, eloquent phrases of this glowering giant from the coal mines were wine and stimulant to the hopes of a leaderless mass. His name became a watchword. Men, yet under the surveillance of spies, wrote his name on girders and walls of factories and inscribed it defiantly on company union ballots. The Flint sit-down strikers' paper wrote with confidence, "John L. Lewis is coming to Detroit to see to it that the auto workers are not deprived of their civil rights." A worker sent a Detroit daily a sarcastic letter: "Boy, do I hate this man Lewis. We used to get sixty cents an hour. . . . My raise amounted to eighty cents a day, or sixteen dollars a month, and out of that I pay one dollar a month in dues. Do I hate this man John L. Lewis!" In 1936, pictures of Lewis and Roosevelt hung side by side in a million union halls and workers' homes. In 1937, the photographs of Lewis alone remained. Wherever he went, at public meetings and in the streets of cities, men and women fought to clasp his hand, to touch his coat. In the annals of labor leadership in the United States, Lewis' name came to stand by those of Debs and Gompers; Debs, the tribune of the people, defeated and a failure in his time only by the great measure of his idealism; Gompers, the organizer, narrow and unscrupulous, yet persistent in his service to the upper strata of labor. Lewis in the years of the second great upheaval combined Debs' eloquence and idealism, though not his economic and political radicalism, and Gompers' organizing genius. The miners' leader created a greater movement than either, and at the close of the first stage of his movement he towered high as the most able and influential leader American labor had yet produced.

V

While the C.I.O. proposed no departure in economic principles, it did not lack an immediate program. The conference of more than 300 leaders of Committee affiliates which met at Atlantic City in October adopted a series of resolutions which for the first time gave a rounded picture of the social objectives of the movement. Three themes stood out: security of employment, adequacy of income, and the maintenance of civil liberties and democratic rights.

The "right to a job" was iterated with a significance which the back-to-work movements had not intended. To effect and maintain this right, national and state legislative programs were set forth. At the top of the list stood a demand for federal legislation for the licensing of all business enterprises engaged in interstate commerce. Each company or corporation, to retain its license, would have to comply with a code securing the rights and privileges accorded labor by the Wagner Act and other labor laws of the nation. Federal wage-and-hour legislation was urged, with the stipulation that minimum pay rates and maximum working-hours were to be scaled so as to absorb all unemployed and afford all workers a "decent standard of living." For workers awaiting reëmployment, the federal government was to continue the Works Progress Administration and the Public Works Administration with increased funds which would leave no worker in economic need. For the unemployed youth, both work and opportunities for education were urged. Turning to the Federal Social Security legislation, salient amendments were proposed. The old-age pension system was to be extended to provide benefits for workers permanently disabled, as well as for needy widows and orphans, regardless of the age of the deceased. Benefits, it was urged, should start in 1939 instead of 1942, and the monthly benefits payable during the earlier years should be liberalized. The conference proposed rewriting of the unemployment insurance sections to make the act apply to workers unemployed for any legitimate reason, which would include strikes or lockouts. A health-insurance program to provide adequate cash and medical benefits should be added, the resolution demanded. The entire unemployment-insurance program, the C.I.O. unions urged, should be extended to include domestic servants, agricultural and maritime workers within its scope.

A program to be pressed by the C.I.O. in state legislatures included bills for state labor relations boards patterned after the Wagner Act in the nation; limiting the authority of the courts to issue injunctions in labor disputes; prohibiting the eviction of unemployed persons or strikers; prohibiting local laws which abridge civil rights; limiting and regulating appointments of deputy sheriffs and prohibiting payment by private corporations for deputy sheriffs; limiting and regulating activities of private detectives, private police, and private guards; incorporating collective-bargaining provisions in contracts between the state and private employers of labor; and, finally, a bill safeguarding the payment of wages as prior claims on employers. To stimulate employment in the building trades and indirectly in other industries, the conference urged the immediate appointment of state housing authorities under the federal Wagner-Steagall Housing Act.

To offset the criticism of employers of the alleged irresponsibility of the C.I.O., the conference unanimously expressed "its firm policy as being one committed to the determined adherence of its contract obligations and responsibilities." Employers who sign with C.I.O. unions, it was pledged, "will receive the complete coöperation and support of the unions affiliated with the C.I.O. in carrying through the full administration of such collective bargaining and wage agreements." A resolution addressed to a farm program "recognized the community of economic interest between the industrial workers and the farmers." Efforts to create antagonism between farm and city workers were denounced, and it was declared that "farmers and farm workers are entitled to their fair share in the national income; and legislation seeking stabilization of farm prices at not less than cost or production will have the hearty support of the C.I.O."

The C.I.O.'s preoccupation with democracy and civil liberties was indicated in a score of resolutions touching on international as well as domestic issues. The encroachments of Fascist nations on democratic countries was denounced, and C.I.O. members were urged to join a boycott of Japanese manufactures. The growth of vigilante movements, interference of public officials to nullify labor rights to assemble, organize, and strike, were declared a menace to all democratic institutions, as well as to the rights of labor. Federal anti-lynching legislation was endorsed. Governors were urged to refuse to permit the use of the National Guard as strike-breaking agencies. The American Newspaper Publishers 'Association was attacked for raising the issue of "freedom of the press" as a smoke screen to fight unionization of their employees, and the C.I.O.'s unions were called upon "to foster and support a free press by every honorable means at their disposal." Congress was urged to investigate alleged undemocratic control of radio facilities by the Federal Communications Commission "and the lobby maintained by the communications companies." The conduct of the Chicago police in the Memorial Day massacre was attacked, the La Follette Committee urged to continue its probing of private espionage systems, and all unions exhorted to wage a ceaseless fight to win freedom for Tom Mooney and Warren K. Billings.

VI

Professor Norman H. Ware wrote in his introduction to his study of the Knights of Labor:

"They [the Knights] had one major idea or sentiment—the idea of solidarity. There was no expression that so caught the popular imagination of the time as the motto of the Order, 'An injury to one is the concern of all.' It is not a new idea, but one that is never old. It was a shibboleth, a catchword, but it is in such terms that men think, and if. men must think in such terms, this one was better than most. The idea, of course, was not enough. Some way had to be found to work it out. The Knights tried one way and failed, but it is pertinent to ask, who has found another way and succeeded? . . . The Order tried to teach the American wage-earner that he was a wage-earner first and a bricklayer, carpenter, miner, shoemaker after. . . . This meant that the Order was teaching something that was not so in the hope that sometime it would be. It failed, and its failure was perhaps a part of the general failure of democracy— or is it humanity?"

The C.I.O. represents the newest, and the greatest, effort of American labor to teach and practice the lessons of solidarity. It is not loaded down with the Knights' excess baggage and lack of direction. Since the half a century when the Knights rose to influence and, almost immediately after, to decline, the tendencies they foresaw have become large realities. The growth of machine production and the erasing of demarcations of skill and craft have given

[297]

millions of mass-production workers one hopeful thing in common—the necessity and possibility of solidarity.

The groping of the unskilled and semi-skilled workers need not be a movement apart. The C.I.O. harbored no ill-will toward the craftsmen; on the contrary, the millions of new unionists asked only for assistance so that in their new-found strength they might take their place beside the remaining craft unions in a unified labor front. They proposed that all should share the benefits of a wider labor movement.

Coupled with its challenge to craft divisions, the C.I.O. also espoused a new concept of government's responsibility toward labor. It did not accept the primitive "voluntarism" of the A.F. of L., which held that although government might serve industrial ownership in a hundred and one ways, labor must stand in proud, if ragged, aloofness. The "voluntarism" of the Federation had received several jolts, even within its own ranks since 1933, but there were indications of a reaction back to the purity of Samuel Gompers' day. Lewis and the C.I.O., on the other hand, not only saw government as a legitimate instrument for labor's emancipation from poverty and unemployment; they envisaged the possibility of labor, together with liberal and progressive fellow travelers, taking a hand in government.

The significance of the new labor movement has not been lost on those on the other side of the fence. William S. Knudsen, truly representative of business and industrial ownership, indicated this when he told a meeting of New England industrialists in October, 1937: "Men will band together on the basis of craft, and with some sense, the idea being hundreds of years old. . . . But to say that a toolmaker or a first-class grinder should concern himself with the plight of his union brother who is pushing a truck is taking a pretty general viewpoint. This is one of the dangers of the industrial union as far as strikes are concerned. A strike binds everybody in a shop to take up the dispute of somebody they are not at all interested in. . . ."

The advantages of a labor movement divided into self-centered segments were obvious, from the point of view of the employing class. As against the view expressed by Knudsen, the C.I.O. had again posed the slogan of solidarity. Millions of workers joined the C.I.O. with a pledge:

"I do sincerely promise, of my own free will, to bear true allegiance to, and keep inviolate, the principles of the Committee for Industrial Organization; never to discriminate against a fellow worker on account of creed, color, or nationality; to defend freedom of thought, whether expressed by tongue or pen; to defend on all occasions and to the extent of my ability the members of our organization. . . . That I will not accept a brother's job who is idle for advancing the interests of the union or seeking better remuneration for his labor; and as only by standing together can workers improve their lot, I promise to cease work at any time I am called upon by the organization to do so. And I further promise to help and assist all brothers in adversity, and to have all eligible workers join the Union that we may all be able to enjoy the fruits of our labor; and that I will never knowingly wrong a brother or see him wronged, if I can prevent it."

SOURCES

GENERAL

American Federation of Labor. Convention Proceedings, A.F. of L. Washington, D. C.
American Federation of Labor Weekly News Service. A.F. of L.
Federated Press. Daily news sheets. New York.
National Labor Board. Decisions. Washington, 1935.
National Labor Relations Board. Decisions (mimeographed). Washington, 1935, 1936, 1937.
New York Post.
New York Times.
Union News Service. Committee for Industrial Organization. Washington.

CHAPTER I

American Labor Year Book, 1917-1918. New York.
History of Labor in the United States. Vol. 2. John R. *Commons and associates,* New York, 1918. Vol. 3. Selig Perlman and Philip Taft. New York, 1936.
Labor Movement in the United States, 1860 to 1895. Norman H. Ware. New York, 1929.
Samuel Gompers. Rowland H. Harvey. Stanford University, California, 1935.
Seventy Years of Life and Labor. Samuel Gompers. New York, 1926.

The Teamster. Organ of the International Brotherhood of Teamsters. Indianapolis, 1933.
Book of Facts for Shipyard Workers. Industrial Union of Marine and Shipbuilding Workers. Camden, 1935.
"Labor Had Better Watch Out Or It Will Lose Everything." Matthew Woll. *Liberty Magazine.* February, 1936. New York.
"Labor Politics and Labor Education." John Dewey. *The New Republic.* January 9, 1929. New York.
The Carpenter. Organ of the Brotherhood of Carpenters and Joiners. Indianapolis, 1936-1937.

CHAPTER II

A.F. of L. Convention Proceedings, 1900 to 1933.
American Labor Struggles. Samuel Yellen. New York, 1935.
History of Labor in the United States. Vol. 3.
Labor and Steel. Horace B. Davis. New York, 1933.
Labor in Modern Industrial Society. Norman H. Ware. New York, 1935.
Labor Movement in the United States, 1860 to 1895.
Samuel Gompers. Rowland H. Harvey.

CHAPTER III

A.F. of L. Convention Proceedings, 1932 to 1936.
"Coal Labor Legislation: A Case." W. Jett Lauck. *Annals of the American Academy of Political and Social Science,* March, 1936. Philadelphia.
"Collective Bargaining and Section 7 (b) of NIRA." Solomon Barkin, *The Annals.* March, 1936. Philadelphia.
Industrial Unionism in the American Labor Movement. Theresa Wolfson and Abraham Weiss. New York, 1936.
Labor Organizations in the Automobile Manufacturing Industry. Anthony Luchek. Earhart Fellowship Report. University of Michigan. 1935 (unpublished).
Steel Dictator. Harvey O'Connor. New York, 1935.
Strikes Under the New Deal. Maurice Goldbloom, John Herling, Joel Seidman, Elizabeth Yard. New York, 1935.
"The Clash Over Industrial Unionism." John A. Fitch. *Survey Graphic,* January, 1936. New York.
United Textile Workers of America. Convention Proceedings, 1934. New York.

CHAPTER IV

A.F. of L. Convention Proceedings, 1933 to 1936.
Labor Organizations in the Automobile Manufacturing Industry.
"The Radio Workers and the A.F. of L." James B. Carey. *The Advance.* August, 1936. New York.
United Automobile Workers. Proceedings of the First Constitutional Convention. Detroit, 1935.
United Rubber Workers of America. Proceedings of the First Constitutional Convention. Akron, 1935.

CHAPTER V

A.F. of L. Convention Proceedings, 1934 and 1935.

CHAPTER VI

A.F. of L. Convention Proceedings. 1936.

Journal of the Amalgamated Association of Iron, Steel and Tin Workers. Pittsburgh, 1936.

Proceedings of the Executive Council in the Matter of Charges Filed by the Metal Trades Department Against the C.I.O. A.F. of L. 1936.

CHAPTER VII

Flint Auto Worker. Published by the United Automobile Workers of America. Detroit, 1936-1937.

Handbook of Labor Statistics. United States Department of Labor. Washington, 1936.

How the Rubber Workers Won. C.I.O. 1936.

"Profile of General Motors." Samuel Romer. *The Nation.* January 23, 1937. New York.

United Rubber Worker. Organ of the United Rubber Workers of America. Akron, 1936.

CHAPTER VIII

"*Sit-Down.*" Joel Seidman. New York, 1937.

"Sit-Down as a Weapon Now Widely Debated." Louis Stark. *New York Times.* February 28, 1937.

"Sit-Down's Legality Debated." Dean Dinwoodey. *New York Times.* January 17, 1937.

Sit-Down Strikes. A Survey by WPA Project on Study of Labor Laws, under direction of Daniel L. Horowitz. New York, 1937 (uncompleted and unpublished).

"The Case for the Sit-Down Strike." Leon Green. *The New Republic.* March 24, 1937. New York.

United Automobile Worker. 1936-1937.

United Rubber Worker. 1936-1937.

CHAPTER IX

"Big Steel, Little Steel, and C.I.O." Benjamin Stolberg. *The Nation,* July 31, 1937.

Chicago Memorial Day Incident. Report of the Committee on Education and Labor of the U. S. Senate. Government Printing Office. Washington, 1937.

Governmental Protection of Labor's Right to Organize. National Labor Relations Board. 1936.

Johnstown Democrat, May, June, July, 1937. Johnstown, Pa.

Johnstown Tribune, May, June, July, 1937. Johnstown, Pa.

SOURCES

Journal of the Amalgamated Association of Iron, Steel and Tin Workers. 1936-1937.
"Republic Sticks to Its Guns." Rose M. Stein. *The Nation,* June 12, 1937.
Steel Labor. Organ of the Steel Workers Organizing Committee. Pittsburgh, 1936-1937.
The Real Issues. Republic Steel Corporation. Cleveland, 1937.
Youngstown Vindicator. May, June, July, 1937. Youngstown, Pa.

CHAPTER X

A.F. of L. Convention Proceedings. 1937.
Back to Work Movements. A Study by Philip Taft under direction of David J. Saposs. Washington, 1937 (unpublished).
Bulletin. Organ of the Metal Trades Department of the A.F. of L. 1936-1937. Washington.
Daily Worker. October 11 and 12, 1937. New York.
Herald Tribune. New York, 1937.
"How Much Democracy Is There in the P.M.A.?" Gerry Allard. *The Socialist Call.* May 28, 1936. New York.
"I Break Strikes"—The Technique of Pearl L. Bergoff. Edward Levinson. New York, 1935.
Independent Unions. A Study by Ralph Hetzel under direction of David J. Saposs. Washington, 1937 (unpublished).
Join the C.I.O. and Help Build a Soviet America. Constitutional Educational League. New Haven, 1937.
Justice. Organ of the International Ladies' Garment Workers Union. July, 1937. New York.
National Industrial Conference Board. Service Letter. Vol. X, No. 8. New York, 1937.
Steel Labor. 1937.
The Hell of Herrin Rages Again. Constitutional Educational League. 1937.
The Progressive Miner. Organ of the Progressive Miners of America. 1936-1937. Gillespie, Illinois.
World-Telegram. New York, 1937.

CHAPTER XI

"All Work and No Pay." Walter Davenport. *Collier's,* November 13, 1937. New York.
Collective Bargaining in the Steel Industry: 1937. Industrial Relations Section, Princeton University. Princeton, N. J., 1937.
Industrial Union of Marine and Shipbuilding Workers Union. Convention Proceedings. Camden, 1937.
Maritime Unity. Joseph Curran. New York, 1937.

[303]

Maritime Voice of the Pacific. Organ of the Sailors' Union of the Pacific. San Francisco, 1937.

Mine, Mill and Smelter Workers International Union. Convention Proceedings. Butte, 1937.

Oil Workers International Union. Convention Proceedings. Washington, 1937.

Peoples Press. United Electrical and Radio Workers' edition. New York, 1937.

Plight of the Share-Cropper. Norman Thomas. New York, 1936.

Reports of John Brophy, James B. Carey, Joseph Curran, John Eddy, Sherman H. Dalrymple, Homer Martin, Philip Murray, Michael J. Quill, Samuel Wolchak and Lewis Merrill to the Conference of C.I.O. Unions at Atlantic City, October, 1937. C.I.O. (mimeographed).

Southern Tenant Farmers' Union. Convention Proceedings. Memphis, 1937.

Steel Labor. Pittsburgh, 1937.

The Advance. 1937. Organ of the Amalgamated Clothing Workers of America. New York, 1937.

The Conveyor. Organ of the West Side Local, United Automobile Workers. Detroit, 1937.

The Guild Reporter. Organ of the American Newspaper Guild. New York, 1936-1937.

The I.S.U. Pilot. Organ of Rank and File Groups in the International Seamen's Union. New York, 1936-1937.

The Pilot. Organ of the National Maritime Union. New York, 1937.

The Shape-Up. Organ of the Rank and File Committee, International Longshoremen's Association. New York, 1936-1937.

The Sharecroppers' Voice. Organ of the Southern Tenant Farmers' Union. Memphis, 1936-1937.

The Shipyard Worker. Organ of the Industrial Union of Marine and Shipbuilding Workers Union. Camden, 1937.

The Textile Worker of New England. Organ of the Textile Workers' Organizing Committee. Boston, 1937.

The Timber Worker. Organ of the Sawmill and Timber Workers' Union. 1936-1937. Aberdeen, Washington.

The Transport Worker. Organ of the Transport Workers of America. New York, 1936-1937.

"These Fellows Just Thrive on Trouble." (The Founding of the Transport Workers Union.) David Davidson, *New York Post.* New York. July 2, 1937.

T.W.O.C. Parade. Southern Organ of the T.W.O.C. Atlanta, 1937.

United Automobile Worker. Detroit. 1937.

United Automobile Workers of America. Convention Proceedings. 1936-1937. Detroit.

United Electrical and Radio Workers' Union. Convention Proceedings. New York, 1937.

United Rubber Worker. 1936-1937.

United Rubber Workers. Souvenir Program for Convention. Akron, 1937.

United Rubber Workers of America. Convention Proceedings. 1936-1937. Akron.

CHAPTER XII

C.I.O. Resolutions Adopted at Atlantic City Conference in October, 1937. C.I.O. Washington (mimeographed).

"John L. Lewis," *Fortune.* October, 1936. New York.

John L. Lewis' Address Before Conference of C.I.O. Unions at Atlantic City. October, 1937. C.I.O. Washington.

"John L. Lewis—An Interview." Selden Rodman, *Common Sense,* January, 1936. New York.

"Lewis Challenges the Individualist." F. Raymond Daniell. *New York Times Magazine.* October 24, 1937. New York.

Rules for Industrial Union Councils. C.I.O. 1937. Washington.

The Labor Movement in the United States, 1860 to 1895.

APPENDIX

I. TRENDS IN TRADE UNIONISM—1933 TO 1937[1]

Industry and Union	Employees in Industry[2]	1933— A.F. of L.	1934— A.F. of L.	1935— A.F. of L.	1936— A.F. of L.	1936— C.I.O.	1937— A.F. of L.	1937— C.I.O.
A. Agri., Forestry, Fishing..........	2,968,485							
Cannery & Agri. Wks.	2,771,264[3]							100,000
Sheep Shearers of N.A.		600	800	1,100	900		800	
Woodworkers of America	472,870[4]							100,000
B. Extraction of Minerals........	919,141							
Mine, Mill & Smelter Wks.	122,844	13,000	49,000[5]	14,600		16,000		45,000
Mine Wkrs. of A., United........	621,661	300,000	300,000	400,000		525,000		600,000
Oil Field Workers..........	105,224	3,000	12,500	42,800		49,500		100,000
Quarry Workers..........	65,288	2,100	2,000	2,000	2,000		2,000	
C. Manufacturing & Mechanical	13,549,817							
(Building Trades)								
Asbestos Workers..........		3,300	3,100	4,300	4,400		5,500	
Bricklayers & Masons..........	170,963	45,800	45,800	65,000	65,000		65,000	
Bridge & Structural Iron........	28,966	10,000	16,000	16,000	16,000		22,700	
Carpenters & Joiners..........	991,461	205,800	200,000	200,000	300,000		300,000	
Electrical Workers..........	284,928	94,100	113,500	130,000	170,000		171,200	
Elevator Constructors..........		10,200	10,200	10,200	10,200		10,200	
Engineers, Operating..........	256,078	35,000	35,000	35,000	35,000		42,000	
Granite Cutters..........	38,956	5,000	5,000	5,000	5,000		5,000	
Hod Carriers, Common Lab's....	710,156	52,100	44,200	52,300	65,400		65,400	
Lathers..........		8,100	8,100	8,100	8,100		8,100	
Marble & Stone Polishers........	36,044	6,200	5,500	5,500	5,500		5,500	
Painters & Paperhangers..........	557,259	59,300	57,800	65,600	66,500		80,100	
Plasterers..........	85,480	22,600	18,000	18,000	18,000		18,400	
Plumbers & Steamfitters..........	243,751	45,000	45,000	34,000	33,000		33,000	
Roofers..........	23,636	4,000	4,000	4,000	4,000		4,000	
Sheet Metal Workers..........	80,400	17,500	16,000	16,000	16,000		16,200	

I. TRENDS IN TRADE UNIONISM—1933 TO 1937—(Continued)

Industry and Union	Employees in Industry[2]	1933 A.F.of L.	1934 A.F.of L.	1935 A.F.of L.	1936 A.F.of L.	1936 C.I.O.	1937 A.F.of L.	1937 C.I.O.
(Chemical & Allied Ind's)......	269,375							
Powder and High Explosives Wks..	10,951	100	100	100	100		200	
(Cigars and Tobacco)........	124,296							
Cigarmakers..........		9,800	7,000	7,000	7,000		7,000	
Tobacco Workers......		2,600	8,300	10,400	8,500		11,000	
(Clay, Glass & Stone).......	242,007							
Brick & Clay Workers.......	72,427	100	1,400	1,600	1,000		5,500	
Glass Bottle Blowers......		6,000	6,000	6,000	6,200		18,800	
Glass Cutters League......		600	1,000	1,200	1,200		1,300	
Flat Glass Workers......			800	10,000		10,000		14,000
Flint Glass Workers......		3,600	6,100	6,100	4,800		5,300	
Paving Cutters......		2,200	2,200	2,100	2,000		2,000	
Potters......	34,525	4,500	7,900	10,000	10,400		11,000	
Stone Cutters......	28,888	5,600	5,600	5,700	5,200		5,000	
(Clothing Trades)........	1,107,311							
Boot & Shoe Workers........	228,317	13,400	19,200	25,900	27,000		29,300	
Shoe Workers, United........	228,317							52,000
Clothing Wks., Amalga'ted....			83,300	100,000		150,000		200,000
Fur Workers.........		4,000	2,000	3,000	15,000			40,000
Garment Workers, United......		39,500	37,000	37,100	40,600		39,500	
Glove Workers........	19,624	500	3,400	3,500	2,200		1,700	
Hat, Cap, Millinery Wks.		14,600	19,800	21,400	22,100[6]	22,100[6]	23,900[6]	23,900[6]
Ladies Garment Workers......		25,000	150,000	160,000		225,000		252,000
(Food and Liquor)........	420,102							
Bakery, Confect'y Wks.	231,085	15,900	18,100	21,800	26,100		32,500	
Brewery Workers......		16,000	25,500	41,700	42,000		42,000	
Meat Cutters & Butchers......	96,104	11,100	19,500	19,800	19,400		30,000	
(Furniture and Woodworking).....	510,966							
Furniture Wks., United......								30,000

Wood Carvers		800	800	600	400		400	
Coopers		700	2,500	2,900	2,500		2,600	
Upholsterers	51,542	6,500	6,500	6,500	8,500		10,200	
(Jewelry Trades)	38,662							
Diamond Workers		300	200	200	400		300	
Jewelry Workers		800	4,900	5,500	5,300		6,000	8,250
(Leather Manufacture)	306,119							
Leather Wks. Ass'n								
Leather Wks., United		800	3,000	2,700	2,500		2,500	
Pocketbook, Novelty Wks.							500	
(Metals & Machinery)		25,000[5]	100,000[6]	50,000[5]		55,000		
Aluminum Workers	140,469							14,000
Automobile Wks., United	49,923							375,000
Die Casting Workers								3,400
Blacksmiths, Drop Forgers		5,000	5,000	5,000	5,000		5,000	
Boilermakers, Shipbuilders		14,200	14,300	15,300	15,500		18,000	
Carmen, Railway		59,200	55,000	55,000	58,300		65,000	
Engravers, Metal		500	300	300	200		200	
Firemen and Oilers	158,504	9,200	10,100	14,900	20,700		23,600	
Foundry Enployees		500	2,000	3,200	3,700		3,500	
Horseshoers		100	100	100	100		200	
Iron, Steel & Tin Wks.	865,912	4,600	5,500	8,600		9,200		9,200
Machinists	774,701	65,000	82,000	92,500	113,700		138,000	
Marine & Shipbuilding Wks.	37,321					10,000		20,000
Metal Polishers		1,400	3,500	4,000	4,600		5,600	
Molders	105,158	6,000	8,800	11,800	15,900		22,200	
Patternmakers	29,750	7,000	7,000	2,500	2,600		4,200	
Steel Wks. Organizing Com.	865,912					113,700[7]		510,000[7]
Stove Mounters		600	1,500	2,000	2,300		3,000	
Wire Weavers		300	300	300	300		300	
(Paper and Printing)	497,188							
Bookbinders		10,700	11,900	11,700	11,600		13,100	

I. TRENDS IN TRADE UNIONISM—1933 TO 1937—(Continued)

Industry and Union	Employees in Industry[2]	1933—A.F. of L.	1934—A.F. of L.	1935—A.F. of L.	1936—A.F. of L.	1936—C.I.O.	1937—A.F. of L.	1937—C.I.O.
Papermakers		2,300	11,500	9,000	6,600		11,600	
Pulp & Paper Mill Wks.	115,667	5,000	6,900	8,500	9,100		15,700	
Wallpaper Crafts		550	500	600	500		900	
Engravers, Photo	19,437	8,700	8,600	8,700	8,800		9,100	
Lithographers	8,868	5,200	5,800	6,700	6,900		7,200	
Printing Pressmen	42,143	35,300	32,000	32,000	32,000		33,700	
Printers, Die Stampers		1,000	1,200	1,400	1,300		1,000	
Sideographers		100	100	100	100		100	
Stereotypers & Electrotypers	7,824	8,200	8,000	7,900	8,100		8,300	
Typographical Union	183,632	73,800	73,100	73,400	73,300[6]	73,300[6]	75,500[6]	75,500[6]
(Rubber Manufacture)	109,958							
Rubber Workers, United	109,958	40,000[5]	60,000[5]	4,000[5]		25,000		78,000
(Textile Industries)	937,903							
Textile Wkrs., United	937,903	15,000	300,000[5]	79,200				
Textile Wkrs. Org'ing Com.	937,903					100,000		450,000[8]
Textile Operatives, Fed. of	937,903						6,000	
(Miscellaneous Manufacture)								
Electrical & Radio Wks.	12,108	10,544[5]		30,000[5]	100	33,000		130,000
Broom & Whisk Makers		200	100	100	100		100	
D. Transportation, Communication	3,368,162							
Marine Engineers								
Masters, Mates & Pilots	24,485	2,500	2,000	2,200	2,500		2,900	
Maritime Union, National	64,700[9]							5,000
Seamen's Union, Intern'l	64,700[9]	6,000	5,000	12,500	20,000		14,200	51,300
Longshoremen	73,954	23,400	34,300	40,000	40,660			
Longshoremen & Warehousemen							61,400	17,000
Air Line Pilots	6,097	600	700	700	800		900	
Street & Elec. R'way Emplo's	151,372	71,200	70,000	73,400	75,700		76,700	
Transport Workers Union								87,800

Teamsters	1,584,560[10]	71,300	95,500	137,000	161,000	210,000	
R'way & Steamship Clerks	435,058	60,000	60,000	72,500	87,500	89,200	
Conductors, Sleeping Car		2,000	2,000	2,000	2,000	1,900	
Maintenance of Way Employees	92,217	27,800	31,200	33,500	35,700	41,800	
Switchmen	27,648	6,300	7,300	8,000	8,500	8,900	
Porters, Pullman					1,200	5,500	
Communications Association	327,836[11]						14,000
Telegraphers, Commercial	67,821[12]	2,200	2,000	2,000	2,000	2,000	
Telegraphers, Railroad		35,000	35,000	35,000	35,000	35,000	
E. Government Service	689,463[13]						
Fire Fighters	73,088	18,000	19,700	23,500	25,500	29,100	
Gov't Empl's, Amer. Fed. of		4,000	8,300	13,900	22,200	21,400	5,000
Federal Employees, United							30,000
State, County & Municipal							
State, County, Municipal (C.I.O.)						11,400	
Letter Carriers	121,333	55,000	51,700	50,000	50,000	52,500	
Mail Assn., Railway	25,608	20,000	19,200	19,100	19,300	21,000	
Post Office Clerks, Nat'l Fed.		36,000	33,300	32,000	32,000	36,000	
F. Clerical, Commercial Service	6,721,169						
Bill Posters & Billers	401,991	1,600	1,400	1,400	1,400	1,400	
Retail Clerks Protec. Ass'n	401,991	5,000	5,800	7,200	10,300	18,500	
Retail Employees, United	3,738,838						40,000
Office Workers, United							25,000
G. Professional, Semi-Pro'al, Amusements	2,273,446						
Actors and Artistes	75,296	3,300	3,100	4,300	4,400	5,500	
Architects, Engineers and Technicians	377,895					10,000	7,000
Draftsmen	79,922	700	1,000	1,200	1,200	1,400	
Newspaper Guild, American	51,844		3,000[5]	4,000[5]			
Stage, Motion Picture Wks.		24,000	24,000	24,000	24,000	24,200	
Teachers	1,044,016	7,000	8,500	12,000	12,700	15,400	15,000

I. TRENDS IN TRADE UNIONISM—1933 TO 1937—(Concluded)

Industry and Union	Employees in Industry[2]	1933— A.F. of L.	1934— A.F. of L.	1935— A.F. of L.	1936— A.F. of L.	1936— C.I.O.	1937— A.F. of L.	1937— C.I.O.
Musicians..........	165,128[14]	100,000	100,000	100,000	100,000		100,000	
H. Domestic & Personal Service......	4,546,220							
Barbers...........	374,290	32,000	39,300	32,000	32,000		40,800	
Building Service Employees.........	439,171	18,000	19,200	27,500	35,000		42,500	
Hotel and Restaurant Wks.........	627,460[15]	22,700	37,800	57,000	73,800		107,100	
Laundry Wks...........	220,131	5,000	5,300	6,000	6,000		7,000	
Cleaning & Dye House Wks........	65,183						4,800	
I. Miscellaneous								
Local Trade and Federal Unions...		89,083	111,489	83,153		232,700	
Local Industrial Unions...........								200,000

1 The membership of the A.F. of L. unions, unless otherwise indicated, is the average monthly membership represented by payment of per capita to the Federation. The membership of the C.I.O. unions, unless otherwise indicated, is the dues-paying membership in December, 1936, and October, 1937, as given by executives of the respective unions.

2 Based on the Fifteenth Census of the U. S. 1930. An effort has been made to select the number of employees coming within the jurisdictions of the respective unions. Wherever possible, foremen and overseers have been excluded.

3 Includes only wage-working farmers and employees in fruit and vegetable canneries.

4 Includes lumbermen, raftsmen, wood-choppers, and workers in saw and planing mills.

5 Statements of union executives.

6 Affiliation listed by both A.F. of L. and C.I.O.

7 Includes dues-payers and signers of cards authorizing union to act as spokesman.

8 Includes dues-payers, signers of cards authorizing union to act as spokesman, and members of United Textile Workers.

9 Deck hands only.

10 Includes drivers and haulers on motor and wagon transportation.

11 Includes radio operators, telegraph messengers, telegraphers and telephone operators.

12 Includes railroad telegraphers.

13 Does not include clerks, etc., otherwise classified, nor soldiers and sailors.

14 Includes teachers of music.

15 Waiters.

APPENDIX

II. EXTENT OF UNION ORGANIZATION IN THE U. S.

	1933	*1935*	*1937*
Organizable Workers	35,026,903[1]	35,026,903[1]	35,026,903[1]
A.F. of L.	2,126,796[2]	3,045,347[2]	3,441,340[3]
Unaffiliated Unions	655,500[4]	571,500[4]	518,397[5]
C.I.O.			3,727,350[6]
Total Organized Workers	2,782,296	3,616,847	7,687,087
Percentage of Workers Organized	.078	.106	.219

[1] Based on Fifteenth U. S. Census, 1930.
[2] Average monthly dues-paying members reported by the A.F. of L.
[3] "Membership" reported by the A.F. of L. as of November 19, 1937.
[4] From Leo Wolman's *Ebb and Flow of Trade Unionism.*
[5] 1936 membership as given in *Handbook of American Trade Unions,* 1936 edition.
[6] Based on Table I, Trends in Trade Unionism—1933 to 1937.

INDEX

Addes, George, 66, 104, 117, 269
Agricultural, Packing and Allied Wks. of America, United Cannery, 241-243
Agricultural Workers, 56, 83
Altiere, Louis, 101
Aluminum Workers, 50, 56, 83-85, 98, 108, 110
Aluminum Workers of America, 255-256
American Federation of Labor, Cincinnati Conference (1937), 135-136
 Conventions: 1886, 30-31; 1900, 40-41; 1924, 4; 1925, 6; 1932, 49-50; 1933, 53-54; 1934, 82-88, 108, 120; 1935, 97-117; 1936, 130-133; 1937, 224, 233-235
 Executive Council, 4-6, 17, 22, 49, 72, 80-83, 85, 87-88, 90-95, 97-98, 102, 105, 107, 109, 111, 118, 120, 122-136, 147, 180, 224, 234-235
 Finances, 80-82, 135
 Membership, 1900, 40; 1904, 40; 1909, 42; 1912, 42; 1916, 43; 1918, 43; 1920, 43, 47; 1923, 47; 1933, 48, 53, 79; 1934, 79, 80; 1935, 80; 1936, 235; 1937, 235, 278
American Federationist, 80-81, 106-107, 226
American Iron and Steel Institute, 26, 69, 190-191, 201, 273
American Liberty League, 142
American Plan, 46
American Railway Union, 36-39
American Woolen Co., 240
Anaconda Copper Co., 56, 78
Apex Hosiery Co., 184
Architects, Engineers, Chemists and Technicians, Federation of, 249

Arizona State Federation of Labor, 134
Associated Automobile Workers, 59, 147
Associated Press, 142, 247
Automobile Chamber of Commerce, 57, 61, 153
Automobile Code, 57-61
Automobile Labor Board, 59, 62-67, 71
Automobile workers, 18, 41-42, 47, 50, 56, 57-67, 80, 84-85, 108, 110
Automobile Workers of America International Union, 88-93, 95, 97, 104, 115, 117, 120-121, 125, 127, 131, 146-168, 175-179, 181, 214, 226, 255, 266-271, 276, 278, 282
Automotive Industrial Workers Ass'n, 59-60, 147
Auto Workers Union, 60

"Back to Work Movements," 204-206, 211, 218-220
Bakery and Confectionery Workers International Union, 104, 235
Bates, H. C., 87, 126
Beck, David A., 264
Beedie, William C., 127
Belmont, August, 31
Bendix Brake Co., 147-148, 171-172
Bennett, Harry H., 214
Bergoff, Pearl L., 146, 219-220
Bernard, John T., Congressman, 184, 254
Berry, George L., 87
Bethlehem Steel Corp., 201, 203-208, 216-218, 230, 272
Bieretz, E. D., 127
Bittner, Van A., 103, 114, 189, 194, 198, 285